THE VIOLENCE OF SCRIPTURE

Overcoming the Old Testament's Troubling Legacy

ERIC A. SEIBERT

Fortress Press

Minneapolis

THE VIOLENCE OF SCRIPTURE
Overcoming the Old Testament's Troubling Legacy

Cover image © iStockphoto.com / Robert Ridder
Cover design: Joe Vaughan
Book design: PerfecType, Nashville, TN

Library of Congress Cataloging-in-Publication Data

Seibert, Eric A., 1969–
 The violence of Scripture : overcoming the Old Testament's troubling legacy / Eric A. Seibert.
   p. cm.
 Includes bibliographical references (p.   ) and indexes.
 ISBN 978-0-8006-9825-6 (pbk. : alk. paper) — ISBN 978-1-4514-2432-4
(ebook)
 1. Violence in the Bible. 2. Bible. O.T.—Criticism, interpretation, etc. 3. Bible.
O.T.—Hermeneutics. I. Title.
 BS1199.V56S45 2012
 221.8'3036—dc23
                              2012007894

Manufactured in the U.S.A.
16 15 14 13 12 1 2 3 4 5 6 7 8 9 10

Contents

To my Dad and Mom,
Laverne and Kathy,

for giving me a wonderful childhood,
loving me unconditionally,
supporting me always,
and reading what I write.

I love you!

Acknowledgments

I would like to express my gratitude to some of the people who have, directly or indirectly, contributed to this book (with apologies to anyone whose name I inadvertently omit). A number of people—many with very busy schedules and lots of other obligations—set time aside to read and comment on a draft of this manuscript, or portions of it. I wish to thank each of the following individuals for investing their time and energy in this way: Terry Brensinger, Julia O'Brien, Doug Miller, Hannah Pratt (who deserves special thanks for compiling the indexes with great care and skill), Morgan Scott, Elisa Seibert, Doug Sider, Louis Stulman, and Darrell Winger. This book is so much better because of your suggestions and input. Thank you! Of course, all remaining imperfections and shortcomings are mine alone, and I take full responsibility for the assumptions I make, the approach I take, and the conclusions I propose. None of these individuals should be held liable for any of the book's remaining deficiencies.

I am very fortunate to be employed at a place like Messiah College and am thankful for the opportunities it provides for teaching and writing. I am especially grateful to the College for the internal grants I received, the scholarship chair I was awarded, and the workload reallocation program in which I participated. These awards helped fund this project and some of them provided valuable release time to complete it. It would have been impossible to finish the book on time without this assistance.

I would like to thank Barb Syvertson from Interlibrary Loan at Murray Library for helping me secure many resources for this project along the way. What a wonderful service you render! Thanks also to Michael Rice for helping me locate an online resource when my searching skills faltered. To my colleagues in the Biblical and Religious Studies Department, I owe a special word of thanks for the way you have supported me through some trying times since the publication of my previous book. I value your friendship and camaraderie more than you know.

I also want to thank John Anderson for pointing me to some important resources. I really hope you like this book! To Elizabeth Sobrevilla, thank you for your good questions and continued interest in the project. You are encouraging. To my parents, to whom this book is dedicated, I want to express my gratitude for the hours of quality childcare you rendered so freely and frequently. Thank you for giving me time and space to work on this book. I am also grateful to the many, many scholars and authors whose works I have utilized in preparing this book. You have taught me a great deal, and I have tried my best to give credit where credit is due. Thanks also to two of my former students, whose work I quote in the book.

I want to thank Fortress Press for partnering with me again on another book project. I appreciate the good people there and owe a special word of thanks to Neil Elliott. Thank you for all the help you have given me along the way to see this project through to completion. It is deeply appreciated. Also, to Marissa Wold, thank you for your patience and for your help in the production phase of this project.

Words are inadequate to express my thanks to my wife and best friend, Elisa, for enduring endless conversations about the violence of Scripture, which she did with characteristic good grace and real interest. Her very careful reading of this manuscript (some parts more than once!) and very helpful suggestions along the way have improved the book in countless ways. You are a gem! I also want to say thank you to my two young children, Nathan and Rebecca, for being patient with a book-writing Daddy. You bring me such immense joy and remind me of the really important things in life. Thanks for being such wonderful kids!

I am hopeful this book will be helpful to many readers who struggle with the violence of Scripture, and with violent readings of Scripture, and yet are not willing to give up on these texts. To you I offer the assurance that there are other ways, and better ways, to read the Bible. I trust this book will be a useful guide for the journey.

CHAPTER 1

Introduction:
The Bible Should Never Be Used
to Harm Others

Humans have an amazing capacity to demonize their enemies, portraying them as the epitome of evil who must be eliminated at all cost. Time and time again "civilized" Christian people have committed genocide, practiced slavery, and in other ways demeaned "uncivilized" peoples because they saw them as evil. *Using the Bible to justify this kind of behavior must stop.*

—ESTHER EPP-TIESSEN[1]

The Mystic River Massacre

On May 26, 1637, New England settlers attacked and burned a Pequot village, massacring approximately "700 elderly men and defenseless women and children."[2] It was an utterly unjustifiable act of cold-blooded killing and unmitigated brutality. How could Puritans justify such carnage? By appealing to Scripture! John Higginson wrote a treatise defending the war against the Pequot generally, and the massacre at the village at Mystic River particularly, on the basis of Judges 20. This chapter in Judges describes intertribal warfare in which the Benjaminites are nearly annihilated by their fellow Israelites. According to Laura Donaldson, this particular Old Testament passage "provided the early settlers of New England with all the legitimation they needed to wage war against the Pequot."[3]

John Underhill, who was second in command on the fateful day of the massacre, also attempts to justify the slaughter by appealing to the Old Testament. He does so by alluding to David's war with the Ammonites in 2 Samuel 12.[4] In an apparent effort to respond to some criticism of the Mystic River massacre, Underhill writes:

> Great and doleful was the bloody sight to the view of young soldiers that never had been in war, to see so many souls lie gasping on the ground, so thick, in some places, that you could hardly pass along. It may be demanded, Why should you be so furious? (as some have said). Should not Christians have more mercy and compassion? But I would refer you to David's war. When a people is grown to such a height of blood, and sin against God and man . . . he [God] hath no respect to persons, but harrows them, and saws them, and puts them to the sword, and the most terriblest death that may be. Sometimes the Scripture declareth women and children must perish with their parents. Sometimes the case alters; but we will not dispute it now. We have sufficient light from the Word of God for our proceedings.[5]

As Matthew Kruer has noted: "The Puritans' worldview was rooted in a Scripture that contained spectacular episodes of mass violence, and . . . these precedents provided a ready justification for those who sought to retroactively account for their ferocity."[6] When the Old Testament is used to justify the killing of hundreds of "elderly men and defenseless women and children," something has clearly gone terribly wrong!

Do No Harm

The premise of this book is simple and straightforward: the Bible should never be used to inspire, promote, or justify acts of violence. This means, among other things, that the Bible should not be read in ways that oppress or otherwise harm people. Yet, tragically, this is how the Bible has often been used in the past, and it is how it continues to be used by many people today.

In recent years, a number of books have appeared, highlighting the destructive way the Bible has been used to hurt others.[7] These books, with such provocative titles as *The Sins of Scripture* and *The Savage Text*, help people recognize how the Bible has often been read in ways that foster injustice, oppression, and death.[8] Biblical texts have been used to justify such things as warfare and genocide, violence against women, child abuse, religious intolerance, capital punishment, slavery, bigotry, and racism. The Old Testament has frequently been used in these ways, resulting in what I refer to as "the Old Testament's troubling legacy." As the subtitle of this book suggests, overcoming this troubling legacy is one of my primary concerns.

As we will see, the Old Testament's troubling legacy is intricately connected to its many violent texts. It is difficult to read the Old Testament for very long without bumping into passages that depict or describe violence in some way. Many of these passages portray violence positively and sanction various acts of violence. Tragically, many of these texts have been used to inspire, encourage, and legitimate all sorts of violence against others over the years.

Like the Old Testament, the New Testament is also extremely problematic in this regard. It too has been used to inspire, encourage, and legitimate all sorts of violent acts and attitudes, and has been used to oppress, afflict, and harm countless individuals and groups over the years.[9] For example, some people have used New Testament texts to perpetrate violent acts against women and children and to legitimate immoral practices like slavery.[10] A handful of New Testament texts that speak disparagingly of "the Jews" have also contributed to an enormous amount of antisemitism, the tragic consequences of which are all too familiar.[11] Other passages, such as those related to the atonement and eschatological judgment, have led to distorted views of God and even caused some people to reject Christianity altogether.[12] Clearly, the Bible's troubling legacy is not confined to the Old Testament. The New Testament is problematic as well.

That said, one may wonder why I have chosen to focus exclusively on the *Old Testament* in this book. First, given the scope and magnitude of the problem at hand, it seemed wise to limit my discussion to one part of the Bible rather than trying to do too much. Second, it made sense for me to focus exclusively on the Old Testament since this is my area of specialization. I feel much better equipped to deal with the problem as it appears in this part of the Bible given my particular training. Third, since the majority of the teaching I do is from the Old Testament, this is the context in which the problem most naturally arises for me.

Although this book focuses on the Old Testament, I believe many of the reading strategies that will be presented are equally effective in dealing with the New Testament's troubling legacy. My hope is that people will find ways to use what is offered here to help them read both the Old *and* the New Testament in ethically responsible ways.

The Purpose of This Book

I have written this book with two particular objectives in mind. First, since I believe the Bible should never be used to harm people, I will advocate reading the Old Testament *nonviolently* in an effort to overcome the Old Testament's troubling legacy. This involves reading in a way that values all people, promotes justice, and facilitates liberation. It requires reading in an ethically responsible manner, one that utilizes various strategies for critiquing, rather than perpetuating, the Old Testament's positive portrayals of violence. Reading nonviolently means resisting all readings that—wittingly or unwittingly—cause harm, justify oppression, sanction killing, or in some way reinforce the value and "virtue" of violence. Ultimately, this way of approaching the Old Testament results in readings that are liberating and life-giving rather than oppressive and deadly.

Second, and relatedly, I have written this book to offer some guidance for dealing with violent Old Testament texts that sanction, and sometimes even celebrate, certain acts of violence. Since these texts are often the source of the problem, it is crucial to discuss how they should be handled. For example, what should we do when we encounter passages containing divinely sanctioned violence, such as the command to kill every last Canaanite? How should we respond to passages that sanction rape and other acts of violence against women? What principles should guide our interpretation and application of passages that endorse stoning rebellious children (Deut. 21:18-21), blasphemers (Lev. 24:16), and wayward worshipers (Deut. 17:2-7)? Since many people do not know what to do with violent texts like these, they often do nothing with them. While this is understandable, it is not terribly helpful. In light of the enormous influence these texts have had on readers over the years, and given the considerable harm they have done, it is unwise to ignore them.[13] Violent texts must be confronted honestly and directly. In this book, I will offer specific guidelines for how to read such texts responsibly by critiquing the violence in them while still considering how these troubling texts can be used constructively.

This book addresses issues that are significant to both religious professionals and lay readers. Since it is designed to be accessible to a wide range of individuals, I have tried to write at a level that will appeal to both general readers *and* to those with some formal training in biblical studies, theology, and related disciplines. While the book provides a good starting point for people who are wrestling with these issues for the first time, there is also much here for those who have reflected on these questions previously. Although I do not envision my primary audience being scholars already committed to—and engaged in—an ethical critique of Scripture, I hope that even these individuals will benefit from some of what they find in the pages that follow.

A Difficult—But Worthwhile—Journey

This book is going to deal with some of the most violent and unsavory parts of the Old Testament, parts that make many readers squeamish and are often quickly bypassed for greener pastures. If you have never lingered long over these troublesome texts, some of what you are about to read will be disturbing. As Cheryl Kirk-Duggan acknowledges: "While many read the Bible for spiritual direction and personal devotion, to unearth the violence and know the impact of that violence requires a reading that can be uncomfortable for those seeking simple or easy answers."[14] Yet, given the harm these texts have caused, simplistic answers are not only inadequate, they are dangerous. The presence of violence in the Bible constitutes a serious problem, one that needs to be confronted with eyes wide open.

As we proceed, we will need to ask some hard questions. We will also need to look at some passages in new ways. At times, this may feel uncomfortable. Reading nonviolently will require us to voice our opposition to positive portrayals of violence and to certain assumptions about violence embedded in these texts. This act of "reading against the grain" may feel unnatural to some readers, especially those who have never questioned or critiqued the biblical text in this way before. It will require them to rethink their view of the Bible and their understanding of how Scripture functions authoritatively.[15] But this way of reading is precisely what is needed to overcome the Old Testament's troubling legacy. Given the concerns some may have about this way of reading the Bible, it may help for me to share a few words about my own faith commitment and view of Scripture before proceeding any further.

My Faith Commitment and View of Scripture

Sometimes people who focus on the violence of Scripture, or who emphasize certain problems with the Bible, do so in an effort to disparage the Bible and discredit Christianity. That is certainly *not* my intention. I am a committed Christian who actively participates in the life of the church and affirms the essential role of Scripture for Christian faith and practice. Thus, I write as one who deeply values Scripture, loves the church, and desires to see Christians use the Bible in a way that deepens their faith and strengthens their resolve to love God and others.

I have had an interest in the Bible for as long as I can remember. I was raised in a Christian home, attended church regularly, and decided to follow Jesus at an early age. The value and importance of the Bible were impressed upon me at home and in church, and my respect for the Bible, both the Old and New Testaments, is deep and profound. I continue to be amazed at how much influence these texts exert over many of my most fundamental convictions and beliefs. The Bible has played an indispensable role in my life in that regard. Reading the Bible has been a life-giving and faith-affirming experience for me, and I am convinced it is one of the most significant ways God communicates with people today. Scripture has been—and continues to be—formative and foundational in my life in many respects.

Yet, ironically, my love for the Bible is precisely what eventually led me to have such substantial difficulties with it. The more I read and studied the Bible, the more I realized how challenging some parts of it were for those wanting to use it as a guide for faithful living and theological reflection. For all its benefits, I began to recognize that the Bible was not without some significant problems. I discovered that the Bible sometimes promotes values that are objectionable, encourages behaviors that are unethical, and portrays God in ways that are unacceptable.

Unfortunately, some readers uncritically embrace these problematic perspectives, internalize the text's accommodating attitudes toward violence, and then use these texts to hurt others. Far too many people have been abused, oppressed, violated, and victimized by those who read the Bible this way. As one who loves Scripture and loathes violence, I find this to be terribly distressing. Therefore, I have written this book to encourage people to read the Old Testament more ethically and less violently, in ways that help rather than harm.

Since I will be urging throughout this book that people read the Old Testament nonviolently, I should also describe my personal convictions as they relate to violence and nonviolence. As a lifelong member of the Brethren in Christ Church, a denomination rooted in the Anabaptist, Pietist, and Wesleyan traditions, I embrace the church's strong commitment to nonviolence, peacemaking, and reconciliation. Personally, I regard all forms of violence as inappropriate for Christians, and I cannot condone the use of violence in any situation. We have been created to love and serve one another, not to harm each other. Part of what makes violence so problematic—and destructive—is that it harms both the victim *and* the perpetrator. I am especially suspicious of any attempt to make violence appear virtuous, and I agree with Walter Wink's assessment that "redemptive violence" is a myth.[16] Even when violence is used for such noble ends as protecting innocent lives, it sows the seeds of future violence and is never capable of producing the kind of lasting peace (*shalom*) God desires for humanity. Therefore, I come to the Bible with a strong presumption against violence.

For the record, I should note that my strong presumption against violence does *not* imply that I think Christians should stand helplessly on the sidelines and do nothing in the face of evil. On the contrary, I am deeply committed to active, nonviolent peacemaking. I believe we are obligated to do all within our power to set things right. But we are not to do this by returning evil for evil (Rom. 12:17). Rather, we should try to "overcome evil with good" by engaging in a wide array of creative, nonviolent strategies (Rom. 12:21).[17] My interest in reading the Old Testament nonviolently represents an attempt to read the Bible in a way that is congruent with my views about violence and nonviolence.

I realize that many people will take exception to my views here. Christians hold many different perspectives about the ethics and morality of violence. Some Christians believe going to war is fully compatible with their Christian faith, while others regard it as a fundamental violation of their most basic Christian commitments. Some Christians approve of the use of torture, violence in self-defense, and capital punishment, while others find one or all of these forms of violence at variance with the teachings of Jesus. There is no single "Christian position" on any these issues. I recognize that and respect those with differing views.

The good news here is that it is not necessary to share my particular views about violence to benefit from this book. Even those who do not categorically oppose all forms of violence are still quite likely to object to certain violent texts in the Old Testament. There are many expressions of "virtuous" violence in the Old Testament that are equally problematic to just-war theorists as to pacifists, to people who advocate total nonviolence as to those who allow Christians to use lethal force in certain situations. Moreover, all readers—religious and otherwise—should be concerned about the way people have appealed to the Old Testament to justify various acts of violence and oppression. Thus, this book has much to offer those who are distressed about the way the Bible has been used to harm others, even if their views about violence differ considerably from my own.

Is It Okay to Critique the Bible?

Reading the Old Testament nonviolently will involve looking at some of the most violent, difficult, and morally offensive texts in the entire Bible. This will require a certain degree of honesty about the problematic dimensions of these texts and a willingness to critique positive portrayals of violence. Still, many readers—even those who feel some tension between the Bible's evaluation of violence and their own—may feel uncomfortable with the idea of critiquing the violence of Scripture. That is understandable since it runs contrary to the way many of us have been taught to read the Bible. We have been taught to listen to the Bible rather than to question it, to accept its values rather than to critique them. Therefore, it may help to say a few words about the appropriateness of engaging the Bible in this way.

First, it is important to keep in mind that the Old Testament does not speak with one voice on the issue of violence. Rather, the Old Testament contains enormous diversity. This is to be expected since the Old Testament was produced over a period of approximately eight hundred years (950–150 BCE) and represents a conversation that spans centuries. It includes many different voices and perspectives on a wide range of issues and, as one might expect, these do not always agree with one another. This is certainly true when it comes to various views about violence. The Old Testament says so many different things about violence that it is impossible to speak about "the Old Testament view on violence." There is no such thing. There are many Old Testament views and perspectives on violence, and some of these are diametrically opposed to each other. Invariably, readers will find themselves agreeing with some Old Testament assumptions about violence while at the same time disregarding others.

Second, one should remember that God allowed human beings to play a central role in the formation of the Bible.[18] The Bible was neither written by God nor divinely dictated. It did not drop out of the sky as a complete collection of sixty-six books. Rather, over hundreds of years, God worked through human writers who shaped and reshaped the texts that are now included in our Bible. While Christians can—and certainly do!—differ over how involved God was in the formation of Scripture, this much is clear: human beings were intimately involved in writing, transmitting, preserving, and translating the various texts we find in the Bible. Given the Bible we now have, and the enormous diversity it contains, it would seem that God allowed human beings considerable freedom in this process. Since people were free to shape these texts in various ways, it comes as no surprise that they reflect the particular social and historical contexts of their writers. Nor is it surprising that the values and beliefs embedded in these texts reflect the worldview of these ancient writers and redactors.

It is not difficult to see that the people who formed the Bible had a radically different worldview from ours in many respects, and they commonly held assumptions and beliefs we no longer do. Their ethical standards, morals, and values often differ from those we accept today. In addition, the way they thought about God—particularly the way they understood God's action in the world—does not always correspond very well to the way many modern people of faith conceive of God or God's role in the world. Yet all these very human assumptions, beliefs, and perspectives are part and parcel of the Old Testament as it now stands. While some of these notions are certainly compatible with Christian faith and practice, others are not. This requires us to engage in a critical reading of the Bible.

While some might worry that critiquing the Bible in this way is tantamount to critiquing God, I do not believe that to be the case. To state the obvious, the Bible is not God! On the contrary, the Bible is a culturally conditioned collection of sacred texts that bear the marks of human involvement from beginning to end. Apparently, God was pleased to work through people who were free to include their own culturally relevant thoughts, ideas, and perspectives. While some of these reveal certain "truths" about God, the world, and humanity, others are not so transcendent. Rather, they simply reflect certain commonly held ideas and beliefs of the time. Therefore, we read the Old Testament faithfully and responsibly not by embracing everything it says but by developing a principled approach that allows us to evaluate its claims carefully and critically. We do so with an eye toward accepting what we can and resisting what we must. The humanness of these texts demands it of us.

Third, those who feel some anxiety about "critiquing" certain aspects of the Old Testament should keep in mind that it is likely they have already been doing this for some time, whether they realize it or not. People routinely engage in a critique of the Old Testament's ethics and values. For example, most Christians today condemn the practice of slavery and regard polygamy as immoral. While the Old Testament presents slavery and polygamy as acceptable, today's readers beg to differ—and rightly so! Modern Christians do critique these ancient practices and judge them as inappropriate today. What I am suggesting here is that we simply apply this same kind of ethical critique to violent Old Testament texts. Doing so is a natural extension of the way we already read and evaluate other things in the Old Testament.

At this point, it is necessary to make a *very important* distinction. The purpose of engaging in an ethical critique of violence in the Old Testament is *not* to pass judgment upon ancient Israel. I am not interested in judging the morality of ancient Israel's behavior, let alone condemning it. Rather, I want to determine the extent to which the Old Testament's assumptions about violence and violent practices should inform our own. Had I lived in ancient Israel, I have every reason to believe I would have shared their assumptions about violence. I probably would have thought that certain kinds of offenses merited death and presumably would have believed that warfare was morally acceptable and God-ordained. It is doubtful I would have even thought to question it. But since I am not living in ancient Israel, I have a moral obligation to raise questions about the accommodating attitude toward violence found in many of these texts. So again, my interest in engaging in an ethical critique is not to judge Israelites, but to consider the extent to which their views should, or should not, be ours.

Finally, for those who worry that critiquing the Old Testament is somehow impious or irreverent, I would argue just the opposite. There is nothing dishonorable about wrestling vigorously with these texts and disagreeing with some of the values, assumptions, and perspectives they offer. In fact, we must do this if our reading is to be relevant and faithful. Given the negative ways these texts have often been used, it would be wrong *not* to evaluate them in this way. Engaging in an ethical critique of the Old Testament honors God and demonstrates our deep respect for Scripture by caring enough about it to enter into a spirited conversation with it. In fact, the Old Testament itself bears witness to this kind of engaged critique as later writers have sometimes significantly reworked and challenged earlier texts and traditions.[19] This should encourage us as we do likewise.

Hopefully, this discussion has been reassuring to those who might have some misgivings about engaging in an ethical critique of the Old Testament. Later, I will say more about why this kind of critical dialogue with the Old Testament is not only appropriate but absolutely indispensible.[20]

Some Definitions

Since violence is a central concern of this book, it may help to offer a working definition before going further. Violence is a notoriously difficult term to define, and there seem to be almost as many definitions of violence as there are manifestations of it.[21] Though my definition is provisional, I offer it here to provide some sense of how I am using the term in this book. For the purposes of this study, I consider violence to be *physical, emotional, or psychological harm done to a person by an individual (or individuals), institution, or structure that results in injury, oppression, or death*.[22] My definition of violence is not limited to physical harm since some forms of violence involve no physical contact and leave no bodily scars but do immense social, emotional, and psychological damage all the same.

The definition of violence offered here is broad enough to encompass a wide range of harmful behaviors, including everything from verbal assault to mass murder. It also includes the kind of harm done to women and children by violent ideologies such as patriarchy and sexism, ideologies that find many expressions within the pages of the Old Testament. Thus, while much of the following discussion revolves around rather obvious and indisputable forms of violence, like killing others, my interests are much broader. I am concerned about all forms of violence, not just those that are most visible or that express themselves physically. Some of the most insidious forms of violence are often less recognizable to many people but are still enormously harmful.

Throughout this study, I will refer to certain Old Testament passages as "violent texts." I will be using this phrase rather loosely to refer to a wide range of passages that (a) describe acts of violence (for example, rape, murder, warfare); (b) prescribe violent sanctions for certain behaviors (for example, laws demanding capital punishment for such things as adultery, Sabbath-breaking, and kidnapping); (c) pronounce violence against others (like many judgment oracles in prophetic literature); (d) yearn for violence to come upon adversaries (as in imprecatory Psalms); or (e) contain violent ideologies (such as patriarchy, ethnocentrism, and so forth) that devalue certain individuals or groups.

Admittedly, referring to these passages as "violent texts" is not entirely satisfactory since texts themselves are not violent. They are mere words on a page, not autonomous agents. Although violent texts, like violent movies, have the power to *portray* violence, they do not, in and of themselves, have the power to *perpetrate* it. Violent texts do not kill people any more than violent movies do. Although both might be a source of "inspiration" for such diabolical deeds, neither a text nor a film can actually kill. Thus, when I speak of a text being violent, I am saying something about both its content and its capacity to be read in ways that may encourage violence. As John Collins reminds us, "it is important to bear in mind . . . that the line between actual killing and verbal, symbolic, or imaginary violence is thin and permeable."[23] We should be very careful not to underestimate the enormous influence these texts can have on readers, one that frequently results in rather accommodating views toward violence. We will consider the relationship between violent *texts* and violent *acts* more carefully later when we discuss how these texts affect the way readers think about the propriety of violence.[24]

Finally, while I am aware that the designation "Old Testament" is problematic in certain respects, I have chosen to use it since I am writing from a Christian perspective and since this designation is the one most commonly used by Christian readers to refer to the first part of the Bible. In light of that, it also made sense to use this designation since the Old Testament's troubling legacy is, tragically, largely attributable to *Christian* readers.

The Old Testament's Troubling Legacy Is Not Its Only Legacy

Writing a book that focuses on some of the most difficult and morally problematic parts of the Old Testament is not without certain risks. Some people, especially those who are generally unfamiliar with the Old Testament, might conclude that virtually every Old Testament passage is terribly violent and ethically unacceptable. That would hardly be accurate. Likewise, given this book's emphasis on the Old Testament's *troubling* legacy, some might fail to appreciate its very positive legacy. The Old Testament is not always problematic, nor is reading it a certain recipe for disaster, one that inexorably leads to acts of violence and oppression. On the contrary, the Old Testament has been a source of tremendous comfort, hope, and encouragement to readers down through the ages. Many people (myself included!) could testify to the positive impact reading and studying the Old Testament has had on their lives. As I wrote elsewhere regarding my own encounter with the Old Testament:

> During . . . eight years in college and seminary, the Old Testament came alive for me and profoundly shaped my understanding of God, the world, and humanity in more ways than I can recall. I came to appreciate how central trusting God is to Christian faith. I learned how dangerous it is for people to create their own solutions apart from God. I witnessed God's deep and abiding desire to be in relationship with people and observed how time and again God tenaciously stuck with the Israelites even *after* they repeatedly messed up. In short, I realized the Old Testament was teeming with theological insight and wisdom.[25]

I regard the Old Testament as an invaluable resource for theological reflection and spiritual growth. I love to teach and preach from the Old Testament because I find it so relevant and applicable to our world. It has much to offer those who want to know more about what life with God is like and who desire to be in relationship with the creator of all things. The Old Testament serves as a reminder of how important it is to be faithful and obedient to God and urges us to seek God diligently as we trust God to guide and direct our steps. Without the Old Testament, my theology would be greatly impoverished and my understanding of the life of faith seriously diminished. Thus, I am extremely grateful the Old Testament is part of the canon.

My deep appreciation of the Old Testament could be echoed and amplified by countless readers across the centuries who have also found the Old Testament to be faith building and spiritually edifying. They could bear eloquent witness to the enormous value of the Old Testament in both their personal lives and their corporate experiences of worship. Some have found tremendous encouragement and solace in the words of the psalmist, and some have been inspired by the Old

Testament's vision of justice. The story of deliverance in the Exodus narrative, for example, has been especially powerful for African Americans and Latin Americans striving for liberation. Others have been stirred to action by the Old Testament's insistence upon caring for the poor and the needy. Still others could speak of how their core convictions about God, the world, and human relationships have been formed through their encounters with these texts. In these and many other ways, the Old Testament has yielded much positive fruit. It is important to keep this firmly in mind, especially when reading a book like this. When we speak of the Old Testament's troubling legacy, we are telling only *part* of the story.

Given the general disregard of the Old Testament by many Christians today, its positive virtues need to be extolled loudly and often. People need to know how beneficial these texts have been to the church and how incredibly valuable they continue to be. People should be encouraged to read the Old Testament and should allow it to challenge their assumptions and broaden their horizons. When I teach the Old Testament to undergraduate students, one of my sincere hopes is that they will have a greater appreciation for it by the end of the course than they had at the beginning. The Old Testament is a marvelous collection of texts, a rich resource that can inspire, instruct, challenge, and convict us. We ignore it at our own peril.[26]

Still, despite all the positive things that can be said about the Old Testament— and there are many—and despite its ongoing value and relevance for the church, problems remain. The tragic reality is that the Old Testament continues to exert a harmful influence upon many people today. Regardless of how much good the Old Testament has done, or how beneficial reading it may be, its troubling legacy continues to have adverse consequences that must be acknowledged and addressed. To that troubling legacy we now turn our attention.

PART 1

Exploring the Old Testament's Troubling Legacy

CHAPTER 2

The Old Testament's Troubling Legacy

Biblical words have been used not only to kill, but even to justify that killing. . . . Quotations from the Bible have been cited to bless the bloodiest of wars.

—JOHN SHELBY SPONG[1]

Texts do *more than they* say.

—DAVID M. GUNN AND DANNA NOLAN FEWELL[2]

The Old Testament has often been read violently, in ways that have done enormous harm to people. Time and again, it has been used to sanction violence, promote injustice, and justify moral atrocities. People have appealed to the Old Testament to marginalize, oppress, and dominate others. This way of using and abusing the Old Testament has a long and ugly history, one that stretches all the way from the ancient world to the present day. Tragically, as in the case of the Mystic River massacre, the people responsible for these violent readings have often been Christians who have used the Old Testament to rationalize and legitimate horrible acts of violence against others.

Before we can overcome this troubling legacy, we must first understand something of its scope and severity. Therefore, this chapter is devoted to exploring some of the ways the Old Testament has been used to justify violence against others. Although the examples given in this chapter are not meant to be exhaustive, they are representative of the harmful effects certain Old Testament texts have had over the years. Since we will only be able to deal briefly with each of the categories presented in this chapter, those who want a more extended discussion are encouraged to consult the sources mentioned in the notes.

Justifying War

Throughout history, numerous people have appropriated Old Testament language and imagery to support the cause of war and have drawn analogies between ancient Israel's wars and their own. While many examples could be noted, a few should suffice.

Of all the wars ever fought, the Crusades represent one of the most shameful chapters in Christian history. Attempting to recapture Jerusalem and other lands under Muslim control, Christians launched a series of military campaigns in which they committed unspeakable atrocities against Muslims (and others).[3] For instance, when Jerusalem was recaptured on July 15, 1099, at the end of the first crusade, the crusaders brutally killed thousands of Muslims. Several eyewitness accounts of this event have been preserved for us. One comes from Raymond of Agiles, who wrote:

> Some of our men (and this was more merciful) cut off the heads of their enemies; others shot them with arrows, so that they fell from the towers; others tortured them longer by casting them into the flames. Piles of heads, hands, and feet were to be seen in the streets of the city. It was necessary to pick one's way over the bodies of men and horses. . . . [I]n the temple and portico of Solomon, men rode in blood up to their knees and the bridle reins. Indeed, it was a just and splendid judgment of God, that this place should be filled with the blood of the unbelievers, when it had suffered so long from their blasphemies.[4]

These Christian conquerors, who had ravaged the inhabitants of the city and had done such carnage, rejoiced and sang, fully confident that God was pleased with their actions. What led them to think that the slaughter of thousands of Muslims would please God? How could these Christians justify such barbarism? The answer, in part, was the Old Testament.[5]

Joseph Lynch argues that the Old Testament played a key role in legitimizing the Crusades. According to Lynch: "The crusades, especially the First Crusade, are not comprehensible without factoring in the Old Testament, which permeated not just the language but the self-view and behavior of the warriors."[6] Although Lynch is careful to say that "the Old Testament did not 'cause' the First Crusade or its violence," he believes "the Old Testament narratives framed the anonymous knight's understanding of the crusade, and gave him and other contemporary historians (and maybe the participants) a way to talk about and to justify war."[7]

Sometimes, particular Old Testament texts were used to encourage people to take up arms or to support the Crusades. Pope Gregory VII, who was instrumental in rallying the troops prior to the first crusade, and who has been called "the most militant of the reforming popes," was especially fond of Jeremiah 48:10: "Accursed is the one who keeps back the sword from bloodshed."[8] Psalm 79, which opens with words of lamentation over the ruined state of Jerusalem, was another important text and became part of the daily mass.[9] Prior to the fifth crusade, James of Vitry sought to rally participants by appealing to the devotion and dedication of Old Testament warriors. In a sermon preached circa 1213–18, James asks: "Is there anyone consumed by zeal for the house of the Lord? . . . Where is the zeal and dagger of Phinehas? Where is Ehud's sharpened sword? Where is Shamgar's ploughshare; and the jawbone of an ass in Samson's hand?"[10] James was firmly convinced that Christians had a moral obligation to retake Jerusalem, and he did not hesitate to use the Old Testament to encourage participation.

But the Crusades are just one of many examples that demonstrate how influential the Old Testament has been in making war palatable for many Christians. During the American Civil War, both Union and Confederate forces appealed to the Old Testament in an attempt "to justify their cause."[11] As Abraham Lincoln famously said in his second inaugural address: "Both read the same Bible, and pray to the same God; and each invokes His aid against the other." During World War I, renowned biblical scholar Hermann Gunkel directed Germans to the Old Testament, convinced its warriors and military ethos were especially instructive to the German state. As William Klassen observes: "Gunkel used Old Testament literature to demonstrate that the Israelites had war heroes and a definite war piety which had specific relevance for Germany during the first World War."[12] This penchant for finding support and encouragement for war from the pages of the Old Testament is attested throughout much of church history.[13] Christians have repeatedly used the Old Testament to justify the practice of war and their participation in it.

For many Christians, God's frequent involvement in war in the Old Testament suggests that war, in and of itself, is not inherently evil. Since God (reportedly) sanctioned war in the past, using it to punish evildoers and save people from oppression, they believe God must not be categorically opposed to warfare and killing. Following this logic, they conclude that God's (apparent) approval of war in the past suggests that God sometimes still approves of war today. Many Christians find this line of reasoning very persuasive.

This was certainly true for Richard Hays, who is now professor of New Testament at Duke Divinity School. Although Hays now regards "killing enemies" as unjustifiable, he did not always think that way.[14] When he was younger, Hays understood "the holy war texts," passages like Deuteronomy 20 and 1 Samuel 15, much the way Karl Barth did. Hays writes: "Barth took these passages as indicators that we cannot constrain God's freedom to command, even to command violent action."[15] For Hays, this belief directly influenced his views about war. "Thinking along similar lines," writes Hays, "I, as a young Christian during the Vietnam War era, found myself unable to justify claiming conscientious objector status because I could not claim that I would never fight; God might command me, as he had commanded Saul, to slay an enemy."[16] Hays was prepared to go to war and to kill because of the presence of divinely sanctioned warfare in the Old Testament. It is a sober reminder of the powerful—and sometimes harmful—influence biblical texts can exert over people in the modern world.[17]

Legitimating Colonialism

Some of the worst abuses of the Old Testament have been perpetrated by colonizers intent on ruling others and exploiting their resources.[18] Throughout history, colonizers have appealed to Scripture to support acts of aggression, theft, and oppression. Old Testament texts that claim God gave the Israelites a particular land to possess, and that God sanctioned the slaughter of others, have all too frequently been used to justify some of the worst moral atrocities ever committed. Lust for land and resources caused colonizers to engage in despicable acts of deception and violence against indigenous people living on land they wanted to occupy. Time and again, all this death and destruction was "justified" biblically because many colonizers believed they had a divine mandate to dominate others and take control of their land.

An especially toxic text in this regard is the conquest narrative in Joshua 6–11. As John Collins observes: "One of the most troubling aspects of this biblical story is the way it has been used, analogically, over the centuries as *a legitimating paradigm of violent conquest*."[19] Similarly, Esther Epp-Tiessen writes:

> The conquest paradigm portrayed in the book of Joshua and related texts has contributed to untold human suffering over the millennia. Much of this suffering has been perpetrated by Christians. Peoples who have understood and appropriated these texts to provide divine sanction for the conquest of others have turned the Bible into an instrument of oppression. It is imperative that Christians today honestly acknowledge and repent of this legacy.[20]

It is difficult to overestimate how much damage such readings of the Old Testament have done to countless individuals. Michael Prior has written extensively about this in his book *The Bible and Colonialism: A Moral Critique*. According to Prior, this way of using Scripture not only harms people but leads to a general disregard of the Bible itself. He writes: "The application of the Bible in defense of the Crusades, Spanish and Portuguese colonialism, South African apartheid and political Zionism has been a calamity, leading to the suffering and humiliation of millions of people, and to the loss of respect for the Bible as having something significant to contribute to humanity."[21] This is clearly what has happened for many Palestinian Christians with respect to the Old Testament. According to Naim Ateek:

> Before the creation of the State [of Israel], the Old Testament was considered to be an essential part of Christian Scripture, pointing and witnessing to Jesus. Since the creation of the State, some Jewish and Christian interpreters have read the Old Testament largely as a Zionist text to such an extent that it has become almost repugnant to Palestinian Christians. As a result, the Old Testament has generally fallen into disuse among both clergy and laity.[22]

Using the Bible to support colonial aspirations is not only terribly misguided, it is immoral. It turns the Bible into a deadly weapon, one that does considerable—and sometimes irreparable—harm to the colonized. Whenever the Old Testament is pressed into the service of selfish agendas, that benefit one group of people while hurting another, it is surely being used in ways God never intended.

Supporting Slavery

It is well documented that slavery in America was justified—and also contested—on biblical grounds.[23] The Old Testament, in particular, provided the necessary rationale for legitimating the practice of slavery.[24] A key text used by proslavery apologists was Gen. 9:20-27. This passage, which comes on the heels of the flood narrative, contains a rather unflattering story of Noah and his youngest son, Ham. As the story goes, Noah gets drunk, takes off his clothes, and sleeps naked in his tent. When Ham sees his father in this state, he immediately tells his two brothers. They enter the tent walking backward, so as not to see Noah's nakedness, and cover their father with a piece of clothing. When Noah wakes up and realizes what Ham has done, he curses Ham's son, Canaan, saying, "Cursed be Canaan; lowest of slaves shall he be to his brothers" (Gen. 9:25).[25]

Stephen Haynes devotes considerable attention to this passage in his book *Noah's Curse: The Biblical Justification of American Slavery*.[26] While proslavery advocates interpreted this passage in various ways, all agreed this text clearly and undeniably justified the enslavement of Africans. As Haynes puts it: "For Southern proslavery intellectuals Ham's act of gazing on his father's nakedness and Noah's subsequent curse of the descendants of Ham and Canaan to be 'servants of servants' were held to be definitive proof that the enslavement of black Africans was God's will."[27] Genesis 9 was repeatedly used in proslavery arguments to make this very point.

Another oft-cited text was Lev. 25:44-46. James Evans claims this passage was "quoted in almost every proslavery defense and almost never refuted in the abolitionist response."[28] It was particularly useful to the proslavery cause because it spoke of taking *non-Hebrew* slaves "from the nations around you" that could be kept in perpetuity. This was unlike the law stipulating that *Hebrew* slaves had to be released periodically (Exod. 21:2). This distinction was very convenient for Southern slaveholders who had no interest in releasing their slaves who were, like the slaves referred to in Leveticus 25, from other nations.

Old Testament passages like these were frequently used to justify the institution of slavery in the antebellum South. They provided a religious rationale for owning slaves and were instrumental in rendering this oppressive practice as something that was not just acceptable but divinely ordained. Using the Old Testament for such devastating and inhumane purposes constitutes a truly troubling legacy indeed.

Encouraging Violence against Women

Many Old Testament texts have contributed to the abuse, degradation, and harm of women for centuries. Some of these texts portray women negatively, while others justify various forms of violence against them. Describing the problematic nature of these texts in the Old Testament, Kathleen O'Connor writes:

> The texts encourage violence toward women. . . . Some biblical texts actually command the subordination of women, convey hatred of women (misogyny), or put God in the role as the abuser of women. Some texts appear to support and condone physical abuse of women and wives, and in some prophetic texts, God participates in and authorizes it (cf. Jer. 13:22-27). Such texts have been used to condone domestic violence against women and children similarly to the way biblical texts were once used to support slavery.[29]

Clearly, this represents a significant problem.

In the West, the Old Testament has profoundly shaped attitudes toward women, and more often than not, the Old Testament's influence in this regard has not been good. Genesis 3 has been one of the most harmful texts in this regard. In fact, according to Pamela Milne: "No biblical story has had a more profound negative impact on women throughout history than the story of Eve."[30] Similarly, Alice Ogden Bellis contends that this story, "more than any other, has been used as a theological base for sexism."[31] To cite just one historical example of the lethal effects this text (along with others) has had, consider the witch hunts that caused so much harm to women. Milne writes:

> A work entitled *Malleus Maleficarum* (*Hammer against Witches*), written by two Dominican priests, Heinrich Kraemer and Jakob Sprenger, published in 1486 for use during the Inquisition, uses Genesis 3 among other biblical texts to depict women as evil, feebleminded and lustful. This work provided the

principle [*sic*] theological justification for the persecution of women as witches. In the years following publication, thousands of women were accused of, and executed for, practicing witchcraft.[32]

Yet, lest we think such problems are a thing of the past, Milne reminds us that "it is still not at all uncommon to find the bible [*sic*] being used to promote the notion that women are, by divine design, secondary and inferior to men."[33] This is exceedingly dangerous! Using the Bible to suggest that women are "secondary and inferior" paves the way for all sorts of religiously sanctioned violence and oppression.

Later, I will have much more to say about various kinds of difficulties the Old Testament creates for women. Suffice it to say for now that the patriarchal nature of the Old Testament constitutes an enormous problem for women, one with a long, ugly history that continues to manifest itself in many unseemly ways even today.

Harming Children

The Old Testament does not typically exhibit a very high regard for the well-being of children, nor should we expect it to given the cultural context in which it was produced. In the ancient world, children were treated as second-class citizens with no legal rights. They were extremely vulnerable and completely dependent on the care, protection, and provision of their parents, particularly their father. Children are often invisible casualties in Old Testament stories of war, natural disaster, and divine judgment.[34] Unfortunately, their voices and concerns are almost never heard in the pages of Scripture.

There are numerous Old Testament passages that actually sanction acts of violence against children. These include such things as legal materials prescribing capital punishment for rebellious children and for those who encourage people to worship other gods, and proverbs advising a severe beating as a form of godly discipline.[35] Texts like these are particularly dangerous for children since they can all too easily be used by adults to justify contemporary acts of violence against children.[36] The same is true of various Old Testament narratives. For example, Andreas Michel claims that Genesis 19, a passage describing an incestuous relationship between Lot and his two daughters, "has . . . been used as a religious legitimation by fathers who have abused their daughters."[37] The story of Abraham's near sacrifice of his son Isaac in Genesis 22 has also had negative repercussions for children.[38]

Those who advocate spanking children, which I would argue is a form of violence, frequently appeal to the Old Testament for support. In his popular parenting book, *Shepherding Your Child's Heart*, Tedd Tripp not only promotes spanking, he contends it is commanded by God. Using a handful of passages from the book of Proverbs (22:15; 23:14; 29:15), Tripp argues that "the rod" (spanking done by a parent) "must be used" since "God has mandated its use."[39] Therefore, parents who fail to use the rod are not only being disobedient to God, they are putting their children at great risk since the rod "drives foolishness from the heart of a child" and ultimately provides a means to "rescue" that child "from death."[40] Accordingly, the rod is seen as "a God-given remedy" to the "child's dangerous state."[41]

Tripp realizes there are various reasons parents might be hesitant to spank their children. He even admits his own reluctance to do so. Nevertheless, Tripp says he did so out of love *and* a conviction that God commanded it. He writes:

> I would have never spanked them had I not been persuaded by the Word of God that God called me to this task. It is not my personality. Margy and I were exposed to some teaching from the book of Proverbs that convinced us that spanking had a valid place in parenting. We became persuaded that failure to spank would be unfaithfulness to their souls.[42]

Tripp decided to deny his God-given parental intuition and to spank his children—even when he did not want to—because the Old Testament "told" him to. While some might find this laudable, it strikes me as extremely dangerous. When reading the Old Testament makes us more, rather than less, likely to hit our children, something is surely amiss.[43]

Condemning Gays and Lesbians

Another way the Bible has been used violently is to condemn those who experience same-sex attraction. The Old Testament, in particular, has frequently been read in ways that have been enormously harmful to gays and lesbians, and the church has often failed to respond compassionately to members of the LGBTQ (lesbian-gay-bisexual-transgender-queer/questioning) community. Historically, the church has done a poor job of extending hospitality and welcome to individuals who come out and are honest about their sexual orientation and/or feelings of same-sex attraction.[44] To make matters worse, Christians have blamed gays and lesbians for many societal ills and tragedies such as the AIDS epidemic, the attacks of 9/11, Hurricane Katrina, and the deaths of American servicemen and women. The Westboro Baptist Church in Kansas is particularly notorious in this regard and regularly pickets at military funerals with offensive placards. Their web address (godhatesfags.com) leaves no doubt about where they stand.

Homosexuality is clearly one of the most contentious and divisive issues in the church today.[45] Christians have very different views about people whose sexual orientation and behavior fall outside of the traditionally accepted norms privileging heterosexuals.[46] They also differ considerably over what the Bible "says" about homosexuality and how the Bible should be used to inform our sexual ethics.

Those who are convinced the Bible condemns same-sex behavior often appeal to the book of Leviticus to support their position. Two verses from the book of Leviticus (18:22 and 20:13) have been particularly harmful for gays and lesbians. These verses describe sexual intercourse between men as being "an abomination" punishable by death. Gary Comstock considers "the legacy of the Levitical prohibitions" in his sobering book *Violence against Lesbians and Gay Men*.[47] He cites a number of official declarations (one as early as 342 CE) that referred to Leviticus when prescribing either punishment or death for homosexuals. For example, some legislation in colonial America included "a word-for-word translation of Leviticus 20:13."[48] Comstock also provides a number of contemporary examples that demonstrate how "Leviticus has continued to be used to shape and justify social policy and practice toward lesbians and gay men" in ways that are decidedly unfavorable toward these individuals.[49]

In her recent book *Hate Thy Neighbor: How the Bible Is Misused to Condemn Homosexuality*, Linda Patterson discusses several prominent Christian leaders—Jerry Falwell, Pat Roberson, James Dobson, and Rick Warren—and two church bodies—the Catholic Church and the Southern Baptist Convention—who have spoken out against homosexuality publically, and sometimes in very ugly ways.[50] What surprised Patterson, "given the vitriolic and unwavering judgment of Christian leaders and churches regarding the supposed depravity of homosexuality," was the paucity of verses that even address the issue.[51] Very few biblical texts speak directly about same-sex behavior, and virtually all that do are found in the Old Testament.[52] Although there is considerable difference of opinion over what these verses mean for us today, that has not stopped some interpreters from making bold declarations about "what the Bible teaches" on this subject.[53]

Tragically, this handful of texts has encouraged and reinforced very unchristian attitudes toward women and men who experience same-sex attraction, especially when that attraction translates into behavior. These texts have often been used to devalue, demean, and demonize gays and lesbians and have encouraged bigotry, hatred, oppression, and exclusion. In the worst cases, they have even served as justification for acts of violence.[54] Whenever someone's reading of the Old Testament encourages attitudes and actions like these, it perpetuates the Old Testament's troubling legacy and does considerable harm.[55]

Distorting the Character of God

Finally, one of the Old Testament's most harmful legacies has been the negative impact it has had on people's view of God. Within the pages of the Old Testament, one meets a God who instantly annihilates individuals, massacres large numbers of people, and commands genocide. God frequently behaves violently in the Old Testament and many readers are troubled by it. The "God of the Old Testament" often seems to be an angry, vindictive deity determined to punish sinners and evildoers severely. Many Old Testament portrayals of God are unflattering, to say the least, and do not inspire worship. While many Christians revere the Bible and recognize its potential to draw people closer to God, Old Testament portrayals of God have sometimes had exactly the opposite effect.

David Plotz, a self-described agnostic Jew, spent about a year reading through the Hebrew Bible (Old Testament), something he had never done before. Along the way, he recorded his reflections and later published them in a book. In his concluding chapter, Plotz expresses deep reservations about the God of the Old Testament in no uncertain terms:

> After reading about the genocides, the plagues, the murders, the mass enslavements, the ruthless vengeance for minor sins (or no sin at all), and all that smiting—every bit of it directly performed, authorized, or approved by God—I can only conclude that the God of the Hebrew Bible, if He existed, was awful, cruel, and capricious. He gives us moments of beauty—sublime beauty and grace!—but taken as a whole, He is no God I want to obey, and no God I can love.[56]

Similar sentiments have been expressed by the new atheists.[57] They too emphasize how nasty and violent God appears in the Old Testament. They find "the Old Testament God" completely detestable and unworthy of anyone's devotion. Richard Dawkins minces no words when offering his perspective:

> The God of the Old Testament is arguably the most unpleasant character in all fiction: jealous and proud of it; a petty, unjust, unforgiving control-freak; a vindictive, bloodthirsty ethnic cleanser; a misogynistic, homophobic, racist, infanticidal, genocidal, filiacidal, pestilential, megalomaniacal, sadomasochistic, capriciously malevolent bully.[58]

Though Dawkins's characterization is obviously one-sided, it is impossible to deny that God engages in an enormous amount of violence in the Old Testament and is often portrayed in ways that are fundamentally at odds with how a good number of Christians think about God.[59]

Over the years, many Christians have been bothered by problematic portrayals of God and have struggled to reconcile God's more questionable actions in the Old Testament with more complimentary views found elsewhere in the Bible. In my previous book, *Disturbing Divine Behavior: Troubling Old Testament Images of God*, I discuss these problematic portrayals and offer a way to deal responsibly with them.[60] Taken at face value, these portrayals can hinder efforts to understand what God is really like. When certain passages make God appear violent, vengeful, and vindictive, thus obscuring God's grace and goodness, they can distort our view of God and lead us to think of God in ways that are, quite frankly, unworthy of God. This creates serious theological problems for people who try to use the Bible to understand God's character. For some Christians, these problems become so overwhelming that they precipitate a faith crisis or, in the most serious cases, a loss of faith altogether. This is also part of the Old Testament's troubling legacy.

While other troubling legacies could be discussed—such as the way the Old Testament has been used to defend capital punishment and to encourage racism[61]—the examples we have considered are sufficient to illustrate the nature of the problem at hand.[62] It is deeply troubling to see how often the Old Testament has been used to harm others and, in the most egregious cases, to kill them. As a Christian, I am horrified by the way these sacred texts have been wielded against women, gays and lesbians, ethnic minorities, children, people of other faiths, indigenous populations, and many, many others. When people commit atrocities in the name of God and find justification for their behavior in the Old Testament, we have a serious problem on our hands.

Text or Reader: Who Is to Blame?

When we see people using the Old Testament to justify their violent behavior, we are naturally inclined to accuse them of misinterpreting the Bible—and sometimes they are. For example, those who use the story of Israel's conquest of Canaan to justify killing and colonizing people are obviously misusing the Bible in the worst sort of way. Likewise, anyone who adopts the Old Testament's patriarchal preferences as a guide for gender relations today fundamentally misunderstands how to read and apply these texts responsibly. But should the blame for interpretive misadventures like these be laid solely at the feet of interpreters? When people read and interpret the Bible violently, is the fault theirs alone? Are they guilty of twisting Scripture, of making it say something it was never intended to say? Have they used the Bible against its will? *Or, is the Bible itself partly to blame?*

Some would say, "Absolutely not!" They would insist there is nothing "wrong" with the Bible. As they see it, the texts are not at fault, only the people who misuse them. To paraphrase that well-worn saying about guns and violence, they might insist, "Texts don't kill people—people kill people!" While I understand this impulse to defend the Bible and exonerate it from charges of wrongdoing, I do not believe the Bible is free from blame. As Terence Fretheim so helpfully puts it:

> One of the first things the church ought to admit . . . is the long history of negative effects many biblical texts about God have had on our life together. With all the emphasis these days on what a text *does* to the reader, we should be absolutely clear: among the things the Bible has *done* is to contribute to the oppression of women, the abuse of children, the rape of the environment, and

the glorification of war. . . . Simply to assume that everything the Bible does is good or is good for you serves neither Bible nor church well.

One might claim that the problem is due to the distorted readings of sinful interpreters and not to the texts themselves, and that is often the case, but the texts cannot be freed from complicity in these matters. The texts *themselves* fail us at times, perhaps even often. The patriarchal bias *is* pervasive; God *is* represented as abuser and a killer of children; God *is* said to command the rape of women and the wholesale destruction of cities, including children and animals. To shrink from making such statements is dishonest. To pretend that such texts are not there, or to try to rationalize our way out of them (as I have sometimes done), is to bury our heads in the sand.[63]

Fretheim is right to emphasize the "complicity" of the Bible in "the long history of negative effects" these texts have had upon us. The texts themselves *are* problematic.[64] They sometimes "fail us." To admit this is not to disparage the Bible or to deny its power and authority. Rather, it is to recognize that for all the truth the Bible contains, it is not always a perfect guide when it comes to matters of ethics, morality, and theology.[65]

In the following two chapters, we will need to consider more carefully *which* texts are problematic and just *how* they fail us. Beyond that, we will need to give attention to how to read the Bible in ways that are ethically, morally, and theologically sound. For now, suffice it to say that the problem is much bigger than just a matter of interpretation.[66] The Old Testament *itself* is part of the problem. Therefore, it is vitally important to pay attention to *how* we read. By reading nonviolently, in ways that expose and critique violent ideologies embedded in the Old Testament, we refuse to endorse the violence of these texts and reject all attempts to use such texts to harm or oppress others. As we will see, this represents an important step in overcoming the Old Testament's troubling legacy.

CHAPTER 3

The Pervasive Presence of "Virtuous" Violence in the Old Testament

There exists within the Bible a degree of violence and praise of violence that is surpassed by no other ancient book.

—Michael Prior[1]

Violence appears early and often in the Old Testament. Stories of killing and kidnapping, rape and murder, war and genocide line its pages. Virtually every book of the Old Testament contains some mention of violence, and violence features very prominently in several of them. It is an integral part of many of the most well-known and beloved Bible stories: Noah and the ark, Joshua and the Battle of Jericho, David and Goliath, Daniel and the lions' den—to name just a few!

In his book *The Blood of Abel*, Mark McEntire contends that "the plot of the Hebrew Bible pivots on acts of violence," something he believes "illustrates that violence is a central, if not the central, issue for the entire text."[2] Whether it is a battle report, a story describing an individual's violent behavior, or a prophetic speech pronouncing impending divine judgment, violent words, themes, and images run throughout much of the Old Testament.

According to Raymund Schwager, "over *six hundred* passages" in the Old Testament "explicitly talk about nations, kings, or individuals attacking, destroying, and killing others."[3] He claims that "no other human activity or experience is mentioned as often."[4] In Schwager's estimation, the prevalence of human violence is eclipsed only by references to divine violence in the Old Testament.

The theme of God's bloody vengeance occurs in the Old Testament even more frequently than the problem of human violence. Approximately *one thousand passages* speak of Yahweh's blazing anger, of his punishments by death and destruction, and how like a consuming fire he passes judgment, takes revenge, and threatens annihilation. . . . No other topic is as often mentioned as God's bloody works.[5]

Although one does not find blood dripping from every page, the pervasiveness of violence in the Old Testament is undeniable. In the words of Athalya Brenner: "The legacy of violence . . . permeates the whole of the Hebrew Bible."[6]

The Old Testament's Appraisal of Violence

At the risk of grossly oversimplifying the complex representation of violence in the Old Testament, and with full acknowledgment that language is ambiguous, texts are indeterminate, and authorial intent is often difficult to discern, I want to suggest that the vast amount of violence in the Old Testament is portrayed in one of two ways: positively or negatively. I will refer to violence that is portrayed positively and approved of in some way as "virtuous" violence.[7] This violence is portrayed as being appropriate, justified, and perhaps even praiseworthy. It is sanctioned and sometimes celebrated in the text. Those who engage in acts of "virtuous" violence enjoy God's blessing and are understood to be acting in ways that are congruent with God's intentions. "Wrongful" violence, on the other hand, is violence that is portrayed negatively and disapproved of in the text. Wrongful violence includes violent acts the text portrays as being inappropriate, unjustified, and condemnable. It is unsanctioned and unacceptable, and those who engage in such behavior do so without divine approval.

A cursory look at violent texts in the Old Testament reveals that the difference between wrongful and "virtuous" violence is not simply based on the *kind* of violence being done. For example, while taking another person's life is sometimes strongly condemned, as in the case of Cain killing Abel (Genesis 4), other times it is highly praised, as we see when Jael kills Sisera (Judges 4–5). Similarly, while Israel's participation in war is often regarded as an act of faithful obedience (Josh. 11:21-23; 2 Sam. 5:25), this is not always the case (Num. 14:36-45). Thus, what renders an act of violence as good or bad in the Old Testament often has less to do with the kind of violence involved and more to do with who does it, to whom, and why.

Obviously, some violent Old Testament texts do not fall neatly into one category or the other. In these instances, it becomes difficult, if not impossible, to determine how ancient readers were expected to view the violence in question. Still, the fact remains that a considerable amount of violence in the Old Testament is portrayed as either good or bad, right or wrong, acceptable or unacceptable.

This chapter will focus primarily on various examples of "virtuous" violence in the Old Testament. These texts, which commend, condone, and celebrate acts of violence, have frequently been used to harm others and thus bear much responsibility for the Old Testament's troubling legacy. In what follows, we will differentiate more carefully between wrongful violence and "virtuous" violence, look at some representative passages in which violence is portrayed positively, and consider why "virtuous" violence is so pervasive throughout the Old Testament.

Wrongful Violence

Two of the most well-known stories of wrongful violence in the Old Testament are the story of Cain and Abel and the story of David and Bathsheba. According to Genesis 4, Cain and his brother Abel bring an offering to the Lord corresponding to their respective livelihoods. Cain, the farmer, brings some fruit; Abel, the herdsman, brings a lamb. For reasons not entirely clear, God accepts Abel's offering but not Cain's, and Cain becomes "very angry."[8] God then confronts Cain and cautions him, saying, "Sin is lurking at the door; its desire is for you, but you must master it" (Gen. 4:7b). Cain fails to heed the warning and kills his brother Abel when they are out in a field. Once Abel is dead, God's displeasure is clearly evident. God curses Cain and informs him of what is to come: "When you till the ground, it will no longer yield to you its strength; you will be a fugitive and a wanderer on the earth" (Gen. 4:12). In this way, Cain's violent behavior is clearly condemned, and he is punished for it. There can be little doubt that readers are to regard Cain's murder of Abel as an act of unsanctioned, or wrongful, violence.

The same kind of conclusion is easy to draw with regard to David's dishonorable—and deadly—dealings with Uriah in 2 Samuel 11. After David commits adultery with Uriah's wife, Bathsheba, and tries, but fails, to cover his tracks, he issues a lethal executive order that amounts to murder-by-proxy. David commands Joab to put Uriah in a vulnerable position in battle to ensure he will be killed, and this is precisely what happens (2 Sam. 11:15). At the end of this sordid story, we read the following narrative comment: "But the thing that David had done displeased the LORD" (2 Sam. 12:1). This perspective is confirmed by the prophet Nathan, who confronts the wayward king and asks, "Why have you despised the word of the LORD, to do what is evil in his sight?" (2 Sam. 12:9a). God's severe displeasure over David's dastardly deeds is unmistakable in the text. David has surely done wrong.[9]

In addition to numerous Old Testament narratives like these that clearly condemn certain acts of violence, other texts speak more generally about God's disapproving attitude toward violence. God is described as one who "hates the lover of violence" (Ps. 11:5) and the "hands that shed innocent blood" (Prov. 6:17).[10]

Numerous prophetic texts also condemn violence. Judah's violence raises God's ire (Ezek. 8:17), and Jeremiah tells the people not to do violence to the alien, orphan, and widow (Jer. 22:3). Various prophets proclaim that foreign nations who are violent toward Israel can expect very harsh consequences in return (Joel 3:19; Obed. 1:10; Hab. 2:8). In these instances, and others, certain acts of violence are clearly portrayed as sinful and wrong.

Whenever the Old Testament condemns acts of violence, most readers readily agree. After all, who wants to come to Cain's defense and argue that killing his brother was virtuous? Or who—except perhaps Machiavelli—would judge David's plan to eliminate Uriah as the right course of action? We naturally—almost instinctively—recognize these violent acts as immoral and have no difficulty embracing the text's negative evaluation of such behavior. The wrongness of these acts is so obvious that, in many cases, we quickly and easily align our perspective with the text's.

If violence was *always* regarded as an undesirable activity in the Old Testament, and if violent acts were *always* condemned in the text, the Old Testament's legacy would be very different indeed! But the unfortunate reality is that the Old Testament does *not* always censure violent acts or violent individuals. On the contrary, the Old Testament often sanctions and blesses them. Through the years, these violence-friendly texts have exerted considerable influence over the way Christians—and others—have thought about the morality of violence.

"Virtuous" Violence

As we will see momentarily, the notion of "virtuous" violence is conveyed in many ways throughout the Old Testament. But before looking at a number of Old Testament passages that portray violence positively, I want to say a brief word about the use of the word *virtuous* to describe this kind of violence. I realize that using this designation carries some risk since it might give the impression that I actually regard some of the Old Testament's violence as "virtuous." That is *not* the case. I am only using this designation descriptively, to identify violent acts and attitudes that find approval within the pages of the Old Testament. I am *not* using it to indicate my agreement with the text's positive assessment of violence in any of these instances. To keep this important distinction in mind, I will consistently place the word *virtuous* in quotation marks when referring to "virtuous" violence.

A Hammer and a Slingshot: Celebrating Two Killers

To begin, I want to focus on two narratives that contain obvious examples of "virtuous" violence. In both passages, one person kills another, and in both passages, this violent act is regarded as praiseworthy. The first story, found in Judges 4–5, involves a conflict between Israelites and Canaanites. Having been oppressed by the Canaanites for twenty long years, the Israelites cry out to God and are assured that help will come, though not through conventional means. Accompanied by the Israelite prophetess Deborah, Barak goes to battle against the Canaanite commander Sisera.

The battle is a complete disaster for the Canaanites under Sisera's command, and Sisera makes his escape by abandoning his chariot and running away from the battlefield (Judg. 4:12-16). He takes refuge in the tent of a Kenite woman named Jael, presumably assuming this would be a safe place to hide given the friendly relations that existed between Canaanites and Kenites. Before the exhausted commander falls asleep, he instructs Jael to stand guard at the entrance of her tent and to tell anyone who might ask that nobody is inside. But Jael has other ideas.

> Jael wife of Heber took a tent peg, and took a hammer in her hand, and went softly to him and drove the peg into his temple, until it went down into the ground—he was lying fast asleep from weariness—and he died. Then, as Barak came in pursuit of Sisera, Jael went out to meet him, and said to him, "Come, and I will show you the man whom you are seeking." So he went into her tent; and there was Sisera lying dead, with the tent peg in his temple. (Judg. 4:21-22)

Of special interest for our purposes is the praise heaped upon Jael for her bold and bloody deed. In a song of victory, Deborah and Barak exclaim:

> Most blessed of women be Jael, the wife of Heber the Kenite, of tent-dwelling women most blessed. . . . She put her hand to the tent peg and her right hand to the workmen's mallet; she struck Sisera a blow, she crushed his head, she shattered and pierced his temple. He sank, he fell, he lay still at her feet . . . where he sank, there he fell dead. (Judg. 5:24-27)

Jael's actions, violent and treacherous though they be, are considered worthy of celebration. The text exhibits no hint of disapproval with her behavior. Rather, Jael receives nothing but unqualified praise and admiration for slaying Sisera. As the text portrays it, her act of violence is "virtuous."

The second story, that of David and Goliath, is one of the most well-known in the entire Old Testament (1 Samuel 17). This story is a study in contrasts. David, a young shepherd boy who is not even part of the Israelite army, plans to fight Goliath, a seasoned Philistine warrior who is armed to the teeth. In fact, when David first proposes fighting Goliath, King Saul discourages him by saying, "You are not able to go against this Philistine to fight with him; for you are just a boy, and he has been a warrior from his youth" (1 Sam. 17:33). David is not deterred. He confronts this mocking Philistine and declares:

You come to me with sword and spear and javelin; but I come to you in the name of the Lord of hosts, the God of the armies of Israel, whom you have defied. This very day the Lord will deliver you into my hand, and I will strike you down and cut off your head; and I will give the dead bodies of the Philistine army this very day to the birds of the air and to the wild animals of the earth, so that all the earth may know that there is a God in Israel, and that all this assembly may know that the Lord does not save by sword and spear; for the battle is the Lord's and he will give you into our hand. (1 Sam. 17:45-47)

Then, with sling in hand, David lodges a stone in Goliath's forehead, causing him to fall down. David then quickly takes Goliath's sword, cuts off the Philistine's head, and carries it to Jerusalem.

The literary context of this story suggests we are to view David's actions as being pleasing to, and empowered by, God.[11] Prior to his encounter with Goliath, David had been anointed by the prophet Samuel at which point we are told "the spirit of the Lord came mightily upon David from that day forward" (1 Sam. 16:13). Then, when David confronts Goliath, he claims that God will give him the victory when he boldly declares: "This very day the Lord will deliver you into my hand" (1 Sam. 17:46). The text suggests God stands behind David's victory over Goliath, and most readers tend to agree. Most people believe God wanted David to kill Goliath and enabled him to do so, and most interpreters describe David's actions as admirable, indicating no discomfort with his behavior.[12] By doing so, they reinforce a key ideological assumption undergirding this captivating story, namely, that violence can be "virtuous."

These two stories of "virtuous" violence raise a lot of important questions. Should we applaud Jael's use of deception and lethal violence to eliminate an enemy of Israel? Should we commend her for her death-dealing blows? Should we agree that killing a Canaanite commander makes her "most blessed of women"?[13] Likewise, should we praise David for killing Goliath? Is David's violent victory over this Philistine the kind of act we should celebrate? Does it make David a heroic figure, worthy of our admiration and respect, or does it make him a murderer with bloodstained hands?

More generally, these stories cause us to reflect on the impact violent texts have on modern readers. What do texts like these do to us when we read them? How do they influence our views about violence? How do they shape our attitudes about others? These are very important questions, and we will return to them later.

Divine Involvement in "Virtuous" Violence

Many Old Testament narratives, prophetic texts, and laws contain examples of "virtuous" violence that are directly related to God's activity. In these instances, we can distinguish between violence God *commits* and violence God *commands*. Whenever God is portrayed as the sole agent (or essentially the sole agent) of a violent act, we can refer to that as an act of divine violence. Whenever *people* commit acts of violence God has ostensibly authorized, we can describe that as divinely sanctioned violence. Obviously, some violent acts in the Old Testament involve *both* divine violence and divinely sanctioned violence. In the conquest of Canaan, for example, divinely sanctioned violence (God commands Israel to exterminate all Canaanites) goes hand in hand with acts of divine violence (God fights with Israel by knocking over walls and hurling down hailstones from heaven). Since God's involvement in acts of "virtuous" violence are so pervasive throughout the Old Testament, it is worth considering a number of examples of both divine violence and divinely sanctioned violence to further illustrate how Old Testament writers sanctioned various acts of violence.

DIVINE VIOLENCE

Some of the most dramatic examples of "virtuous" violence in the Old Testament are those in which God kills countless numbers of people in overwhelming acts of divine violence. A few of the most notorious examples include the flood narrative, in which God depopulates the planet (Gen. 6:9—8:22); the destruction of Sodom and Gomorrah, in which God kills virtually every inhabitant (Gen. 19:12–26); and the devastation of Egypt, in which God destroys plants and animals, kills every first-born Egyptian, and drowns the Egyptian army (Exod. 7:14—12:32; 14:26-31). In various ways, each of these narratives suggests that God's actions were fully justified ("the earth was filled with violence," the inhabitants of Sodom and Gomorrah were terribly wicked, and the Egyptians had enslaved and oppressed the Hebrew people).

In some cases, God's violent behavior is explicitly praised. For example, after God drowns the Egyptian army in the Red Sea, the Israelites—who are safe on the other side—see the bodies of dead Egyptian soldiers washing up on shore (Exod. 14:30). They respond by singing a song of praise to God for this unprecedented act of divine violence.

> Then Moses and the Israelites sang this song to the LORD: "I will sing to the LORD, for he has triumphed gloriously; horse and rider he has thrown into the sea. Your right hand, O LORD, glorious in power—your right hand, O LORD, shattered the enemy. In the greatness of your majesty you overthrew your adversaries." (Exod. 15:1, 6-7a cf. vv. 19-21)

The writer displays no uneasiness with this overwhelming act of divine violence and regards God's behavior as completely praiseworthy.[14] It constitutes an example of "virtuous" violence that is hard to miss. But is it really appropriate to rejoice over the death of one's enemies? Is mass murder ever cause for celebration?

Of course, God's violence in the Old Testament is not limited to mass killing and large-scale slaughter. Sometimes God is portrayed as being directly responsible for the death of a particular "sinner." Such acts of divine violence include the execution of Er and Onan (Gen. 38:7-10), the incineration of Nadab and Abihu (Lev. 10:1-2), the smiting of Nabal (1 Sam. 25:38), and the elimination of Uzzah (2 Sam. 6:6-7). Regardless of whether God's behavior is explicitly justified in the text, most readers regard such divine violence as "virtuous" simply because God is the one doing it.

DIVINELY SANCTIONED VIOLENCE

In addition to numerous passages containing divine violence, many others contain examples of divinely sanctioned violence. Some of this violence is prescriptive in nature, such as the roughly forty Old Testament laws that stipulate death for various offenses: kidnapping (Exod. 21:16), cursing a parent (Exod. 21:17), working on the Sabbath (Exod. 31:15), adultery (Lev. 20:10), bestiality (Lev. 20:15), sorcery (Lev. 20:27), blasphemy (Lev. 24:16a), and murder (Lev. 24:17), among other things. Since all these laws were purportedly given by God, killing offenders would be considered divinely sanctioned in these cases and, therefore, "virtuous."

Many other examples of divinely sanctioned violence in the Old Testament involve the practice of war. Whenever God commands Israel to fight, readers are expected to regard Israel's warfare as "virtuous" because God willed it. Likewise, whenever the text claims God gave Israel victory in battle, readers are expected to agree that the Israelites fought and killed their enemies with God's blessing and approval.[15] Many divinely sanctioned wars, such as Israel's war against the Midianites (Num. 31:2) and later against the Amalekites (1 Sam. 15:2), are described as divine judgment upon foreign nations for their transgressions.[16] Other wars, like many of those in the Book of Judges, were ostensibly sanctioned by God in order to liberate Israel from their oppressors. God appointed "judges"—military deliverers like Othniel, Ehud, Barak, Gideon, and Jephthah—to lead the people of Israel in battle and free them from oppression.[17] In all these examples, warfare and killing receives divine approval in the text.

The most extreme form of divinely sanctioned warfare in the Old Testament called for the utter annihilation of a particular group of people. The conquest of Canaan is the most notorious example. According to the book of Deuteronomy, God commanded the Israelites to annihilate the Canaanites, leaving no survivors. Consider these chilling instructions given to the Israelites just prior to entering Canaan:

> When the LORD your God brings you into the land that you are about to enter and occupy, and he clears away many nations before you . . . then you must utterly destroy them. Make no covenant with them and show them no mercy. (Deut. 7:1-2)

As for the towns of these peoples that the LORD your God is giving you as an inheritance, you must not let anything that breathes remain alive. You shall annihilate them . . . just as the LORD your God has commanded. (Deut. 20:16-17)

Every Canaanite—from the oldest to the youngest—was to be killed. As the text portrays it, Israel's indiscriminate slaughter of Canaanite men, women, and children represented "virtuous" acts of obedience to God (see also Josh. 11:16-23).

Portraying acts of genocide as "virtuous" should be particularly disturbing to modern readers, especially in the wake of more recent atrocities like the Shoah (Holocaust), the Rwandan genocide, and the genocide in Darfur. As we have seen, Old Testament texts portraying divinely sanctioned genocide have had a nasty after-life and have been used to sanction an enormous amount of violence and killing. We will need to revisit these texts later to consider how we might avoid perpetuating their violent legacy.[18]

The Old Testament also contains numerous examples of divinely sanctioned violence against Israelites who worshiped "other gods." One particularly memorable story appears in Numbers 25 when the people of Israel are camped on the plains of Moab, just prior to entering the land of Canaan. When some Israelites begin having sex with Moabite women and worshiping their gods (Num. 25:2), the divine response is swift and severe:

The LORD said to Moses, "Take all the chiefs of the people, and impale them in the sun before the LORD, in order that the fierce anger of the LORD may turn away from Israel." And Moses said to the judges of Israel, "Each of you shall kill any of your people who have yoked themselves to the Baal of Peor." (Num. 25:4-5)

As soon as Moses finishes speaking, an Israelite man named Zimri brings a Midianite woman named Cozbi "into his family" and does so "in the sight of Moses and in the sight of the whole congregation of the Israelites" (Num. 25:6). This prompts Phinehas, Aaron's grandson, to leap into action. With spear in hand, he follows them into a tent and thrusts the spear "through the belly" of both of them (Num. 25:8). This violent act not only stops a plague—one that had already claimed twenty-four thousand lives (Num. 25:8-9)—it elicits a very positive reaction from God, who says to Moses:

Phinehas . . . has turned back my wrath from the Israelites by manifesting such zeal among them on my behalf that in my jealousy I did not consume the Israelites. Therefore say, "I hereby grant him my covenant of peace. It shall be for him and for his descendants after him a covenant of perpetual priesthood, because he was zealous for his God, and made atonement for the Israelites." (Num. 25:11-13)

According to this text, God is so pleased by Phinehas's decisive act of violence that God decides to reward Phinehas for it!

Another example of divinely sanctioned violence related to the worship of other gods is found in 2 Kings 10. This chapter describes certain events that took place during the reign of Jehu, an Israelite king who ruled during the latter part of the ninth century BCE. After annihilating the entire dynasty of Ahab in a series of massacres (2 Kgs. 10:1-17), Jehu invites all the worshipers of Baal to come to a "great sacrifice" (2 Kgs. 10:19). But they are invited under false pretenses. Little did they know they were the ones to be sacrificed!

> Jehu sent word throughout all Israel; all the worshipers of Baal came, so that there was no one left who did not come. They entered the temple of Baal, until the temple of Baal was filled from wall to wall. . . . As soon as he had finished presenting the burnt offering, Jehu said to the guards and to the officers, "Come in and kill them; let no one escape." So they put them to the sword. (2 Kgs. 10:21, 25a)

The narrator clearly approves of Jehu's purge. This is indicated by the summary statement following this episode which reads: "Thus Jehu wiped out Baal from Israel" (2 Kgs. 10:28). This positive evaluation is contrasted to Jehu's failings in other matters in the following verse (2 Kgs. 10:29). The narrator's perspective appears to be in line with God's since the text seems to suggest God also approved of this massacre.[19]

> The LORD said to Jehu, "Because you have done well in carrying out what I consider right, and in accordance with all that was in my heart have dealt with the house of Ahab, your sons of the fourth generation shall sit on the throne of Israel." (2 Kgs. 10:30)

God commends Jehu for killing Baal worshipers—and Ahab's family—in a chapter replete with "virtuous" violence.

In addition to narratives like these, there are legal materials providing divine sanction for killing Israelites who tried to persuade fellow Israelites to worship other gods. Prophets and diviners who tried to lead others astray in this way were to be "put to death" (Deut. 13:5), as were family members or close friends. In fact, if family or friends tried to lead you astray, you were instructed to execute them yourself!

> Show them no pity or compassion. . . . You shall surely kill them; your own hand shall be first against them to execute them, and afterwards the hand of all the people. Stone them to death for trying to turn you away from the LORD your God (Deut. 13:8b-10a).

Deuteronomy 13 also speaks of "scoundrels" who might lead an entire town astray, in which case Israelites were instructed to "put the inhabitants of that town to the sword, utterly destroying it and everything in it—even putting its livestock to the sword" (Deut. 13:15). Encouraging Israelites to worship other gods was very dangerous business! Doing so could get you killed since God commanded it.[20]

While many Christians probably resonate with biblical texts stressing the importance of exclusive devotion to God, the idea of killing those who worship a different God—or who try to persuade others to do so—is problematic, to say the least. Even though most Christians do not regard these texts as mandating them to kill their Muslim, Hindu, or Buddhist neighbors, such texts can easily encourage attitudes of suspicion and distrust. They invite us to regard those who worship other gods as dangerous people to be avoided at all costs. In this way, such texts have the potential to foster a climate of hostility rather than hospitality toward those whose religious convictions differ from our own. In a world that is already riddled with too many accounts of religiously motivated violence, texts like these need to be handled very carefully.

Structural Violence as "Virtuous" Violence

So far, the examples of "virtuous" violence we have considered involve sanctioned killing of one kind or another. The reader is expected to agree that the death of this person or that group was necessary and right. But the notion of "virtuous" violence in the Old Testament is much broader than this. It is not confined to specific acts of lethal violence. If that were the case, our task would be somewhat more manageable. We could simply identify and isolate all the offending texts. In reality, things are far more complex.

Earlier, I defined "virtuous" violence as violence that is regarded as appropriate, justified, and sometimes even praiseworthy. Some of the most basic structures and practices of ancient Israelite society would fall under this definition since they were inherently violent yet regarded as completely acceptable. Slavery and patriarchy are two noteworthy examples. It was considered normal for Israelites to own slaves and for men to dominate women in various ways. This was simply the "natural" order of things, the way things were. While some Old Testament texts contain legislation regulating the practice of slavery, for example, none directly challenges the morality of it. Slavery was simply a given in ancient Israel.

Likewise, Israelite society was thoroughly patriarchal, and this too was regarded as perfectly acceptable. Time and again, Old Testament texts endorse patriarchal perspectives that are, to a greater or lesser degree, inherently violent. Even though some of these texts do not describe physical acts of violence against women, they are violent just the same. In fact, some of the texts that have done the most harm to women, such as Genesis 3, are completely devoid of physical violence. Nevertheless, they convey and condone patriarchal perspectives that have had—and continue to have—oppressive effects on women around the world. This constitutes a huge problem for modern readers of the Bible, especially those who are concerned about the well-being of women. Later, we will devote considerable attention to the problem of patriarchy in the Old Testament and what can be done to address it.

The approval of slavery and patriarchy remind us that "virtuous" violence in the Old Testament is not just limited to the more tangible and obvious expressions of harm done to others. It can manifest itself in many ways. While some of these may be harder to see than others, they are no less problematic.

A Few Words about Ambiguity: Virtuous or Not?

As noted earlier, it is not always clear whether the violence portrayed in certain texts is being condoned or condemned, or whether it is being presented with any particular ethical evaluation at all. In these more ambiguous cases, it is difficult to know how ancient readers would have reacted to the textual violence they encountered. A classic example of this ambiguity is found in the story of Jephthah's daughter (Judges 11). Jephthah is one of several spirit-empowered "judges" God appointed to deliver Israel from foreign oppressors. Just before leaving to fight the Ammonites in an effort to reclaim "Israelite" territory, Jephthah makes a vow to the Lord:

> If you will give the Ammonites into my hand, then whoever comes out of the doors of my house to meet me, when I return victorious from the Ammonites, shall be the LORD's, to be offered up by me as a burnt offering. (Judg. 11:30-31)

Having uttered these words, Jephthah goes off to battle and soundly defeats the Ammonites (vv. 32-33). But tragically, upon his victorious return home, his daughter—and only child—is the one who comes out of the house to greet him (v. 34). Nevertheless, true to his vow, Jephthah sacrifices her as a burnt offering to the Lord (v. 39).[21]

There is no direct evaluation of Jephthah's violent act in the text, making it difficult to ascertain how readers were expected to regard his behavior. Does the writer envision this as an act of wrongful violence (Jephthah should have broken his stupid vow and spared his daughter)? Or did the writer consider this an example of "virtuous" violence (Jephthah was a righteous man, true to his vow even though it cost him—not to mention his daughter!—dearly)? Then again, perhaps the writer was being intentionally ambiguous. How is the reader to decide? Commentators differ, and readers are left wondering how to evaluate this truly horrifying act of violence. As John Thompson observes:

Judges 11 is filled with foolishness and tragedy: an honorable daughter is needlessly slain by her soldier father. What's worse, her father's death-dealing act seems to be related, somehow, to his anointing with the spirit of God. So, was her death divinely arranged? Maybe, but the text is not very clear. And, adding further to the cruel ambiguity, there is virtually nothing in the text of Judges 11 that says whether Jephthah was right or wrong—much less whether we should go and do likewise.[22]

In the absence of any specific condemnation of Jephthah's behavior, it is possible to regard the sacrifice of Jephthah's daughter as an example of "virtuous" violence, and this is precisely how some have interpreted it over the years. Since ambiguous texts such as Judges 11 can be read in this way, they have also contributed to the Old Testament's troubling legacy.

Judging Violence as "Virtuous" Because of Who Does It

What do modern readers do when they encounter texts, like the one just noted, that do not explicitly condone or condemn the violence they contain? How do they make a judgment one way or the other? While this obviously differs from reader to reader, a key factor in making that decision relates to the reader's view of who is doing the violence and who is receiving it.

Over time, people who grow up in church or synagogue become familiar with many of the foundational stories and key people in the Old Testament. In the process, they learn to differentiate between the "good guys (and gals)" and the "bad guys (and gals)." Individuals like Moses, Deborah, David, Solomon, and Esther are heralded as heroes and heroines and routinely placed in the good category. Others, including Lot, Delilah, Saul, Jezebel, and Manasseh, are seen as sinful and, in some cases, exceedingly wicked. They are categorized as "bad people." Readers often generalize in similar ways with regard to various nations. Israelites are good; Canaanites are bad, for example.

Obviously, this way of classifying people (and nations) in the Old Testament is overly simplistic. Most individuals are far more complex, and many of their stories can easily yield both positive and negative readings, depending on who reads the story and how. This is especially true of certain "high-profile" individuals in the Bible, such as Saul, David, and Solomon.

Still, the average reader tends to categorize many people in the Bible as basically "good" or "bad." Doing so invariably influences the reader's attitude toward the violence these individuals do and toward the violence done to them. For example, when "good" individuals engage in acts of violence against others, most readers give them the benefit of the doubt and assume that what they did was right *unless* their actions are explicitly condemned in the text. This is especially true when these "heroes of the faith" are involved in killing non-Israelites, people often portrayed as Israel's enemies and thus "deserving" of death.

To illustrate this, consider the way many readers think about David. In the eyes of many, David is one of the "good guys" of the Bible. David is highly revered, and many readers rank him right up there with the likes of Moses and Elijah. Therefore, whatever David does (with the obvious exception of his behavior in 2 Samuel 11) meets with approval by many readers. Yet, David is one of the most violent men in the entire Old Testament, directly responsible for tens of thousands of deaths. According to one estimate, David's "body count" in 1 and 2 Samuel is somewhere in the neighborhood of 140 thousand men.[23] While this total is obviously exaggerated, it undoubtedly reflects a very real reality: David was a very violent man.[24]

Still, most readers simply assume that David's violence is "virtuous" without really giving it a second thought. Why? Because it is David who does it! Many readers sincerely believe David was "a man after his [God's] own heart" (1 Sam. 13:14). Similarly, they resonate with the astonishing claim that "David did what was right in the sight of the LORD, and did not turn aside from anything that he [the LORD] commanded him all the days of his life, except in the matter of Uriah the Hittite" (1 Kgs. 15:5). Texts like these clearly put David on a pedestal, and many readers are reluctant to take him down. People's perceptions about David's "godly" character profoundly influence the way they evaluate his behavior.

In his New York Times bestseller *The Good Book*, Peter Gomes recounts a dramatic incident that illustrates just how resistant some people are to hearing any criticism of a figure like David. He writes:

> In a debate in the Israeli Parliament in December 1995, Foreign Minister Shimon Peres said that he disapproved of some of the practices of King David, particularly of his conquest of other peoples, and his seduction of a married woman, Bathsheba, whose husband, Uriah the Hittite, David sent to his death. . . . According to an account in *The New York Times* of December 15, 1995, outraged Orthodox rabbis screamed at the foreign minister to "shut up." Another shouted, "You will not give out grades to King David!" A third man flew into such a rage of apoplexy that he had to be treated for hypertension in the parliamentary infirmary, and a motion was introduced condemning the government for having besmirched the "sweet psalmist of Israel."[25]

Such reverence for David, a reverence that is felt just as keenly by many Christian readers as by Jewish ones, makes it exceedingly difficult for some readers to criticize his violent deeds. For that reason, they regard David's violence as "virtuous" and make similar assessments of the violence done by other Old Testament "heroes" and "heroines."

This same tendency to regard violence as "virtuous" applies to the way many people view Israel's struggle with other nations. In such cases, most readers tend to read *with* Israel and *against* others. Unless the text offers clear signals to the contrary, their default mode is to regard the Israelites as the "good guys" (since they are regarded as God's chosen people) and their opponents as the "bad guys." Although the Old Testament provides some sympathetic treatments of non-Israelites—Ruth, the Moabitess, for example—many of Israel's neighbors are routinely demonized. This creates certain alliances within readers who then side with the Israelites while adopting the text's negative perspective of Israel's neighbors. In this way, readers are conditioned to see Israel's violence against other nations as "virtuous" even when no explicit comment is made to that effect. This effectively compounds the amount of "virtuous" violence many people find in the Old Testament.

The Pervasiveness of "Virtuous" Violence

Although we have been able to consider only a handful of Old Testament passages containing "virtuous" violence in this chapter, these should suffice to illustrate the various kinds of texts under consideration here. One reason I devoted so much time to a discussion of "virtuous" violence was to emphasize just how pervasive it is in the Old Testament. Many people are unaware of how frequently it appears throughout the Old Testament. Even many Christians who have gone to church for years are not always cognizant of just how ubiquitous this kind of violence is in the Old Testament. There are various reasons for this. Many of the Old Testament's violent texts are unfamiliar to Christians. For some, it is due to the simple fact that they have never actually read the Old Testament.[26] While most Christians know some Old Testament stories and are familiar with certain key passages, many have never read all the way from Genesis to Malachi.[27]

Another reason many people are not aware of the pervasiveness of "virtuous" violence in the Old Testament is because the church often bypasses the Old Testament's more violent and difficult passages.[28] In church traditions that follow the Common Lectionary, for example, the vast majority of violent texts are never used in worship since they are excluded from the designated readings.[29] According to John Thompson: "The Revised Common Lectionary . . . bypasses with surgical precision not only . . . fragmentary imprecations in the Psalter, but also virtually every text that pertains to violence against women."[30] Likewise, Barbara Brown Taylor acknowledges that people "who preach from the lectionary have never been confronted with Moses' killing of the 3,000 in the wilderness (Exod. 32:25ff.) or Jephthah's murder of his daughter (Judg. 11:29ff.)" since these passages, and others like them, do not appear in the lectionary.[31] By ignoring these passages, the church (unwittingly?) presents a skewed picture of what the Bible actually contains, and this hinders people from realizing how pervasive violent texts are throughout the Old Testament.

Reinforcing the "Virtue" of "Virtuous" Violence

Obviously, not every violent text is avoided in the life of the church. A number of these texts are used with some regularity. But they are used very "judiciously," in ways that do not draw attention to their more violent and potentially troubling dimensions. One simple way to illustrate this is to consider how we typically refer to these stories. We use innocuous "titles" that gloss over the ugly realities of violence embedded in these texts. For example, we blandly speak about "Noah's Ark" or "Joshua and the Battle of Jericho." But these generic titles hide the grim reality of death and destruction that is part and parcel of these familiar stories.

It is interesting to ponder how our view of these stories might change if we—and the Bibles we read—provided more descriptive titles. What if we referred to Genesis 6–8 as the story of "God's Massacre," rather than the story of "Noah's Ark"? Or what might happen if we stopped speaking of Joshua 6 as the story of "Joshua and the Battle of Jericho" and more appropriately referred to it as the story of "Joshua and the Genocide at Jericho"?[32] At the very least, titles like these would get our attention! They would force us to recognize the violent aspects of these stories and would encourage us to consider their implications.

Still, in most religious contexts, Old Testament stories containing violence are used in ways that obscure, or at least minimize, the violent content they contain. In church and in various church-related publications, these stories are told in ways that tend to focus on the "positive," liberating aspects of the story without acknowledging those dimensions that are deadly, destructive, and therefore decidedly more negative.[33] This results in a very peculiar phenomenon, namely, talking about violent passages without ever talking about the violence they contain.

The church routinely engages in sanitized readings of violent texts, readings that emphasize deliverance and minimize death and destruction. When the story of Israel's exodus from Egypt is retold, for example, the focus tends to be on the Israelites' liberation from their Egyptian oppressors. That is true enough, as far the story goes, but it is only part of the story. The exodus is not just about Israel's deliverance; it is also about Egypt's destruction. According to the text, Israel's deliverance comes at an exceedingly high price: the decimation of Egypt (its waterways, crops, and animals), the death of every firstborn Egyptian, and the drowning of the Egyptian army. It is both a dramatic story of deliverance *and* a disturbing story of divine violence. The two are inseparable.

Still, we are seldom invited to reflect on the violent destruction of Egyptians or to consider their plight. We are not encouraged to feel sympathy for them, either by the text's portrayal or by the story's retelling. But why? Why focus on one part of the story and not the other? Why bypass the violent dimensions of these texts without even giving them a second thought? Shouldn't the catastrophic loss of life in the Exodus narrative trouble us deeply? Emphasizing only the "good parts" of this story—namely, Israel's deliverance from Egypt—without addressing the messy and very violent means used to accomplish this deliverance reinforces the "virtue" of "virtuous" violence. It perpetuates the belief that violence is sometimes not only necessary but completely acceptable. From my perspective, this kind of tacit approval of textual violence is extremely dangerous.

To cite one additional example of how people often engage in a sanitized reading of a very violent text, consider the flood narrative in Genesis. Most discussions of this narrative emphasize God's wonderful deliverance of Noah, his family, and the fortunate animals *inside* the ark without reflecting on the fate of those *outside* the ark, the countless men, women, and children—not to mention innumerable animals—who drowned. Because of this, most readers are trained to see the story in only one way, from only one particular perspective. They have been taught to read the story of Noah's ark (again, notice the innocuous title) from *inside* the ark, as a story about God's merciful preservation of Noah and his family. They have never been encouraged to read the story from *outside* the ark, as a story of death and destruction, where hordes of people desperately struggle to keep their heads above water to no avail. As a result, the story of the catastrophic flood in Genesis 6–8—a flood that annihilates virtually every living creature on the planet—is transformed into a cute and colorful story about Noah's boatload of happy animals. The violent parts of the story, though present, are not directly addressed.

Throughout this book, I will repeatedly emphasize how important it is to consider the view from *outside* the ark, so to speak. We need to see the faces of those being killed in these stories. We need to look deeply into their eyes as we listen to their stories and experience their pain and suffering. Until we have done that, our job is incomplete, and we have not really read the text, or at least not very well. Paying attention to the victims in these texts, and straining to hear their voices, raises serious questions about the "virtue" of "virtuous" violence. It encourages us to critique, rather than condone, acts of violence against others. But here I am getting ahead of myself. The present point is simply this: these stories are often read, retold, and reused in ways that mask their violence and make them seem less violent and less problematic than they really are.

In chapter 4, I will argue that the presence of "virtuous" violence in the Old Testament creates a number of serious problems for modern readers and contributes to the Old Testament's troubling legacy. These problems are compounded when the church engages in sanitized readings of violent texts. When the church behaves as though there is nothing concerning about these texts, when it condones violence it ought to condemn, readers are not well served. If we hope to overcome the Old Testament's troubling legacy, we need to be honest about the problematic nature of violent biblical texts, and we need to find ways to confront and critique various expressions of "virtuous" violence that we encounter there.

CHAPTER 4

The Danger of Reading the Bible

As we hand out Bibles and urge people to read them, it is imperative that we also say, caveat lector, *let the reader beware.*

—Eugene H. Peterson[1]

Because reading changes us in powerful ways, we need to attend carefully to the ways in which we read.

—Carolyn J. Sharp[2]

Take it slowly. This book is dangerous."[3] This warning appears inside the front cover of *Fox in Socks*, a children's book written by Dr. Seuss. Those who read this book are admonished to proceed with caution, not because the book contains "mature" subject matter or politically subversive ideas (it does not), but because reading its tongue-twisting rhymes requires considerable effort and patience. Reading too fast inevitably leads to jumbled words, missed phrases, and intense linguistic frustration.

Although the Bible is a far cry from the fanciful world of Dr. Seuss, I have often wondered if similar words of warning might be well placed just inside the cover of the Bible, albeit for different reasons. Many readers would benefit from heeding such words of caution when they open the Bible and begin to read. We should take it slowly because, whether we realize it or not, the Bible *is* a dangerous book. In fact, Mieke Bal claims that "the Bible, of all books, is the *most* dangerous one, the one that has been endowed with the power to kill."[4]

Admittedly, this is not how most Christians conceive of the Bible. While many would concede that parts of the Bible are difficult to understand, few would say the Bible itself is dangerous. On the contrary, many Christians revere the Bible and regard reading it to be extremely beneficial. In fact, it would not be an exaggeration to say that many Christians believe that reading the Bible is to our spiritual health what exercise and good diet are to our physical health.

Many churches promote Bible reading as an essential part of faithful Christian living. Pastors regularly exhort parishioners to "get into the Word" and to "listen to what God might be saying" to them through the Bible. This encouragement is given enthusiastically, without the slightest hesitation or equivocation. Since the Bible is believed to reveal God's character, God's plan of salvation, and God's will for humanity, reading it is seen as indispensable for Christian growth and maturity. Therefore, believers are not only expected to read it, they are expected to abide by it! Those who approach the Bible with these expectations quite naturally assume that reading it will be an edifying, enriching, and faith-enhancing experience. And quite often, that is precisely what it is. But not always.

The Bible has a dark side that is not often acknowledged by those who regard these texts as Scripture. Those who open the Bible in search of divine wisdom and truth may find themselves confounded by morally difficult passages that violate their own sense of right and wrong. They may encounter depictions of God that are deeply disturbing and fundamentally at odds with their own beliefs about God. They may even discover that some texts they had long assumed were life-giving and liberating are actually quite oppressive.

As we have seen, reading the Bible can have some rather nasty side effects. People have used the Bible to sanction all kinds of awful behavior. Time and again, the Bible has been used to justify injustice, oppression, and killing. Many individuals have suffered serious abuse and significant harm at the hands of "devout" Bible readers. But how can this be? How can the Bible—something so many people believe is profoundly good—sometimes be so terribly bad? Part of the answer has to do with the simple fact that reading the Bible influences us significantly, and it does so in ways that are not always beneficial.

In this chapter, we will consider what the Old Testament *does* to those who read it. More specifically, we will consider how the presence of so much "virtuous" violence in the Old Testament affects readers, often in rather troubling ways. Additionally, it is necessary to consider *how* people actually read the Old Testament. If we are to overcome the Old Testament's troubling legacy, we must pay careful attention to the way these texts are read and applied.

What Does the Bible Do To You?

For better or for worse, people who read the Bible are influenced by it, especially when they regard these texts as authoritative in some sense. The Bible profoundly shapes the way we think about a whole host of issues, not least of which are issues related to gender, power, and violence. Although much of this shaping takes place without realizing it, it happens all the same. As John Barton observes:

> The biblical text works in some way on what we might call the subconscious mind, helping to shape and train it. We should be concerned in this for just *how* the mind is shaped, for there is a variety of material in the Bible . . . and one could end up misshapen, I should think, by attending to the wrong parts of the material. We all know that one can be encouraged in various sorts of malevolence by concentrating on certain parts of the Old Testament to the exclusion of others. . . . Implacable vengeance is not the only teaching in the Old Testament, as people so often suppose; but it is there, and uncontrolled meditation on it could easily help to form a very unchristian character. So there are hazards.[5]

The fact that the Bible shapes our attitudes, assumptions, values, and views at the most fundamental levels, and that it does so very subtly and almost imperceptibly, would be no cause for concern if the Bible contained nothing but wholesome goodness and godly teachings. But, as Barton points out, there are "parts of the Old Testament" that can "easily help to form a very unchristian character. So there are hazards." Reader beware! You cannot—or at least should not—agree with everything you read in the Bible. Some things you find in the Bible are good for you; some are not. Therefore, we must be very careful about *how* we read.

When reading the Bible, it is important to remember that biblical texts are neither neutral nor innocent. Rather, these texts want us to see things from a certain perspective or point of view. In this respect, biblical texts share similarities with modern films. Just as a movie director carefully controls the viewer's gaze, allowing him or her to see only what the director desires, biblical texts attempt to focus the reader's attention on certain things while excluding others. Even though readers often see much more—or something altogether different—from what was originally intended (given the ambiguity of language and the multiple meanings texts are capable of generating), the fact remains that these texts do reflect certain perspectives.

Some of these perspectives simply reflected the writer's worldview and were not intended to be persuasive since it was taken for granted that these were shared assumptions. Other perspectives would not have been shared by all and, in these instances, the writer clearly wanted to convince readers to see things from a certain perspective, namely, the writer's! Writers had no interest in setting disparate points of view side by side, supplying a list of the strengths and weaknesses, and letting readers decide which view they found most compelling. Instead, they tried to convince people that their perspective was the right one.

Another way to put this is to say that biblical texts have ideologies.[6] Mikhail Bakhtin defines ideology as "a deeply held and interlocking set of religious, social, and political beliefs or attitudes about the world and how the world works."[7] In modern usage, the word *ideology* often has rather pejorative connotations. People frequently use the word to refer disparagingly to the beliefs and perspectives of those with whom they disagree. But ideologies are not inherently bad or wrong. In fact, they can be profoundly good and right. Still, as Julia O'Brien reminds us, "ideologies . . . are rarely if ever innocuous."[8] While some ideologies are quite beneficial and worth internalizing, others are not, hence the need for caution. Biblical texts should always be examined and evaluated, never blindly accepted or uncritically embraced. Otherwise, we may find ourselves being taken in by the Bible—seduced by Scripture, as it were—at times when we ought to be resisting. As David Clines warns: "Readers who are not wide awake to the designs that texts have on them (to speak anthropomorphically) find themselves succumbing to the ideology of the texts, adopting that ideology as their own, and finding it obvious and natural and commonsensical."[9] If we read the Old Testament without recognizing the "designs" certain texts have on us, we may unwittingly embrace the claims they make and may find ourselves nodding our head in agreement at the very moment we should be shaking it furiously in protest.

Because of the influence the Bible has upon us, whenever we read it, we should consider not just what these texts *mean*, but what these texts *do*.[10] In fact, some would argue that this is "the fundamental question that should be asked of any text."[11] For example: "What kind of values does it advocate? Is it doing anyone harm? What effect does it have upon its readers? Does it promote hatred and violence? Does it encourage racism, misogyny, colonialism, xenophobia or homophobia? Does it contribute to the general well-being of society or does it have a negative, detrimental effect, perhaps by reinforcing the language of oppression and domination?"[12] When we ask questions like these of certain Old Testament texts, the answers are not always encouraging. This is particularly true when such questions are posed to passages containing "virtuous" violence.

As noted earlier, if the Old Testament's evaluation of violence was always negative, it would be far less worrisome. But, as we have seen, the Old Testament routinely sanctions various acts of violence. Despite the fact that the use of violence is circumscribed and even criticized at various places in the Old Testament,[13] it is often regarded as necessary, unavoidable, and completely acceptable. Assumptions about the propriety and "virtue" of violence were deeply ingrained in Israel's consciousness, and these assumptions are reflected in many Old Testament texts. In passage after passage, the use of violence is portrayed as an appropriate way to resolve conflict, punish human wrongdoing, and carry out God's will. Texts like these—which condone violence and make it appear respectable and even honorable—are especially dangerous for "readers who are not wide awake to the designs that texts have on them."[14]

The Problem of "Virtuous" Violence in the Old Testament

At this point, we can be more specific about why texts like these, texts containing "virtuous" violence, are so problematic. First, to state the obvious, these "violence-friendly" texts, provide all the necessary ingredients for those wishing to find religious justification for their own violent behavior. Authoritative texts that sanction violence, killing, and bloodshed, that marginalize women, children, and foreigners, and that give divine approval to acts of war and genocide, can easily be used to legitimate all sorts of violent acts and attitudes. Tragically, this is precisely what has happened time and time again. As noted in chapter 2, these texts have repeatedly been used to colonize, kill, oppress, and harm countless people in the name of God. They have inspired and legitimated unspeakable acts of violence against others and continue to have very toxic afterlives.[15]

Second, and related to what has just been said, the presence of "virtuous" violence in the Old Testament is dangerous because it makes violence acceptable. The inclusion of so many positive portrayals of violence in the Old Testament can have a profound influence on us. It can encourage us to think that certain forms of violence *are* appropriate and that killing others is sometimes necessary. For example, reading story after story about sinful individuals who are punished by death in the Old Testament sends a powerful message that it is appropriate to kill people who engage in certain kinds of behavior. Even though we might feel rather uncomfortable with the idea of killing someone ourselves, we may be quite sympathetic toward—and perhaps even actively supportive of—others who are willing to do so.

In subtle but insidious ways, Old Testament texts that valorize violence normalize it. Because of this, readers are likely to become more accommodating toward violence. As Adrian Thatcher explains: "The impact is analogous to the watching of violent DVDs. In a tiny number of cases individuals replicate or act out scenes that have disturbed or excited them. The more serious problem is the likely desensitization to violence."[16] When we are desensitized to violence, we are not as bothered by it as we should be.[17] This causes us to become less vigilant and more tolerant of violent attitudes and actions we should resist. While this accommodating attitude toward violence may not cause us to embark on a life of violent crime or transform us into vicious serial killers, it may provide just enough encouragement to make us think it is appropriate to engage in certain forms of violence. It may also cause us to be far less inclined to speak out against it, and this can have a devastating effect on people who are victimized by violence. When this happens, we too are guilty, not because we have engaged in acts of violence, but because we have done nothing to stop them.

Old Testament assumptions about the propriety of violence, if left unchecked and unchallenged, have a tendency to work themselves deep into our souls. When they do, they become extremely hard to dislodge, especially when they are reinforced by contemporary attitudes about the value and necessity of violence. Since our opinions about weighty moral matters, such as capital punishment and war, are undoubtedly influenced by the way we read, interpret, and apply the Old Testament, we must approach these violent texts carefully and critically. Otherwise, the presence of so much "virtuous" violence in the Old Testament can make us far too accommodating toward violence and can shape our values and beliefs in ways that have harmful consequences for others. As we have seen, the cumulative effect of soaking in stories of "virtuous" violence is a church that has come to tolerate—and, at times, even actively support—a considerable amount of violence and killing.

Third, the presence of "virtuous" violence in the Old Testament creates real difficulties for those who look to the Bible for moral guidance. These texts sanction actions and attitudes many people condemn. For example, most Christians would regard genocide and indiscriminate slaughter as morally repugnant. Yet, the Old Testament sanctions these acts on more than one occasion. (See Deut. 2:31—3:7; 7:1-2; 20:16-18; Josh. 6–11; and 1 Sam. 15.) But if the Old Testament sometimes condones what so many Christians condemn, how can these texts provide spiritual or moral guidance for readers today? Texts that portray violence favorably, and suggest that killing for the "right" reasons is pleasing to God, can mislead those who use the Bible for moral guidance and direction.

Obviously, the question of how people actually use Scripture for moral guidance is a complicated one.[18] Regardless of what people may claim, most do not come to the Bible as neutral inquirers on issues of moral significance. Typically, they already have a position—sometimes a highly invested one—on this or that issue and then read the Bible in a way that is compatible with that position. Still, we should not minimize the influence these texts have on how people think, believe, and behave. Individuals who regard the Bible as authoritative, and who read it for moral or ethical guidance, take their cues from the values and perspectives embedded in these texts. Unless a text explicitly condemns the violence it contains, most readers—both laity and clergy—are reluctant to raise their voice in protest. They often regard it as unnecessary and/or undesirable to question, challenge, or critique acts of violence that are portrayed positively in the Old Testament. I find this reluctance to critique the violence of Scripture highly problematic since it essentially condones acts of violence we ought to condemn.

It is not hard to demonstrate that the Old Testament frequently sanctions behaviors most Christians reject as unacceptable for faithful living. There are texts that encourage retribution rather than forgiveness, bigotry rather than religious tolerance, and domination rather than servanthood. In these and numerous other instances, the presence of "virtuous" violence in the Old Testament works at cross-purposes with Christian values the church wants to cultivate in people.[19] This creates significant tension between the ethics of the text and the ethics of the reader. As David Gunn and Danna Fewell put it: "Readers who look to the Bible for spiritual direction and yet disagree with the values found there face a dilemma."[20] What should be done with Old Testament texts that advocate values Christian readers seek to avoid? Can they be used responsibly without endorsing the violent values they promote, or do such texts do more harm than good? Either way, the presence of "virtuous" violence seriously complicates the efforts of those wishing to use the Old Testament as a moral guide.

Finally, "virtuous" violence in the Old Testament creates a unique set of *theological* problems for readers who regard these texts as Scripture. As discussed earlier, a considerable amount of "virtuous" violence in the Old Testament can be classified as divine violence or divinely sanctioned violence. God is routinely portrayed as committing and commanding many violent acts. This raises serious ethical and moral questions about the character of God, especially when the victims of this violence happen to be women, children, and civilians. Did God really say and do the violent things the Old Testament claims? If so, what does that imply about God's character? Can this be reconciled with other images of God in the Bible? If not, what are we to do with these violent images and the passages in which they reside? While the Bible can certainly help us understand God's character, I believe it can also significantly hinder those same efforts. Violent portrayals of God in the Old Testament have the potential to seriously distort people's view of God and can be a real stumbling block to faith.[21]

Reasons like these demonstrate why the presence of "virtuous" violence in the Old Testament constitutes such a serious problem for modern readers. Some have even called for the removal of these violent texts from the Bible altogether.[22] While that is certainly not my position, it serves to underscore the worrisome nature of these passages. These texts have done—and continue to do—enormous harm.

Do Violent Texts Lead to Violent Acts?

Despite what has just been said, some might still question just how much these troublesome texts really influence the way people think and act. Do violent texts actually lead to violent acts?[23] In many ways, this question is similar to asking whether playing violent video games or watching violent movies and television shows increases aggression. An overwhelming number of studies have conclusively answered that question in the affirmative.[24] Engaging in acts of virtual violence and viewing violent programming makes people more aggressive. One recent study claims the same is true with regard to people who are exposed to "scriptural violence."[25]

In this study led by Brad Bushman, participants were instructed to read Judges 19–21, three chapters that contain a considerable amount of violence. Half the group was informed this passage was from the Bible while the other half was told it was from an ancient scroll. Also, half of the group read the text as it appears in the Bible, while the other half read a slightly modified version. The modified version included two extra verses written for the purpose of this study, which provide divine sanction for some of the violence in this narrative. After completing their readings, participants in each group engaged in an exercise designed to measure aggression. As a result, Bushman "found compelling evidence that exposure to a scriptural depiction of violence or to violence authorized by deity can cause readers to behave more aggressively,"[26] since those in the group who thought this was from the Bible, and those in the group with the extra verses adding divine sanction, actually did behave more aggressively. This suggests that violent biblical texts have a real and measurable effect on those who read them.

Still, some caution against overemphasizing the relationship between reading violent texts and engaging in violent acts. For example, Old Testament scholar John Goldingay argues that we should not "overestimate the influence of Scripture in causing people to make war."[27] Obviously, motivations for making war are complex. I would agree that Scripture alone is not the sole reason—or perhaps even the primary reason—why Christians have historically gone to war. Still, unlike Goldingay, I am far less concerned about people *overestimating* "the influence of Scripture" on those who make war, and far more worried about people *underestimating* it. Many people are relatively unaware of the enormous impact these texts have on our ethical and moral decision making. Old Testament texts that portray war positively, and that provide divine sanction for war, have had an enormous influence on Christian attitudes about war. These texts have rendered war acceptable in the minds of many, and have conditioned people to view warfare not only as permissible, but sometimes as noble and praiseworthy. The same thing has happened with respect to other forms of violence in the Old Testament as well.

To be sure, most people do not read violent verses in the Old Testament and then, on the basis of those verses alone, decide to commit lethal acts of violence.[28] Although there are some tragic examples of this kind of direct (mis)application, the impact violent texts have on us is often more subtle, though still quite harmful and destructive. As noted earlier, these texts have a way of desensitizing us to the problematic nature of violence while simultaneously rendering certain expressions of violence as acceptable and even "normal." Unfortunately, this has the potential to make us less resistant to the use of violence and more ready to condone what we ought to be quick to condemn.

Obviously, different people are influenced by violent texts in different ways. This has a lot to do with *who* is reading these texts and *how* they are reading them. Still, it would be naive to think that these texts have no discernable impact on a person's views about violence. People are affected by these texts, *especially* people who regard the Bible as authoritative Scripture. Thus, while one may legitimately debate *how much* influence such texts have on a person's behavior and beliefs, it is hard to deny that a real and significant link exists between textual and actual violence. In big ways and small, violent texts do contribute to violent acts and attitudes.

Moreover, even those who remain unconvinced that there is a *causal* connection between violent texts and violent acts cannont deny that the Old Testament has often been used to justify acts of violence. For centuries, people have used the Old Testament and its violent verses to harm, oppress, and kill others. Considering the potential these verses have to be wielded in such destructive ways, and given the significant influence they have in shaping our views about violence, it becomes exceedingly important to pay careful attention to how we read.

How Do You Read: Violently or Nonviolently?

We can read and interpret the Bible in ways that cause enormous harm, or we can read in ways that result in enormous good. As Tina Pippin observes: "The Bible can be read to support slavery, monarchy, the death penalty, racism, sexism, and a host of other violent relations, *or it can be read to support an opposite set of structures.*"[29] In other words, we can read violently, or we can read nonviolently. We read violently when we adopt the Old Testament's views about "virtuous" violence and accept its insistence that certain kinds of people deserve to be marginalized, oppressed, or even killed. Reading violently is especially dangerous when we interpret and apply these texts in ways that continue to justify acts of violence in the world today. On the other hand, we can choose to read nonviolently, in ways that respect all people— Israelite and Canaanite, women and men, straight and gay, Gentile and Jew. When we read nonviolently, we read in ways that promote justice, liberation, and human dignity. We will have much more to say about *how* to read nonviolently in chapter 5. For now, suffice it to say that reading nonviolently means reading in ways that do no harm.

As I have been saying, overcoming the Old Testament's troubling legacy will require us to pay careful attention to how we read. To illustrate this, consider, for a moment, the issue of slavery. The Bible can quite naturally be read in ways that support slavery since it neither condemns slavery nor considers it morally problematic. In fact, both the Old and New Testament assume slavery is perfectly acceptable and offer laws and directives governing its practice. Thus, a case *for* slavery can—and has—been made from the Bible, and it can be made without misinterpreting Scripture or forcing texts to mean something they were never intended to mean. Yet, virtually all Christians today agree that slavery is not pleasing to God. Slavery dehumanizes people, robs them of dignity, and subjects them to a form of bondage never intended by God. So what should we do with passages that condone practices, like slavery, that we condemn? How should we read them? Must we read *with* the text and accept its ideological assumptions, or should we resist? How we choose to read these violent texts will depend, to a large extent, on the kind of reader we are.

What Kind of Reader Are You?

Reading is a very complicated process, and we, as readers, are terribly complex creatures. Whether we realize it or not, the way we read is influenced by a whole host of factors, including our ethnicity, class, gender, age, sexual orientation, socioeconomic status, and religious affiliation (or lack thereof). We all bring certain assumptions, presuppositions, values, and beliefs to the Bible that inform our reading of it. While many readers are not very aware of how profoundly these factors influence the way they read, one thing is sure: nobody comes to the Bible as a blank page. The purely objective reader does not exist. All of us have biases, proclivities, and idiosyncrasies that shape *and slant* our readings, for better or for worse.

With that in mind, what I am about to say next may seem reductionistic. Without wanting to minimize the diverse array of factors that influence the way we read, I believe most people who read the Bible *as Scripture* do so in one of two ways: compliantly or conversantly. In order to explore the implications of these two rather different approaches to reading the Bible, it will help to describe two fundamentally different types of readers—*compliant* readers and *conversant* readers. The following descriptions are offered as a heuristic device in the spirit of Max Weber's "ideal types."[30]

Compliant Readers

Compliant readers are individuals whose basic instinct is to read the Bible trustingly. Those who read this way accept the Bible's claims, adopt its values, and embrace its assumptions without necessarily giving serious consideration to the implications of their consent. Rather than questioning or challenging the text, compliant readers take what the Bible says—or at least what they think it says—for granted.[31] Their reading is appreciative and accommodating. It is neither confrontational nor contentious. Rather, they embrace the text "as is." Therefore, they choose to agree with—and submit to—the Bible's assessment of things, even when this may be difficult to understand or morally troubling.

For example, when the Bible speaks about violence approvingly, compliant readers are generally willing to agree with that positive assessment. This is especially true when the text explicitly celebrates, sanctions, or otherwise endorses the violence it describes. In these instances, compliant readers tend to be quite willing to adopt the writer's perspective. They nod approvingly as they read Old Testament stories of violence, killing, and warfare that in other contexts would presumably give them pause. But because these stories are in the Bible, and because the Bible approves of them, compliant readers are willing to approve of them as well.

When the Old Testament sanctions Canaanite genocide, for example, these readers feel compelled to agree that it was right for Israelites to slaughter Canaanites, even though they may be deeply troubled by all the bloodshed and killing. Likewise, when the Old Testament claims that the destruction of Judah and Jerusalem by the Babylonians was an act of divine judgment (2 Kgs. 24:1-4), compliant readers accept this theological assessment without seriously questioning it. Whatever misgivings they might have—if any—are left unexpressed. Rather, they maintain a posture of trust and acceptance.

Compliance is typically the default mode of readers who grow up in the church. This is because many churchgoers are routinely taught to revere the Bible rather than to question or challenge it. Their view of the inspiration of Scripture, which often posits a high degree of divine control over the specific content of the Bible, also contributes to their tendency to read compliantly.[32] Since they believe God is largely responsible for what is in the Bible, they assume that the Bible speaks for God and that the Bible's values represent God's values. Therefore, it makes sense why they read compliantly. They believe they are listening to a communiqué from God, albeit through human authors. This way of reading the Bible is strongly encouraged in many Christian circles and, in the minds of many sincere believers, represents the right way to read the Bible.

While I understand this perspective and respect those who read this way, I believe this approach is very dangerous, especially when reading texts containing "virtuous" violence. The dangers of reading compliantly are dramatically illustrated by the following story told by Old Testament seminary professor Cheryl Anderson:

> During the summer of 2005, I was teaching a Bible study class with teenagers who would be high school seniors that fall. I had them do an exercise, the purpose of which was to encourage them, as people of faith, to read the biblical text carefully and ask crucial questions about the messages communicated. We read the Ten Commandments, and I pointed out how slavery is condoned, and we read Judges 19, a particularly heinous story about the gang rape of a woman, and I showed them how one of the underlying messages of the text is that it is better for a woman to be raped than a man. My goal was to get them to see that they already had a sense of who God is and how God is at work in the world that can help them evaluate problematic biblical texts. For one female . . . student in the class, the exercise was a total failure. At one point, she had had enough, and she blurted out, "This is the Word of God. If it says slavery is okay, slavery is okay. If it says rape is okay, rape is okay."[33]

While most people who read compliantly do not take it to this extreme, this story illustrates the inherent dangers of reading under the influence of violent ideologies. Those who do so may find their own judgment impaired as they embrace elements in the text they ought to resist.

Conversant Readers

Conversant readers, on the other hand, are not constrained in the same kind of way. Rather than simply acquiescing to the text, their fundamental disposition is one of active engagement, sustained conversation, and critical evaluation. Conversant readers are ready to engage the Bible in a genuine dialogue whose outcome is not predetermined by the ideology of the biblical text. While they might agree with the views and values espoused in this or that Old Testament text, they are just as likely to disagree. Conversant readers are discerning readers who accept what they can and resist what they must. Although they are willing to embrace what they read when that is warranted,[34] they are equally prepared to resist what they read when it is offensive, dehumanizing, or morally deficient.

While conversant readers can be compliant, they can also be contentious and confrontational. They are comfortable disputing violent texts that breed injustice, foster oppression, and sanction killing. Conversant readers do not feel obligated to agree with texts that violate the most basic dictates of human decency, and they are not prepared to remain obsequiously silent. Rather, they are ready to speak out. Conversant readers realize the importance of carefully and critically evaluating what they read and are not prepared to accept whatever the text claims just because it is in the Bible. They are ready to engage in a lively conversation with the text in an effort to discern right from wrong and to differentiate between what is morally acceptable and what is not.

Unfortunately, those who wish to converse with the Bible this way often receive little guidance from biblical scholars who routinely forgo an ethical critique of these texts. As David Clines explains: "Most biblical scholars . . . regard it as the whole of their task to understand, exegete, explain, and comment on their texts."[35] Yet, Clines believes—as do I—that "there is . . . another distinct project . . . we ought to be engaged [in] as readers of the biblical texts: that of 'critique' or evaluation."[36] Still, most commentators adopt the text's ideology "as their own" and "rarely, if ever, offer a critique of the text."[37] Clines refers to this as their "default mode" and contends that "in confining themselves to 'understanding' and 'explaining' the text they typically screen out or suppress questions of value—and so leave half their proper task unattempted."[38] This should not be! Whether we are trained biblical scholars or interested lay readers, we must not suppress questions of value when we read a biblical text. Rather, we should render some assessment of the assumptions it makes and values it promotes, especially when reading passages containing "virtuous" violence.

Reading the Old Testament nonviolently, as I am advocating, requires the kind of critical engagement conversant readers bring to the text. I realize that people who have never been taught to engage the Bible in this way may initially find this approach disconcerting. That is understandable. Still, I am convinced that this way of reading the Old Testament is absolutely essential if we are to read it responsibly. In the next chapter, I will say more about why I believe this to be so.

There Are Dangers Here . . . But That Is Not All!

Before concluding this chapter, I want to reiterate a point I made earlier, namely, that the Old Testament's troubling legacy is not its only legacy. In spite of some very real dangers involved in reading the Old Testament, there are also tremendous benefits awaiting those who do. Countless Christians could testify to the positive influence the Old Testament has had upon their lives. I would be one of them! They could bear witness to the way God used the Old Testament to speak to them when they needed guidance or encouragement. They could explain how these texts have inspired them to care for the poor and to work for justice. They could describe how various Old Testament passages were an indispensable resource in their struggle for liberation from oppression. People all around the world have benefitted greatly from direct engagement with the Old Testament. Anyone who denies this, or argues that no good comes from reading the Old Testament, is simply uninformed.

Still, for all its benefits, the Old Testament has been responsible for considerable harm, and I think it is important to be completely honest about that fact. Previously, I made a point of saying that people sometimes raise problems with the Bible, or highlight the "bad" parts in an effort to discredit the Bible, Christian faith, or religion generally. By now it should be clear that is *not* my intention. Nor do I wish to discourage people from reading the Old Testament. Heaven forbid! Most people would benefit from *more* Bible reading, not less. The reason I have emphasized the danger of reading the Bible is to help readers avoid certain pitfalls and to encourage them to read more carefully when they open it up.

If we hope to overcome the Old Testament's troubling legacy and avoid perpetuating the kind of violent readings that have caused so much damage, we must learn to read nonviolently. In what follows, I will argue that we need to engage in a critical conversation with the Old Testament and must be ready to confront violent texts and harmful readings wherever they are found. As we do, we can find more appropriate and constructive ways of reading these texts. Doing this will both limit their harmful effects and ensure their ongoing value and significance to the church and broader society.

PART 2

Proposing a Way of Reading the Old Testament Nonviolently

CHAPTER 5

Developing Good Reading Habits:
Becoming Ethically Responsible Readers

Readers of the Bible have a right—and, indeed, a duty—to probe, question, and oppose statements that seem to them to be morally unacceptable. Far from being passive recipients of the text, they are encouraged to become active agents whose duty it is to subject the ethical implications of the Hebrew Bible to critical scrutiny.

—Eryl W. Davies[1]

All too often we equate piety and devotion with passive obedience to the biblical texts. Resistance, however, can be a sign of a deep piety. While devout people do certainly listen to and read the Bible, they also actively engage it.

—Carol Hess[2]

On a number of occasions, I have had the privilege of teaching an undergraduate course called Issues of War, Peace, and Social Justice in Biblical Texts. Throughout the semester, students keep a journal to demonstrate various ways they are engaging the course material. The first assignment for the course includes reading several Old Testament passages containing descriptions of violence and war.[3] After reading the assigned passages, one student made the following journal entry:

I have read through the Bible before and am familiar with the Old Testament war stories, using the word "familiar" loosely here. However, I can honestly say that . . . reading these specific passages in this sequence has been very eye opening. It is astounding that I have never before remarked on how troubling these stories are. The most . . . disturbing passage that we have read thus far has to be Joshua 6-11. Sunday school class very innocently retold this battle as a mighty story of triumph of the Israelites over the city of Jericho. . . . As a child, I never stopped to wonder why exactly Joshua was waging war with this city. The only context in which this story is given is that God told them to do so. Then we learned that the almost crazy actions of the Israelites . . . led them to victory and the "walls came tumbling down". The rest of the story is a mystery because, apparently, the only part worth mentioning was the victory of God's people. Never would we delve into Joshua 6:21, where God instructs the Israelites to destroy any man, woman or child within the walls of Jericho. Perhaps our Sunday school class would not have found this to be such an appealing tale after all.[4]

I appreciate this student's candor, especially her frank admission that despite her familiarity with Old Testament stories about war, they had never bothered her before. This genuinely surprised her. Once she began to see the problematic nature of these passages, she found it hard to believe she had never noticed it before.

What this student heard in church was a very sanitized version of the story of the battle of Jericho, one that emphasized Israel's victory with nary a word about the human carnage that resulted after the walls fell down. But this way of retelling the story is dangerous. It fails to confront the problem of "virtuous" violence in the text and actually exacerbates the problem by tacitly condoning what the Israelites did. It also fails to acknowledge the harmful effects violent texts—like this one—have had on people over the years. This kind of accommodating reading makes it all too easy for people to use violent biblical texts to justify various acts of violence against others.

Three Essential Reading Habits

If we are committed to overcoming the Old Testament's troubling legacy and stopping the harmful effects of violent texts, we need to read differently. For many, this will involve developing some new reading habits, including a willingness (1) to read actively, (2) to question the text, and (3) to engage in an ethical critique of violent ideologies. Since these practices are foundational for reading the Old Testament nonviolently, it is necessary to explore what they entail. Although there is some overlap among these practices, they are progressive, with each one requiring a bit more of the reader.

Reading Actively Rather than Passively

At the most fundamental level, reading the Old Testament nonviolently requires a willingness to read actively rather than passively. "It is time that we give up our practices of passive reading," says Danna Fewell, "and begin 'fighting to find what we must in the holy text.'"[5] Yet, as previously noted, many people read the Bible compliantly, and therefore passively. They affirm what the Bible affirms and condemn what it condemns. Such readers are not likely to raise objections to the presence of "virtuous" violence in the Old Testament. Rather, they do their best to make sense of these texts as they stand.

For some readers, their familiarity with the Bible exacerbates this tendency to read passively. Having heard the stories of the Bible for years, they find themselves virtually inoculated against them. They have grown comfortable with the Bible and come to terms with it. But, as Trappist monk Thomas Merton wisely warns:

> There is, in a word, nothing comfortable about the Bible—until we manage to get so used to it that we make it comfortable for ourselves. But then we are perhaps too used to it and too at home in it. Let us not be too sure we know the Bible just because we have learned not to be astonished at it, just because we have learned not to have problems with it. Have we perhaps learned at the same time not to really pay attention to it? Have we ceased to question the book and be questioned by it? Have we ceased to fight it? Then perhaps our reading is no longer serious.[6]

Reading the Old Testament responsibly requires active engagement with the biblical text. If our reading is to be serious, it must be one that genuinely grapples with the text in all its wonder, mystery, and madness. It is impossible to do this if we come to the Bible as a sponge, indiscriminately soaking up everything we read. Rather, we must engage the Old Testament as a partner in conversation. Rather than passively accepting what it says, we must enter into a dialogue with it. As Eryl W. Davies puts it: "Reading is not an exercise for passive spectators, for it involves a variety of activities, including reflection, judgment, appraisal, assessment, evaluation, and these activities, in turn, inevitably lead to approval or disapproval, acclaim or criticism, acceptance or rejection."[7] Likewise, as Renita Weems observes:

> Reading is not the passive, private, neutral experience that we have previously believed. To read is to be prepared in many respects to fight defensively. It is to be prepared to resist, to avoid, to maneuver around some of the counterproductive impulses within the text. In short, reading does not mean simply surrendering oneself totally to the literary strategies and imaginative worlds of narrators.[8]

Reading nonviolently requires us to read actively, to engage the text with all of our heart, soul, and mind. This is essential if we are to read responsibly and avoid repeating the mistakes of the past.

Questioning Rather than Just Listening

Reading actively will inevitably lead us to ask tough questions about certain things we find in the Bible, such as some of the practices it promotes, the behaviors it sanctions, and the view of God it portrays. Many people of faith are uncomfortable doing this, however. They approach Scripture deferentially and believe that reading the Bible primarily involves listening rather than questioning. Intent to listen and learn, they are reluctant to question and critique. Eager to embrace the biblical message, they are hesitant to contest it. While all that may sound pious, it results in a superficial reading of Scripture, one that fails to grapple with the very real challenges the Bible presents. If we are to read the Old Testament responsibly, we must enter into a spirited conversation with the text, one that allows us to ask questions freely.

Carol Hess speaks eloquently about this need to "converse" with the Bible. Though she recognizes the value of listening to the text, she realizes that listening, by itself, is not enough. She writes:

> To understand the Bible as the word of God means that we converse with it. We listen to it, we try to understand it, we allow ourselves to be challenged; *and also we talk back to it, we argue with it, we critique it.* In the conversation, we hope for mutual transformation, and we open ourselves to new truth emerging from the interaction of conversation partners.[9]

Engaging in this kind of conversation with the Bible is not a sign of disrespect or irreverence. On the contrary, "Conversing with the Bible is an act of caring for the Bible."[10] As Hess goes on to explain:

> We listen to, we speak to, and we converse with the Bible in a relationship characterized by hard dialogue and deep connections. In line with Abraham who argued with God, Jacob who wrestled the angel, and the Syro-Phoenician woman who rebuked Jesus, we do not simply receive our tradition as empty vessels but rather we take part in the traditioning process as genuine agents.[11]

Reading the Bible faithfully means reading it conversantly.

This need to converse with the Bible and to ask questions of it is especially acute when we encounter "virtuous" violence in the Old Testament. When we read texts that promote values that seem ethically or "morally dubious," we have an obligation to stop and ask questions.[12] Danna Fewell refers to this act of questioning as "interruption." She writes: "As a strategy of reading, interruption is a way of stopping and questioning the text—of recognizing that, ethically, something is amiss in what we are being told."[13] This practice of interrupting and questioning is nicely illustrated by William Holladay, who shares this personal story:

> When I was pastor of a congregation many years ago, one of the church school teachers telephoned me one Sunday afternoon; she taught a class of fourth-grade boys, and she said the class had posed a problem she could not answer. They had been studying the events of the book of Joshua, particularly how Joshua led the Israelites to take possession of the land of Canaan. "But," the boys objected, "didn't the land belong to the Canaanites?" "Yes," she admitted. "But that isn't fair!" they all agreed. So here was her question: "What," she asked, "am I to tell the class?" It is indeed a problem, when the ethical sensitivity of a group of nine-year-old boys exceeds that of Joshua.[14]

These young boys were troubled by Israel's conquest of the land because it violated their sense of fairness. They thought it was wrong for one group of people to take land belonging to another. Because something in the story did not seem right, these boys choose to interrupt it. In doing so, they moved from listening to questioning. This is precisely what we must do if we want to read the Old Testament nonviolently. When the Bible portrays violence positively and sanctions behaviors we consider immoral, just listening is not enough. Instead, we need to interrupt and ask questions.

Ethically Critiquing, Rather than Uncritically Approving, Violent Texts

Old Testament texts, especially those that are morally questionable, need to be ethically critiqued rather than uncritically approved. We must weigh and evaluate the claims such texts make to determine whether they should be accepted or rejected. As Weems puts it:

> Reading the Bible should be no less a lively conversation between writer and reader than is reading other pieces of literature. Readers should have the right to question which visions offered by the Bible's writers are worth devoting one's energies to implementing in the world. Those visions readers decide are not worth inhabiting—that is, the ones that call for slaughtering and silencing others—should be critiqued and resisted.[15]

We should not feel compelled to accept violent or oppressive views that are sanctioned in the Old Testament simply because they appear in the Bible. On the contrary, it is our duty to expose and challenge perspectives we regard as inappropriate, unethical, or immoral.

As noted previously, the purpose of this critique is *not* to pass judgment on the Israelites but to raise questions about the extent to which the ethics inscribed in various Old Testament texts can—or should—inform our own. Rather than condemning people for choices made in the distant past, this critique is designed to assist modern readers who want to use the Bible intelligently to make decisions about how to live faithfully in the present.

David Clines argues forcefully that we ought to be engaged in this kind of ethically oriented reading and evaluation of the biblical text. He writes: "We have a responsibility . . . to evaluate the Bible's claims and assumptions, and if we abdicate that responsibility, whether as scholars or as readers-in-general of the Bible, *we are . . . guilty of an ethical fault*."[16] Yet, ironically, this sort of critique is a task that both biblical scholars and general readers have too often left undone. As Clines observes: "Commentators on biblical texts . . . rarely, if ever, offer a critique of the text."[17]

Like Clines, Eryl Davies also advocates an ethically engaged reading of the Bible. Appealing to reader-response criticism, Davies writes:

> Readers . . . have a duty to enter into dialogue with the text and to consider the extent to which the views adumbrated by the biblical authors agree or conflict with their own. As they read Scripture, they must respond as thinking individuals and feel free to draw their own conclusions regarding the validity or otherwise of the text's claims. Their task is to engage in a vigorous debate with the Hebrew Bible, resisting statements that appear morally objectionable, and taking a critical stance against what they may regard as the excesses of the biblical text.[18]

This is precisely the kind of active engagement and ethical critique I believe is necessary when we encounter "virtuous" violence in the Old Testament.[19] Rather than uncritically adopting the text's perspective as our own, we should raise serious questions about the assumptions and values we find there. "As Clines observes," writes Davies, "there is no shortage of material in the Hebrew Bible that demands such ethical critique, for it contains numerous passages that should make us angry and provoke in all, apart from the emotionally anaesthetized, a sense of moral outrage."[20] There is plenty of work to be done here, work that requires us to be "resisting readers," as literary critic Judith Fetterley puts it.[21] Again, to quote Davies at length:

> Resisting readers feel that they have a duty to converse and interact with the text, and believe that literary compositions should be read in an openly critical, rather than in a passively receptive, way. Instead of tacitly accepting the standards of judgment established in the text and capitulating uncritically to its demands, they are prepared to challenge its assumptions, to question its insights, and (if necessary) to discredit its claims. They may want to resist texts that appear to be oppressive or tyrannical and reject demands that they feel should not (and perhaps cannot) be fulfilled. They may want to argue that the tradition underlying a particular text is ethically questionable and that to

accept it as it stands is both morally and intellectually indefensible. In brief, they may want to "read against the grain" of the text.[22]

The practice of "reading against the grain" is one that will be very useful in our effort to read the Old Testament nonviolently. It allows us to see the text from a different angle of vision and enables us to critique—and even reject—certain values and assumptions embedded in the text. Of course, this way of reading the Bible is nothing new. Those who are aware of the Bible's potential for harm, and those who have been harmed by the Bible, particularly women and "minorities," have been reading against the grain for some time now.

One of the reasons engaging in an ethical critique of Scripture is vitally important is because it holds readers accountable for *how* they read. Elizabeth Schüssler Fiorenza speaks of the need for "an *ethics of accountability*,"[23] and Cheryl Anderson, echoing Fiorenza, believes "interpreters have an ethical responsibility to consider the actual consequences of their interpretations."[24] Indeed we do! Unless we actively, intentionally, and deliberately raise questions about the violence of Scripture and ethically critique it, we are likely to perpetuate the Old Testament's troubling legacy in various ways.

Three Guidelines for Engaging in an Ethical Critique

For some people, engaging in an ethical critique of the Old Testament will undoubtedly be the most difficult aspect of reading nonviolently. The idea of evaluating—and in some cases disagreeing with—certain values, beliefs, and assumptions sanctioned in Scripture makes some readers nervous. Some worry that such a critique inevitably leads to moral relativism, a situation without moral absolutes in which interpreters simply decide what is right in their own eyes.[25] That is a valid concern, and one that can be addressed, at least to some extent, by being clear about what governs an ethical critique of Scripture. To that end, I would like to offer three key commitments that guide this critique and that help us determine what constitutes an ethically responsible reading of the Bible. They are the rule of love, a commitment to justice, and a consistent ethic of life.

The Rule of Love: Reading for the Love of God and Others

The rule of love refers to the twin commands to love God and neighbor, which, according to Jesus, are the two greatest commands.[26] In the words of St. Augustine: "Whoever, then, thinks that he understands the Holy Scriptures, or any part of them, but puts such an interpretation upon them as does not tend to build up this two-fold love of God and our neighbor, does not yet understand them as he ought."[27] Whenever we read and interpret the Bible, we should always be asking whether our interpretation increases our love for God and others. If it does not, we should read again. In a statement on the authority and interpretation of the Bible, the Presbyterian Church asserts that "no interpretation of Scripture is correct that leads to or supports contempt for any individual or group of persons either within or outside the church. Such results . . . plainly indicate that the rule of love has not been honored."[28]

A Commitment to Justice: Setting Things Right

Second, an ethical critique of Scripture is guided by a concern for justice. "What does the LORD require of you but to do justice, and to love kindness, and to walk humbly with your God?" (Mic. 6:8b). Our reading and interpretation of the Bible should always foster justice. The Hebrew word typically rendered as "justice" (*mishpat*) is derived from a verb that "means 'to put things right', to intervene in a situation that is wrong, oppressive or out of control and to 'fix' it."[29] *Doing* justice, then, is about setting things right, realigning things that have gotten out of whack. *Reading* justly involves reading *for the sake of* those who have been wronged, oppressed, and violated, for those who are most vulnerable and at risk in our world. Specifically, we should read biblical texts in ways that are liberating and life-giving for the poor, for women, for sexual minorities, for children, and for all who are disadvantaged and marginalized. If our reading is not good news for these individuals, if it does not contribute to their liberation, it is *not* just. Any interpretation of Scripture we offer should always be consistent with this commitment to set things right and to create *shalom*—well-being and wholeness for everyone.[30] As Martin Luther King Jr. once said: "The arc of the moral universe is long, but it bends toward justice." So too should our reading of the Bible.[31]

Rosemary Radford Ruether advocates this way of reading the Bible for the sake of women and proposes using what she calls "the prophetic-liberating tradition of Biblical faith," which she regards "as a norm through which to criticize the Bible."[32] Ruether identifies four essential themes in this tradition: "(1) God's defense and vindication of the oppressed; (2) the critique of the dominant systems of power and their powerholders; (3) the vision of a new age to come in which the present system of injustice is overcome and God's intended reign of peace and justice is installed in history; and (4) finally, the critique of ideology, or of religion."[33] Her rationale for using this particular tradition is because it is "generally accepted" as "the central tradition" in the Bible.[34] Therefore, as Ruether sees it: "The extent to which Biblical texts reflect this normative principle" determines whether "they are regarded as authoritative."[35]

Similarly, I understand the concept of justice as a normative principle that can be used to help us read ethically.[36] Since a deep and abiding concern for justice is evident throughout both the Old and New Testaments, and can be regarded as a central biblical theme, it strikes me as being a useful plumb line to determine whether a reading is ethical or not.[37] When we read the text in ways that advance the full humanity of every individual and promote liberation from every oppressive structure, we can be sure we are reading in the right direction.[38]

A Consistent Ethic of Life: Valuing All People

Third, an ethical critique of Scripture should be guided by "a consistent ethic of life."[39] This means that our readings should be life affirming for *all* people at *every* stage of life, from youngest to oldest and greatest to least. It also means that every single life is valued and valued equally. Valuing all people is rooted in the conviction that all life is precious to God. Theologically speaking, being created in God's image means that people are of infinite worth to God and should be treated with reverence and respect.[40]

This high concern for life is expressed forcefully in one of the core values of the Brethren in Christ Church, which states: "We value all human life and promote forgiveness, understanding, reconciliation, and nonviolent resolution of conflict." As Harriet Bicksler insightfully comments:

> The "all" word is the challenge. Do we really mean all human life—the murderer on death row; the ruthless dictator who massacres his own citizens while amassing great personal wealth; the unborn baby conceived by a rape; the homeless alcoholic who won't accept help; the nasty coworker who is always criticizing? Surely there are limits! We haven't allowed ourselves any escape clauses, however.[41]

Being guided by a consistent ethic of life *hermeneutically* means resisting all readings that condone the use of violence and lethal force against others, even when such force is ostensibly exercised in the name of justice.[42] Valuing *all* human life precludes the possibility of using violence and lethal force against *any* human life. It means consistently choosing life rather than death (Deut. 30:19-20).

While these three guidelines are not foolproof, they enable us to develop a principled approach to reading ethically and serve as helpful boundary markers. Christians will continue to debate what neighborly love looks like, differ over what constitutes justice, and disagree about the appropriateness of using lethal force. Still, reading with these parameters in mind should help us determine what constitutes an ethically responsible reading and what does not. When we read in ways that are consistent with these three principles, it should inspire confidence that we are using the Bible ethically, in ways that please God. When we read in ways that violate these principles, we do well to go back and read again.

Permission to Read Differently

Even with the relative safeguards these guidelines afford, some people will still feel uncomfortable about the idea of questioning the Bible, let alone critiquing it, since they have never been encouraged to read the Bible this way. What can be said to reassure such individuals that engaging in an ethical critique of these texts is completely appropriate and pleasing to God?

First, it helps to recognize that everyone who reads the Bible engages in an ethical critique of it to some degree, whether they realize it or not. To illustrate this, consider again the issue of slavery. Although the Old Testament clearly and unequivocally approves of slavery, few Christians today believe it is morally right to enslave another human being. Such behavior is demeaning, dehumanizing, and fundamentally incompatible with how God wants us to relate to each another. Even though the Old Testament approves of slavery, we do not. To take such a position *is* to engage in an ethical critique of the Old Testament. Recognizing that we already evaluate and critique the Old Testament in some ways, and seeing this as both legitimate and beneficial, should free us to do so in other ways as well.

Second, the enormous amount of diversity within the Old Testament requires us to engage in some process of evaluation and critique. Since the Old Testament does not always speak with one voice on issues of moral and ethical significance, but presents various perspectives that are not always compatible, we need to decide which voices to heed and which to ignore. Contradictory claims in the Old Testament force readers to make choices and to recognize that all parts are not equally authoritative for determining how we should think and live. Anyone who wishes to use the Bible as a reliable guide for modern ethics and morals will need to critique some parts while embracing others.

Third, the Old Testament itself bears witness to a deep and robust tradition of critique, and this should reassure anxious readers. This tradition is evident in Abraham's questions about God's justice in destroying the righteous along with the wicked (Genesis 18), in Moses' dispute with God about God's plan to wipe out the entire nation of Israel (Exodus 32), in the psalmist's cries, and elsewhere. Likewise, there are many instances in which a certain point of view expressed in one part of the Old Testament is challenged in another. To cite just one example, consider how the theology of retribution in Deuteronomy, which claims that obedience to God brings blessing while disobedience brings hardship, is challenged by the innocent suffering of Job. There is clearly an inner-biblical conversation going on within the pages of the Old Testament, and this provides a precedent for engaging in the kind of ethical critique proposed here.[43] As Davies recognizes: "The biblical authors themselves frequently exercise a critical role, questioning past beliefs and querying past judgments. Far from accepting passively the values that they had imbibed, their strategy was to probe, question, modify and even reject some of their inherited traditions."[44] Davies emphasizes that this practice of reading critically is rooted in Scripture itself. It does not "introduce an alien principle into biblical interpretation" but "is a way of interpreting the Bible in its own terms."[45] When we engage in an ethical critique of Scripture, we add our voices to a critical dialogue already started within the pages of Scripture itself.

Fourth, it is important to emphasize that engaging in an ethical critique of the Old Testament does not indicate a lack of respect for the Bible. As Clines puts it: "We need not suppose that reading against the grain of the text is a sign of disrespect for the text."[46] Reading the Old Testament nonviolently, and engaging in the kind of ethical critique required to do so, does not disparage the Old Testament, deny its central importance in the life of faith, or undermine its authority. As Weems writes: "Our criticism does not intend to destroy the Bible, as though that were possible (and whatever that means). Rather, it is to help those of us interested in reading and interpreting the Bible to find ethical ways to read intelligibly and responsibly."[47]

Engaging in a sustained and serious reading of the Old Testament—one that involves elements of critique *and* affirmation—actually demonstrates how important the biblical text is to us. Most of us would hardly bother taking the time to read the Old Testament so critically and carefully if we did not care so much about it. As Thom Stark sees it: "The ability to engage scripture in argument without rejecting its rightful place in the community is a mark of spiritual maturity."[48] Once you realize this, and view engaging in an ethical critique of the Old Testament as a sign of "spiritual maturity" rather than an act of sacrilegious sabotage, it becomes much easier to read this way.

Finally, whenever we engage in an ethically responsible reading of the Bible, we should keep in mind that doing so is a two-way street. Jacqueline Lapsley writes: "Evaluation moves in both directions."[49] Whenever we read the Bible, we should be prepared not only to critique it but to be critiqued *by* it. "As we pass judgment on the Bible," writes Eryl Davies, "we must allow the Bible to pass judgment on us."[50] As we question the Bible, "the Bible also questions us, inviting us to reconsider our priorities, to revise our long-cherished beliefs, and perhaps to re-orient our deeply entrenched ethical positions."[51] Clines also envisions an ethically informed reading of Scripture as something that cuts both ways. It enables the interpreter to challenge aspects of the text that are found wanting and to *be* challenged by aspects of the text that are more inspiring. He writes:

> It is a measure of our commitment to our own standards and values that we
> register disappointment, dismay or disgust when we encounter in the texts
> of ancient Israel ideologies that we judge to be inferior to ours. And it is a
> measure of our open-mindedness and eagerness to learn and do better that we

remark with pleasure, respect and envy values and ideologies within the biblical texts that we judge to be superior to our own.[52]

Thus, while we have an ethical obligation to critique the text, we must always approach the text with humility and openness, prepared to have some of our own beliefs and perspectives challenged as well.

I hope enough has been said to demonstrate both the importance and propriety of engaging in a ethical critique of Scripture. To read this way is an act of loyalty, not treachery. In fact, if the Old Testament is to speak a liberating word for our day, one that is truly transformative and life-giving, we must be willing to engage in an ethical critique of its most violent texts. Such a critique is indispensable for reading the Old Testament nonviolently, which, in turn, is crucial to overcoming the Old Testament's troubling legacy.

But *how*, exactly, do we engage in an ethical critique? What kind of reading strategies can help us challenge "virtuous" violence in our effort to read these texts nonviolently? And after we have engaged in this kind of critique, then what? How can these texts still be read constructively? Some answers to these questions will begin to emerge in the pages that follow.

CHAPTER 6

Reading the Old Testament Nonviolently

Reading is not disinterested. Our interpretation of a text is the result of the kinds of questions we ask, and those questions are determined by our interests (acknowledged or not).

—J. Cheryl Exum[1]

We ignore at our peril the potential for violence built into the Bible.

—Alastair Hunter[2]

At this point, we are ready to discuss how one goes about reading the Old Testament nonviolently. How does one read violent texts in ways that are liberating and life-giving, and that reduce the risk of being used to justify further acts of violence and oppression? Although the approach I develop in this chapter does not constitute a formalized methodology that needs to be applied with exacting rigor and precision, it does involve a commitment to read the Old Testament in a certain way, from a particular perspective. The various reading strategies described in this chapter will provide a number of practical tools that are helpful for reading the Old Testament from this perspective. Although none of these strategies miraculously resolves all of the problems associated with the Old Testament's troubling legacy, when taken together they go a long way toward resisting some of the most harmful effects of these texts.

Those who are familiar with more recent ways of reading the Bible by utilizing various forms of postmodern criticism will recognize much of what follows.[3] Many of the reading strategies I advocate, and the suggestions I offer, are derived from interpretive approaches such as reader-response criticism, feminist criticism, postcolonial criticism, ideological criticism, and deconstruction.[4] I have found these approaches extremely helpful in my efforts to read nonviolently. Although I do not engage in any extensive theoretical or methodological discussion of those approaches in what follows, interested readers are encouraged to consult the more specialized studies referenced in the notes.

Five Steps in Reading Nonviolently

I would like to suggest five steps that work together to help us read nonviolently. While I have arranged these in roughly the order one might use them, I would again emphasize that methodological precision is *not* my intent. The goal here is to develop a way of reading the Old Testament from a certain point of view.

The first three steps—naming, analyzing, and critiquing the violence—are intended to limit and neutralize the harmful effects these texts often have on readers (and others!). The last two—using textual violence constructively and transcending the violence—have more to do with finding ways to use these problematic passages positively. I will argue that those who wish to read the Old Testament responsibly *as Scripture* must be willing to engage in an ethical critique of its violent texts while at same time considering how to read them in ways that enhance faith and affirm life. Doing one without the other is insufficient. The two must go hand in hand.

Step 1: Naming the Violence

Naming the violence we encounter in the Old Testament constitutes a first step toward reading the Old Testament nonviolently. Violent assumptions, attitudes, and actions should be identified and acknowledged as such. This takes patience and practice, but also courage and determination. Many readers would just as soon ignore these troubling texts, or at least the troubling dimensions of them, and pretend they do not exist. But this is not an effective way of dealing with violence in the Old Testament. As Nancy Bowen recognizes: "An ethical response to biblical violence requires naming it, for only then can we take responsibility for it."[5]

Before we can name the violence, we must be able to see it. In some instances, seeing violence is relatively easy since it is such a prominent feature in the text. Numerous Old Testament narratives, poems, and prophetic oracles are laced with violent words, deeds, and images that are—or at least should be—immediately recognizable. We have already considered a number of passages like these, passages in which violence is unmistakable.

Yet, ironically, even in some of the most violent texts, there is a danger of not actually seeing the violence. One reason for this—especially with the most familiar and well-known stories of violence in the Old Testament—is "textual blindness," a phrase I have adapted from Don Everts. Everts talks about "home blindness," a situation in which "we are so used to something being around that we stop seeing it in detail."[6] As Everts explains, "Whether we're talking about a picture hanging on the wall, the patterns of tile in the bathroom or the color of a chair, we all have items we've become 'home blind' to. We see something so often that our brains stop taking note of the details."[7] The same kind of thing sometimes happens with regard to violence in the Old Testament. We have grown so familiar with these violent stories, *and with certain sanitized ways of reading and hearing these stories*, that we fail to notice what they are really saying. We do not observe what is actually in the text (or implied by the text) because we have been conditioned to see it from a particular angle of vision, or through a particular lens, that tends to ignore its violent dimensions in favor of focusing on its more pleasant interpretive possibilities.

But reading nonviolently requires us to see the violence for what it really is and to name it as such. This is especially important when the violent aspects of a text are less obvious or less explicit. It involves reading with special sensitivity to those who are harmed in these texts, even when—and especially when—the text claims they deserved it. Similarly, a concerted effort needs to be made to identify structural forms of violence embedded in these texts. Although these are sometimes more difficult to detect, they can be just as problematic and should be named.

Since violence manifests itself in many forms, when we name the violence, we should be as specific as possible. Rather than simply saying, "This is a story about violence," it would be better to say, "This is a story about genocide, or slavery, or rape," and so on. Naming the violence with this kind of specificity forces it to the surface, where it can be discussed, analyzed, and critiqued. Once it is out in the open for all to see, it can no longer be ignored. Moreover, by naming the violence, we signal our willingness to "take responsibility for it" and to do something about it.

There is another aspect of naming the violence that should be mentioned here as well. This involves naming the violence *of* Scripture in addition to naming the violence *in* Scripture. When we name the violence *of* Scripture, we discuss how certain texts have been used to inspire or legitimate acts of violence against others throughout history. No discussion of Genesis 3 or Joshua 6–11, for example, is complete without acknowledging how problematic these passages have been for women and for those who have been colonized, respectively. The toxic afterlives of violent texts like these should be freely acknowledged. Describing how such texts have been used to harm others, and openly critiquing readings that are oppressive, goes a long way toward preventing them from being used to justify further acts of violence.

Step 2: Analyzing the Violence

Having named the violence, it is then helpful to analyze it from a number of angles by exploring certain questions:

- Who is the source, or agent, of the violence? Is it portrayed as an act of divine or human violence? Is it a combination of both?
- What motivates this violence? Religion? Politics? Revenge? Or is it simply—albeit tragically—a symptom of the structural violence of patriarchy, ethnocentrism, and so forth?
- Whose interests does this violence serve? Who benefits from it, and who is harmed by it? What results from the violence?
- How is this violence evaluated in the text? Does it receive textual approval or condemnation? Is it ambiguous?
- How does this violent text function in its literary context? What purpose(s) does it serve?

Readers will need to decide which of these questions (or others) feels most helpful to pursue when investigating textual violence in various passages. This process of asking questions, and answering the most relevant ones, will provide numerous insights into the nature and function of violence in these texts. For many readers, it will also create some serious cognitive dissonance, if not profound disagreement, with textually sanctioned acts of violence.

When analyzing the violence, it is especially important to determine—insofar as this is possible—if modern readers think the text approves or disapproves of the violence it contains. Are they inclined to regard the violence in question as being sanctioned or unsanctioned by the text? If it seems most readers are likely to conclude that the text condemns the violence and portrays it as a clear case of "wrongful violence," it becomes relatively easy to read that text nonviolently. One can simply amplify the text's own critique and expound upon why this or that act of violence is so harmful and destructive. On the other hand, if most people are likely to regard the violence as sanctioned—regardless of whether the text presents it that way—then it becomes crucial to find ways to critique it. By carefully analyzing the violence, readers are better able to identify where problems exist. This, in turn, will enable them to focus their energy and attention more constructively as they attempt to respond to various challenges these violent texts present.

Step 3: Critiquing the Violence

Since engaging in a critique of "virtuous" violence in the Old Testament is fundamental to reading nonviolently, it requires a more extensive discussion at this point. There are many different ways to critique "virtuous" violence in the Old Testament, and we will consider several different strategies here. What follows is neither an exhaustive list of all possible strategies nor a full-blown discussion of any single strategy. Rather, I have chosen five approaches that illustrate various ways readers can critique "virtuous" violence in the Old Testament. The first two strategies are rooted in the biblical text, while the other three come from outside the text. In one way or another, each of these strategies challenges the "virtue" of "virtuous" violence by resisting the Old Testament's favorable assessment of these violent acts and attitudes.

LOOK FOR INTERNAL CRITIQUES OF VIOLENCE WITHIN VIOLENT TEXTS

One strategy for challenging the "virtue" of "virtuous" violence involves looking for an "internal critique" of violence within the text itself.[8] Some Old Testament passages that *seem* to sanction the violence they describe may actually be doing just the opposite. Therefore, when reading a text that *appears* to contain "virtuous" violence, it is very important to consider whether the text actually endorses the violence it contains. Although a cursory reading of the text may lead many readers to conclude that the violence is portrayed positively, a more careful reading may suggest otherwise. There may be a critique of what seems to be "virtuous" violence within the text itself. In these cases, texts appearing to legitimate certain acts of violence may actually critique them.

Consider, for example, the execution of certain individuals at the beginning of Solomon's reign. According to 1 Kings 2:13-46, Solomon orders the execution of Adonijah, Joab, and Shimei, and in each case, the text appears to justify their execution. But there are subversive undercurrents that suggest more is going on than meets the eye. Did each of these men really deserve to die, as the text seems to claim, or were these actually politically motivated killings disguised as something else? Did the writer *really* approve of Solomon's deadly dealings, or was the writer actually criticizing Solomon's violent behavior? A careful reader can detect hints of critique that cast serious doubt on the propriety of Solomon's execution orders. Elsewhere, I have argued that there are enough clues in the text to suggest the writer disapproved of Solomon's actions and registered this critique covertly to avoid attracting unnecessary attention and possibly becoming another one of Solomon's casualties![9] Apparently, not everyone in Israel viewed Solomon's violence as "virtuous."

To illustrate how an inner-textual critique may be at work in two other texts, consider Elijah's slaughter of the prophets of Baal (1 Kings 18) and the Jews' massacre of Persians (Esther 9). While it is commonly assumed that the Old Testament portrays the violence in these passages as "virtuous," there are indications that both passages actually condemn—or at least severely critique—the violence they describe.

At the end of a dramatic confrontation between the Israelite prophet Elijah and 450 prophets of Baal on Mount Carmel, we read these chilling words:

"Seize the prophets of Baal; do not let one of them escape." Then they seized them; and Elijah brought them down to the Wadi Kishon, and killed them there. (1 Kgs. 18:40)

With typical reticence, the writer provides no details of the actual slaughter, though it takes little imagination to envision the brutal and bloody scene. Many readers regard this bloodbath as a valorous act of violence that was pleasing to God.[10] But not everyone agrees with this favorable assessment.

In a recent essay, Frances Flannery argues that there is "an internal textual critique" of Elijah's excessive violence in this prophetic purge.[11] Her argument is based on a very careful reading of the text, one that pays special attention to its chiastic structure and redactional history. Flannery contends that "1 Kgs 18-19 contains carefully crafted linguistic structures that illuminate an editorial layer severely critiquing Elijah, who commits acts never mandated by God and who fails to perceive a nonviolent alternative offered by God."[12]

Flannery argues that the narrative draws a sharp contrast between the "way" of Obadiah, a top official in Ahab's administration who had saved one hundred prophets of Yahweh by hiding them in caves and providing for their physical needs, and the "way" of the prophet Elijah who brutally slaughters 450 prophets of Baal. This contrast is key to Flannery's reading of the text. She writes:

> The two carefully constructed chiasms stand as a vibrant, internal critique of one of the bloodiest episodes in prophetic sacred history. Obedyahu's nonretributive, pacifistic defense of Yahwism poses an alternate vision for triumphing over an unjust regime, seriously calling into question the displays of power, might, and conflict favored by Eliahu.[13]

If Flannery is correct, if the text really is critiquing the prophet for his use of violence and his failure to behave otherwise, then this particular text becomes far less problematic. While the slaughter of 450 people created in God's image is still horrific, at least the text does not add to the horror by blessing it!

The end of the book of Esther provides another example of a text that many readers believe endorses violence but that may actually subvert it. Toward the end of the book, after Esther exposes a plot to kill all the Jews, she pleads with the king to revoke a decree he had naively issued regarding their destruction (Esth. 3:7-15; 8:3). Although this particular request proves impossible to fulfill, the king permits another edict to be written giving Jews permission to defend themselves with lethal force. Letters were written to this effect and were hastily sent throughout the kingdom. "By these letters the king allowed the Jews who were in every city to assemble and defend their lives, to destroy, to kill, and to annihilate any armed force of any people or province that might attack them, with their children and women, and to plunder their goods" (Esth. 8:11). This edict took effect the very same day the Jews were to be destroyed. Thus, when the fateful day arrived, rather than being annihilated, "the Jews struck down all their enemies with the sword, slaughtering, and destroying them, and did as they pleased to those who hated them. In the citadel of Susa the Jews killed and destroyed five hundred people" (Esth. 9:5-6). At Esther's request, the killing was extended another day, resulting in an additional three hundred casualties (Esth. 9:13-15). This two-day killing spree was followed by "a day of feasting and gladness" (Esth. 9:18).

Outside the Persian capital, similar reprisals took place. "The other Jews who were in the king's provinces also gathered to defend their lives, and gained relief from their enemies, and killed seventy-five thousand (!) of those who hated them" (Esth. 9:16). This was also celebrated with "a day of feasting and gladness" (Esth. 9:17). To commemorate this "auspicious" occasion in perpetuity, these two days of killing were to be celebrated each year as the festival of Purim (Esth. 9:26-28).

At first glance, it would seem that the book of Esther portrays this massacre favorably since Jews are allowed to fight and kill in self-defense in order to protect themselves against people who wanted to kill them. To many readers, it seems like the enemies of the Jews got just what they deserved. But is this what the writer meant to suggest?

Carolyn Sharp thinks not. She marshals four lines of evidence she believes suggests the narrator is *not* "presenting the Jewish slaughter as justifiable."[14] These are as follows: (1) the Jews are portrayed as the ones in power (9:3), not as the underdog, when the killing begins; (2) the first reference to the Jews killing their enemies in Esth. 9:5 has a "semantic excess" of verbs for killing; (3) the phrase used in Esth. 9:5 indicating that the Jews did "as they pleased" to their enemies is also found in Esth. 1:8 and Dan. 8:4 and in both places has negative connotations; and (4) it does not appear that the Persians fight back or resist the Jews, raising questions about whether this is really violence in self-defense as the king's decree allowed.

Additionally, following the lead of Kenneth Craig, Sharp argues that the genre of this book is "carnivalesque," a genre that "relies on hyperbolic ironic renderings."[15] If this is correct, then reading the book of Esther requires paying attention to the way irony functions throughout the book. According to Sharp: "The ironies in the carnivalesque Book of Esther rely on excessiveness as the primary 'key' or tonality of the narrative."[16] Sharp emphasizes a number of "excesses" throughout the story, from the excessive partying at the beginning of the book to the excessive killing at the end. According to Sharp: "Instances of excess in the Book of Esther are not intended to be valorized, nor should they be taken lightly."[17] In fact, she believes that "there is no example of excessiveness that should be read as innocent in this story."[18]

Therefore, since the killing at the end of the book seems excessive in various ways—so many people are killed, the killing does not seem to be done in self-defense, and more time for killing is granted—this indicates that the killing at the end of the book is not being justified, let alone celebrated. As Sharp puts it: "Far from the slaughter being presented as a morally appropriate and justified comeuppance for planned Persian violence, the narrative is signaling that this particular role reversal constitutes *an atrocity that is not to be approved of by the implied audience*."[19] When careful attention is paid to the genre of this book, and to the use of irony and excess, it can help readers discern that the killing spree at the end of Esther is to be regarded as problematic rather than praiseworthy.

Obviously, most examples of "virtuous" violence in the Old Testament appear with no evidence of any internal critique. Still, it is useful to keep this possibility in mind when reading texts that appear to portray violence positively. When such critiques do appear, they assist our efforts to read the Old Testament nonviolently.

USE DISSONANT (NONVIOLENT) VOICES TO UNDERMINE DOMINANT (VIOLENT) ONES

The Old Testament contains many different voices and divergent perspectives on a wide range of issues—exactly what you would expect of a collection of texts produced over hundreds of years. This results in a considerable amount of diversity in the Old Testament. While some may be troubled by this, it is actually an asset for those committed to reading the Old Testament nonviolently. This discordant discourse, reflecting various values and viewpoints, opens a door for engaging in a critique of "virtuous" violence. Readers can use dissonant voices and perspectives to undermine more dominant ones. For example, passages describing the nonviolent resolution of conflict—such as Joseph's forgiveness of his brothers (Genesis 45 and 50) and Abigail's swift intervention that prevents a massacre (1 Samuel 25)—can be brought into conversation with texts that resolve conflict through lethal force. Likewise, texts promoting a more inclusive view of God's grace toward outsiders—like the book of Jonah—can be used to critique others, like Nahum, that anticipate the destruction of foreigners with great delight.

A number of interpreters have suggested the usefulness of this approach for dealing with some of the more problematic parts of the Old Testament. For example, David Gunn and Danna Fewell write: "Because of its multivocal nature, the Bible, despite its biases of gender, race/ethnicity, and class, *makes provision for its own critique*."[20] They continue: "The Bible shows us not merely patriarchy, élitism, and nationalism; it shows us the fragility of these ideologies through irony and counter-voices. Xenophobic Joshua and Ezra are undermined by the book of Ruth. David is countered by Hannah and Rizpah. The patriarchy of Persia is threatened by the single woman Vashti."[21]

Similarly, John Collins believes it is possible "to note the diversity of viewpoints within the Bible and thereby relativize the more problematic ones."[22] While Collins believes this kind of "selective reading . . . does not negate the force of the biblical endorsements of violence," it nevertheless provides a strong countervoice that challenges certain dominant assumptions about the propriety of violence.[23] By reading one biblical text in light of another, new and sometimes confrontational perspectives come to light.[24] When these alternate voices are accented and brought into conversation with positive portrayals of violence, they can be quite subversive, inviting us to reconsider assumptions about the necessity and propriety of violence in certain cases.

This reading strategy should not be crudely conceived as a simplistic attempt to neutralize all the "bad parts" of the Bible by simply citing the "good parts."[25] Nor is it an attempt to say the "bad parts" do not really matter or are not all that problematic. As I have already argued at some length, the "bad parts" are terribly problematic, and we need to be fully honest about the kind of problems they raise. Rather, this reading strategy reminds us that the Old Testament does not speak with one voice when it comes to the issue of violence. We encounter competing perspectives, some of which can be quite helpful in critiquing certain deeply held assumptions about the inevitability and "virtue" of violence. While these alternate perspectives do not make the objectionable parts of the Old Testament disappear, they destabilize them and provide us with resources from within the Bible itself to bolster our critique of "virtuous" violence.[26]

READ WITH THE VICTIMS IN THE TEXT

One of the most effective ways to critique "virtuous" violence in the Old Testament is to read it from the perspective of the victims: individuals in the text—named or unnamed, seen or unseen—who are abused, oppressed, or killed. Reading from this perspective involves reading *with* those who have been marginalized, silenced, and erased by the text. These individuals are often part of the "excluded groups," as Cheryl Anderson calls them, and include women, children, and all those who are ethnically, religiously, or otherwise different from the ideal norm.[27] We seldom hear from these individuals and are rarely allowed to see things from their perspective.

Many victims of violence in the text are virtually invisible. If they are mentioned at all, it is only briefly and in the most general way. Sometimes, the only textual sighting we have of them is as part of a collective group being destroyed. Since we are not allowed to see them as individuals, they remain anonymous. This makes it difficult to develop sympathy toward them, and easy to accept their destruction with little—if any—concern.

But all that changes when we *dare to read the story from their perspective*. When we allow these invisible individuals to materialize—when they become real people with faces and names, families and futures—it becomes much more difficult to endorse the violence done to them. Reading with the victims allows us to read with different questions in mind, and causes us to wonder how the story would sound differently if told by the victims. As we read with the victims, we attempt to see things from their point of view. Recognizing that their voices and concerns are not represented in the text, we do our best to listen and to take their concerns into account. This enables us to see these individuals in a whole new light and raises serious questions about the violence so often praised in these texts.[28]

Reading with the victims of violence opens our eyes to some of the most morally troubling dimensions of these violent texts. It exposes the dreadful underside of these texts, a side that is too often ignored and suppressed. For example, rather than rejoicing with Israelites celebrating the destruction of the Egyptian army in the Red Sea, try grieving with the Egyptian widows and orphans across the Nile. Hear their cries. Experience their pain. Peer into their homes as oil lamps dim and Egyptian toddlers cry themselves to sleep because, "Daddy is not coming home tonight—or ever again!" Reading this way, with the victims of violence, is consistent with our commitment to read the Old Testament in ways that value *all* people. Doing so inevitably challenges the "virtue" of "virtuous" violence.

To further emphasize the importance of this approach and to illustrate what is involved in reading with victims, I briefly want to consider one particular group of individuals who are rarely mentioned explicitly in the Old Testament but who suffer greatly in its pages just the same.

EXCURSUS: READING FOR THE SAKE OF THE CHILDREN

According to one count, there are "almost 200 texts about violence against children in the Hebrew Old Testament."[29] Some of these stories are well known, such as the near sacrifice of Isaac (Gen. 22:1-14), Joseph's mistreatment at the hands of his brothers (Gen. 37:12-28), and the death of every firstborn Egyptian on the night of that first Passover (Exod. 12:29-30). Others are less familiar, such as the story about forty-two boys who are mauled by bears for saying to Elisha, "Go away, baldhead" (2 Kgs. 2:23-24), and the story of an unnamed Israelite girl who was kidnapped and enslaved by the Arameans (2 Kgs. 5:2).

In many Old Testament stories of death and destruction children are often invisible victims of violence. Consider, for example, the flood narrative in Genesis 6–8. According to the story, God "blotted out" (drowned!) every human being on the planet with the exception of eight *adults* in the ark (Gen. 7:23). If everyone perished except those inside the ark—a boat for adults only—that means every teenager, toddler, infant, and unborn baby died in the flood. No children were spared. Many readers never consider this side of the story. This is largely due to the way the story is told in Genesis and retold in books, sermons, and classrooms. Contemporary depictions of the flood narrative in children's Bibles, Christian storybooks, and other media focus on the eight passengers and countless animals who are safe and dry inside the ark. Little, if any, attention is given to the myriad people (not to mention animals!) outside the ark who are struggling to survive against all odds.

But *the view from outside the ark is terribly important*! Reading with the victims requires us to fix our gaze on those ravaged by the floodwaters, many of whom presumably were children. Once you see the faces of these doomed children and hear their cries as they desperately—but hopelessly—try to keep their heads above water, you can never read the story the same way again. If you do not believe me, take a look at some of the disturbing wood engravings depicting the plight of those outside the ark done by nineteenth-century French artist Paul Gustave Doré.[30] Or watch James Cameron's *Titanic* and pay particular attention to the scenes involving children after the ship begins to sink in the North Atlantic. Drowning is horrific and especially heartwrenching when the victims are children. Yet, nary a word is said about their plight or the violent deaths they suffer at the hands of God in the book of Genesis.

In addition to the flood narrative, other stories of mass destruction, such as the destruction of Sodom and Gomorrah (Genesis 19), the Transjordanian massacres in the territories of Sihon and Og (Deuteronomy 2–3), and the Amalekite genocide (1 Samuel 15) display a similar lack of interest in the fate of the children—or virtually any other victim, for that matter. Even though each of these stories assumes the utter annihilation of every single child, these children remain virtually invisible. (This is with the possible exception of Lot's daughters, depending on how old one envisions them being. See Gen. 19:15-16, 30-38.) In some instances, such as the case of the Transjordanian massacres, children are generically noted in passing—"we utterly destroyed them . . . in each city *utterly destroying men, women, and children*" (Deut. 3:6; emphasis mine). Still, we are never introduced to any of these children or encouraged to be concerned about their well-being.

What is especially troubling is that stories like these depict the destruction of children (and others) as divinely sanctioned and thus "virtuous."[31] But is it? Can killing children ever be considered moral? Danna Fewell challenges us to "imagine what might happen if we were to start thinking about these children who are victims of literary and theological exploitation."[32] She wonders what would happen "if we were to start looking for these children . . . hidden between the lines," allowing them "to surface and reshape the meaning of the biblical text."[33] My guess is that many of us would begin to read nonviolently, condemning the violence done against them in no uncertain terms. I believe this is precisely what needs to be done. As Gary Phillips puts it: "Readers of the Bible must read differently, deferentially, deliberately for the children, lest they contribute to the formation of a culture that makes the murder of the innocents natural, inevitable, biblical."[34] Rather than passing over these individuals as voiceless victims, we must allow their voices to *interrupt* our reading of the story. Phillips writes:

> Interruption occurs when particular innocent children disrupt the power biblical texts exercise in shaping our perceptions and informing our world. By

attending to these children's faces and other innocents whose deaths rupture our critical strategies and our memory, we open ourselves to the possibility of saying "No" to all texts, biblical or otherwise, that kill children.[35]

Violence against children is never appropriate, never justifiable, and never virtuous. If we condone textual violence against children, we have been seduced by Scripture. We must resist all such readings as inherently violent and as a violation of our obligation to read critically and ethically. For the sake of the children, we must read these texts nonviolently, in ways that neither legitimate the violence in the text nor justify it in our present context.

Before concluding this excursus and returning to our discussion of various ways to critique "virtuous" violence, I want to comment briefly on an article written by Chris Heard that engages in a deconstructive reading of the book of Habakkuk since it is relevant to the present point of reading with the victims of violence, especially children.[36] In the book of Habakkuk, the prophet is troubled by the current state of affairs in Judah. People are ignoring God's law and behaving violently. Habakkuk wonders why God has not judged the wickedness of Judah (Hab. 1:2-4), and God informs the prophet that punishment is on the way—in the form of the Babylonian army (Hab. 1:5-11). Habakkuk is more disturbed by this news since the Babylonians are even worse than the wicked inhabitants of Judah (Hab. 1:12-17)! But God assures Habakkuk that the Babylonians will also be held responsible for their actions and will be punished in due time (Hab. 2:2-20).

Heard's deconstructive reading of the book of Habakkuk exposes instabilities in the text that make it impossible to differentiate "between just and unjust violence," leaving the reader to wonder whether Yahweh's supposed justice is actually *un*just.[37] Guided by the ethics of deconstruction, Heard is compelled to seek "other Others" in the text.[38] He finds them with help from the Psalter.[39] They are the children of Judah and Babylon. Heard refers to these children, the ones who suffer as a result of God's judgment upon Judah and Babylon, as "the invisible victims of Yahweh's 'justice.'"[40] He believes we have an ethical obligation to hear their voices lest we perpetuate further acts of violence against them.

> A deconstructive reading cannot comfort, clothe, feed, or resurrect those children. But perhaps a deconstructive reading can perform an obligation to those children. Perhaps such a reading could commemorate them, and could thereby discourage cruelty to present and future generations of children. A deconstructive reading cannot undo the disasters of Jerusalem 587 bce or Babylon 539 bce. But perhaps, just perhaps, by opening up the reading of Habakkuk so that the cries of Judahite and Babylonian children may be heard, deconstructive criticism can make some small contribution in resistance against another Jerusalem or Babylon . . . or Dresden, or Hiroshima, or My Lai.[41]

If we are serious about reading with the victims, we will often find ourselves reading for the sake of children whose stories of suffering and death are often submerged in the pages of the Old Testament. Any text that sanctions violence against children for any reason must be subjected to the most rigorous ethical critique.

READ FROM THE MARGINS

Related to this idea of reading *with* victims is the notion of reading *from* the margins. While reading with victims involves reading with ancient individuals victimized *in* the text, reading from the margins involves reading with modern readers often marginalized *by* the text. It involves listening to what our brothers and sisters around the world have to say about these texts and the effect certain readings have on them.

In recent years, a number of significant studies have appeared, urging us to read from the margins and inviting us to listen to those who do.[42] Miguel De La Torre believes that the Bible "must be read with the eyes of the disenfranchised" and that "reading the Bible from the margins liberates not only those who are oppressed but the oppressors as well."[43] Similarly, Cheryl Anderson proposes an "inclusive biblical approach," one that "insists" on hearing the voices of "women, the poor, and the ethnically or religiously 'Other.'"[44] Such an approach "takes into account the perspectives of these groups and the consequences traditional interpretations have had upon them."[45] As we have seen, these "consequences" have historically been quite negative and often extremely violent.

Reading from the margins helps us recognize the harmful nature of these texts and provides further justification for critiquing the violence in them. This is why Esther Epp-Tiessen urges "North American Christians to listen to their Palestinian sisters and brothers in the faith."[46] She believes this is part of the solution for dealing with these violent texts. As Epp-Tiessen sees it: "Listening to the voices of those victimized by the biblical paradigm of conquest and interpreting the troublesome texts through the revelation of Jesus Christ can help redeem the Bible and contribute to justice, peace, and healing between peoples."[47] Since certain Old Testament texts have been used to legitimate the oppression of Palestinians, their reaction to these texts and their approach to reading them merits our special attention.[48] We should listen carefully to those who have been oppressed and victimized by violence.

For example, when reading prophetic texts that utilize images that sexually degrade women and condone violence against them, we should be especially attentive to the impact such texts have on women who have experienced domestic violence and sexual abuse. Renita Weems believes that when we discuss texts using metaphors to portray Israel as a "promiscuous wife," for instance, we "must address the matter of the metaphor's effects on *marginalized readers*." She asks: "*What does it do* to those who have been actually raped and battered, or who live daily with the threat of being raped and battered, to read sacred texts that justify rape and luxuriate obscenely in every detail of a woman's humiliation and battery?"[49] It is a very important question.[50] When we consider the negative impact such texts have on marginalized readers, we are well positioned to offer an incisive critique of these violent texts and images.

Reading from the margins is an especially urgent task for all those who actually live on the margins. They have the most at stake in the way these texts are read and applied. "If history is our guide," writes Emerson Powery, "minority readers have much more to lose if the ancient ideas of the Bible are appropriated in destructive ways."[51] Therefore, those who read from the margins tend to operate with a "hermeneutics of survival."[52] Powery contends that this way of "reading Scripture . . . has become (and, some would argue, has always been) the dominant mode of reading Scripture within many minority communities."[53] If the text is killing you, you need to find a way of dealing with it that allows you to survive. As Renita Weems describes it: "The expression of oppression has forced the marginalized reader to retain the right, as much as possible, to resist those things within the culture and the Bible that one finds obnoxious or antagonistic to one's innate sense of identity and to one's basic instincts for survival."[54] Critiquing "virtuous" violence provides one such means of survival. Reading from the margins, with those who so often experience the Bible as an "instrument of oppression," underscores the importance of resisting the Old Testament's accommodating attitude toward violence wherever it is found.[55]

APPEAL TO COMMONLY ACCEPTED STANDARDS OF MORALITY

In certain cases, one of the most compelling critiques that can be leveled against "virtuous" violence in the Old Testament is a simple appeal to common human decency and morality. There are some actions and behaviors that most people instinctively know are wrong, regardless of why they are done or who does them. Raping women (or men) and killing infants, for example, are violent acts that are routinely condemned by people everywhere. Regardless of one's religious affiliation (or lack thereof), and irrespective of any commitment to nonviolence, most people would judge rape and infanticide as heinous acts of violence that are completely unjustifiable, morally indefensible, and just plain wrong. Any mentally healthy, rationally functioning human being should quickly and easily recognize this.[56]

Therefore, when the Old Testament condones behaviors like these, we should appeal to our collective sense of morality and condemn them in no uncertain terms. While contextualizing these acts may help us understand how the Israelites could have regarded them as acceptable in certain situations, that does not change the fact that these acts are still profoundly wrong. Sexual violence and infanticide are always wrong, and most of us know that intuitively. Widely accepted moral intuitions like these, shared by people all around the world, are some of the best places from which to launch an ethical critique.

Obviously, the five reading strategies just described do not exhaust all the possible ways one might challenge the "virtue" of "virtuous" violence in the Old Testament. Still, they are representative of the various ways one can engage in an ethical critique of these violent texts. They are tools in the ethical reader's toolbox that should be used regularly. While some of these strategies will prove more useful in certain contexts than in others, all of them can help us critique "virtuous" violence as we attempt to overcome the Old Testament's troubling legacy.

Interlude: After Critique, Then What?

From what has been said thus far, it should be obvious that critiquing "virtuous" violence is an indispensable part of reading the Old Testament nonviolently. I cannot overemphasize the importance of this point. These texts have done enormous damage, and they continue to harm people to this day. If we hope to minimize their negative effects, we must be willing to engage in a serious critique of the violence they condone. This critique should be performed frequently, forthrightly, and forcefully. It is an ethical obligation incumbent upon all who desire to read the Old Testament responsibly.

But what happens after critique? What do we do once we have exposed the problematic nature of "virtuous" violence? Is our work finished, or can we still do something constructive with these violent texts? Interpreters differ on the potential usefulness of biblical texts that are judged to be morally deficient. Some try to redeem them in various ways, while others find these texts so offensive and problematic that they reject them completely.

As I see it, the problematic aspects of these texts do not render them unusable or drain them of all theological significance. I do not think we should cavalierly dismiss these texts as theologically worthless just because we find problems in them. Nor should we allow the problematic nature of these passages to overwhelm our ability to hear a word from God in them. There is more to these texts than just the difficulties they raise. Critique is not the final word.

After wrestling with the violence of the text honestly, responsibly, and transparently, and after engaging in a thoroughgoing critique, we should reexamine these texts to determine how we might use them constructively, in spite of their obvious shortcomings. The final two steps in the process of reading nonviolently demonstrate how this might be accomplished.

Step 4: Use Textual Violence Constructively

After critiquing the violent aspects of a particular passage, we may be very eager to move on to other texts that seem less troubling and more edifying. But we should not be too quick to turn away from these problematic passages. Despite the difficulties they raise for us, these texts can be used profitably when they are handled carefully. For example, the violent parts of the Bible can help us see ourselves more clearly and can provide useful insights into the nature and problem of violence itself. Violent texts expose our own violent tendencies and our desperate need for transformation. As Jacqueline Lapsley recognizes: "Part of the need to retain 'texts of terror' in the biblical witness is . . . their painful mimetic quality: they reveal us to ourselves."[57] We see ourselves when we read these texts, and the image is not particularly flattering.

Naming and critiquing textual violence alerts people to the violent and destructive patterns they experience in their own lives. For some readers, this can be self-revelatory. Some victims of abuse, for example, do not realize that what they are experiencing is abuse. They may blame themselves for the violence they endure and may even think their experience is normal ("every husband beats his wife now and then"). One way to use textual violence constructively is to help people recognize that physical and emotional abuse is *always* wrong. It is *never* normal or healthy. As Julia O'Brien observes: "One positive function that recognizing patriarchy in [the book of] Hosea can have is to train readers to see patriarchy in the present. For many people, hearing familiar patterns of relationship called 'sexist' or 'abusive' invites a reconsideration of their own lives."[58] This can be liberating for those who are victims of violence, since "awareness is the first step to change."[59] Becoming aware that what they have experienced—and perhaps still are experiencing—is wrong is a key insight that can empower them to take the necessary steps to get help and to care for themselves.

This new awareness can also have salutary effects on the *perpetrators* of violence as well since the "reconsideration" of which O'Brien speaks can—and should—invite confession and repentance. At the very least, it should prompt those who behave violently to reexamine and reevaluate their violent behavior. Nancy Bowen believes these violent texts can be read "in the manner of confession." As Bowen sees it:

> These difficult texts should be proclaimed and taught within faith communities. They should be treated not as paradigms to follow, though, but as part of our heritage from which to turn away in repentance as we confess that they reveal the sins of sexism, violence, and patriarchy. Another way of saying this is to advocate reading the biblical text as a mirror of identity. What we see in the Bible are stories that tell us that when we demonize the Other (whoever that might be), the result is theological justification of violence and destruction. When we see this dynamic in the text and critique it, we can then consider how contemporary situations also reflect similar dynamics and critique them. Having confessed that these are our sins, we can then repent and turn to another way.[60]

In other words, these texts serve as striking examples of how *not* to live. They expose our own violent attitudes and actions and can prompt us to change our ways.

Thom Stark also believes there are constructive ways to use these texts after critiquing them. He speaks about problematic passages of Scripture as "condemned texts" and believes "their status as condemned is exactly their scriptural value."[61] He understands these passages to function as "negative revelation" and therefore does not advocate ignoring or disregarding them.[62] Rather, he believes they are valuable if we hold them up like a mirror and see ourselves in them, since they reveal what we should *not* be and do.[63] Stark believes that "we must keep these texts in our liturgies, so that God can speak through them, urging us not to be yet another people willing to kill in the name of some land, some ideology, or some god."[64] In this way, these texts serve as a warning that can keep us from repeating the same violent patterns of the past.

One specific way to use these violent texts constructively is to use them as conversation starters to address sensitive issues that are often difficult to discuss. For example, the book of Hosea, which portrays God as an abusive husband, would function quite well as a starting point for discussing domestic violence, an extremely serious problem today. Other passages, such as Joshua 6–11, could be used to help us talk about such issues as the horrors of genocide, the violence of colonization, and the insidious problem of killing in the name of God. The opening chapters of the story of Esther could be used to reflect on "the sexual exploitation of young girls."[65] Cheryl Anderson believes that "if we become more aware of the inherent violence of such biblical texts [like those in Esther] and start to contest it, we will be better able, as people of faith, to confront and contest sexual violence today."[66] If we are willing to focus our attention on the violent ideologies embedded in texts like these, we may find unexpected resources for addressing a wide range of violent behaviors prevalent in the world today.

Step 5: Transcend the Violence

Another way to use problematic texts constructively, after acknowledging and critiquing expressions of "virtuous" violence within them, is to look for important themes and ideas that move beyond the violent dimensions of the text. Jacqueline Lapsley emphasizes this idea as it relates to the problem of patriarchy in the Bible. Although Lapsley is very aware that the patriarchal nature of the Old Testament creates significant problems for many readers, she believes this should not prevent them from seeing other valuable insights in these texts. She writes:

> The difficulties posed by these disturbing aspects of the Bible do not mean that readers of biblical narratives must reductively conclude their interpretations with the lament that "this is a patriarchal text," as though this were the end

result of interpretation or the only responsible interpretation. Many texts are patriarchal in some respects, and are *still about something else as well.*[67]

Lapsley is very interested in discovering "what else might be going on in the text that people who understand themselves as Christian and as feminist would benefit from hearing."[68] She believes that "acknowledging the ideological nature of a text does not disallow the possibility that the reader may discover other interpretations of that same text that are interesting, enlightening, and worth pursuing."[69] Precisely! After we have critiqued the problematic aspects of the text, we are free to consider other interpretations that might prove quite beneficial.

One of the more recent and helpful attempts to grapple with the question of what to do after critique comes from Old Testament professor Julia O'Brien. In her exploration of prophetic metaphors, O'Brien asks: "Is it possible to take seriously the sexism and violence of the Prophetic Books and still find value in them, to refuse to pit appreciation against critique? *Is there a way to do theology after critique*, to let critique inform theological reflection rather than stand as its opponent?"[70] Her answer to these questions is an unequivocal "Yes!" She believes it is both possible and desirable to allow our critique to inform our theological reflection. Rather than seeing critique as antithetical to reading texts constructively, O'Brien insists that we should use our critique to ask questions and explore issues raised by the text.

To illustrate her approach, O'Brien devotes several chapters to various prophetic metaphors. In her chapter titled "God as (Angry) Warrior," she includes a case study of the book of Nahum.[71] The prophet Nahum enthusiastically anticipates the day when God will utterly destroy the hated Assyrians, who were noted for their brutality in the ancient world. Given Israel's demoralizing experience of oppression and subjugation at their hands, one can certainly understand why Israelites would resonate with Nahum's message of judgment. Still, Nahum's description of God as a divine warrior planning to avenge the Assyrians is disturbing, to say the least. At one point, we read:

> I am against you, says the LORD of hosts, and will lift up your skirts over your face; and I will let nations look on your nakedness and kingdoms on your shame. I will throw filth at you and treat you with contempt, and make you a spectacle. (Nah. 3:5-6)

Using the language of sexual abuse to imagine God's judgment is deeply offensive and highly problematic to many readers. The message of Nahum and the way that message is communicated tends to polarize readers, who conclude that "either Nahum is a *bad* book—violent and misogynistic—*or* it is a *good* book, one that champions justice for the oppressed."[72] But O'Brien sees this as a false dichotomy and resists an either/or approach.

Rather than asking whether we like Nahum or whether we are willing to live the way it prescribes, what happens when we consider what pressing human questions this book and its critique invite us to consider? What good can come from reading Nahum, problems and all? How, for example, does ideological critique illumine ancient and modern understandings of anger and justice? And what do the metaphor of the Divine Warrior and its ideological critique suggest for Christian theological formulations?[73]

O'Brien is fully aware of the problems raised by the book of Nahum but does not allow these to keep her from using the text constructively. Instead, she uses an ideological critique of Nahum to engage in significant theological reflection on issues such as anger and justice, issues that are deeply rooted in the text.[74] For example, regarding the issue of justice, O'Brien writes, "Engaging Nahum through the lens of ideological critique makes me more aware of my own potential for defining justice in ways that benefit some at the expense of others; at the same time it reminds me that my own concerns need not be brushed off for the sake of 'bigger issues.' Nahum itself might not be a manifesto for equal justice for all, but my engagement with it in light of ideological critique helps me take up that cause yet again."[75] This type of content-based theological reflection strikes me as a very beneficial way to move beyond critique in an effort to use the book of Nahum constructively, responsibly, and reflectively.

A Final, Very Important Note: Critique and Embrace Must Go Hand in Hand

In this chapter, I have argued that overcoming the Old Testament's violent legacy involves reading nonviolently, and that reading nonviolently requires both critique and embrace. If we hope to be ethically responsible readers, we must critique expressions of "virtuous" violence in the text. But we should not stop there. If all we do is critique these texts, some will wonder why we should bother reading them at all. We must also find ways to use these texts constructively. Yet, this should be done only *after* we have engaged in a thoroughgoing critique. As Katharine Sakenfeld recognizes the value of both critique and embrace for reading the book of Hosea. "If we lift up only the positive imagery of tenderness and restoration in Hosea," writes Sakenfeld, "and do not challenge the negative aspects with which we disagree, we may unintentionally allow both batterers and victims to believe that these biblical verses justify such behavior."[76] That would be tragic. Critique and embrace must go hand in hand. Doing one without the other carries serious risks.

Renita Weems also advocates this approach in her work on the so-called marriage metaphor in the books of Hosea, Jeremiah, and Ezekiel. Early in her study, she writes:

Despite its obscene portrait of women, the metaphor of Israel as promiscuous wife represents an attempt by prophets . . . to call attention to political greed, moral decay, religious syncretism, social disintegration, and egregious national policies. How do we affirm its positive side while simultaneously renouncing its negative effects?[77]

Her answer comes later in the book and serves as a model we can emulate. According to Weems: "Reading texts that terrorize women requires . . . a dual hermeneutic: one that helps a reader to resist the ways in which texts subjugate aspects of a reader's identity, and another that allows a reader to appreciate those aspects of texts that nurture and authorize them in their struggle for personhood."[78] I find this notion of a dual hermeneutic, a both/and approach that includes resistance and appreciation, quite helpful.[79] It strikes me as a very useful posture to adopt when reading problematic passages containing "virtuous" violence.

Unfortunately, we tend to be people of extremes and often emphasize one aspect of these texts at the expense of the other.[80] We either talk incessantly about the positive lessons to be learned from a text (and thereby minimize its problematic nature), or we focus exclusively on the problematic nature of the text (and thereby leave readers wondering what value it possesses). Neither is desirable. The first allows the text to remain dangerous, while the second renders it theologically useless. These two practices must be used together.

The purpose of this chapter has been to describe a general approach to reading the Old Testament nonviolently. In what follows, we will utilize various aspects of this approach to explore Old Testament texts related to genocide, warfare, and violence against women. This will illustrate how reading nonviolently works in specific cases and will highlight the potential this approach has for overcoming the Old Testament's troubling legacy.

PART 3

Applying Nonviolent Reading Strategies to Violent Texts

CHAPTER 7

Confronting Canaanite Genocide and Its Toxic Afterlife

The problem is that the book [of Joshua] endorses, and even promotes the kinds of attitudes and practices that have generated violence and suffering on a massive scale. The story the book tells—of conquest, extermination, and dispossession—is all too familiar to a world reeling from waves of genocidal violence and recovering from the effects of colonial imperialism. Some of these programs of conquest and exclusion have been aided and abetted by Christians who have imitated what they have read in the biblical story.

—L. Daniel Hawk[1]

By any standard of measure, the narrative describing the conquest of Canaan in Joshua 6–11 is one of the most morally troubling texts in the entire Old Testament. Historically, it has also been one of the most toxic. This text has had an extremely harmful afterlife and has been used to provide religious rationale for some of the most heinous acts of violence in human history. People have repeatedly utilized the conquest narrative to justify colonialism and its attendant evils of warfare, killing, theft, and dispossession.[2] As Eryl Davies puts it: "What this text has 'done' is to justify colonialism and exploitation, and to bring untold suffering to countless communities resulting, in some cases, in their virtual annihilation as a people."[3] This narrative has also created enormous theological problems for Christians who have struggled to reconcile its image of a merciless, genocidal God with other images of God in Scripture. After all, what kind of God would order the ruthless and indiscriminate slaughter of Canaanite men, women, and children? If there was ever a text begging to be read nonviolently, this is it!

Calling a Spade a Spade: It Is Genocide

The conquest narrative in Joshua 6–11 is regarded as the fulfillment of the divine promise to Abraham that he and his descendants would one day possess the land of Canaan. As the story goes, all of Abraham's descendants travel to Egypt, where they are eventually enslaved. They cry out to God for help, and God selects Moses to be their deliverer. Speaking from the midst of a burning bush, God tells Moses: "I have come down to deliver them [the Israelites] from the Egyptians, and to bring them up out of that land to a good and broad land . . . to the country of the Canaanites" (Exod. 3:8). Although the Israelites are to inherit land occupied by others (Exod. 3:8, 17), nothing is said at this point about the fate of the indigenous population. But in the book of Deuteronomy, their fate is unmistakably clear: every inhabitant is to be exterminated.[4]

> When the LORD your God brings you into the land that you are about to enter and occupy, and he clears away many nations before you—the Hittites, the Girgashites, the Amorites, the Canaanites, the Perizzites, the Hivites, and the Jebusites, seven nations mightier and more numerous than you—and when the LORD your God gives them over to you and you defeat them, then you must utterly destroy them. Make no covenant with them and show them no mercy. (Deut. 7:1-2)

The command to "utterly destroy" the inhabitants of the land, people who are sometimes collectively referred to as Canaanites, suggests more than just a summons to war; it requires an act of genocide.[5] The picture that emerges from Joshua 6–11 largely seems to confirm this. We are repeatedly informed that people *are* utterly destroyed (Josh. 8:26; 10:1, 28, 35, 37, 39, 40; 11:11, 12, 20, 21), and the text claims that Joshua leaves alive neither survivors (Josh. 10:33) nor those who breathed (Josh. 10:40; 11:11, 14). While this description of total conquest is at variance with other traditions, such as those in the book of Judges and even some within the book of Joshua itself (Josh. 13:1-6a, 13; 17:13), it is hard to escape the conclusion that what is pictured here is genocide.

Still, some interpreters object to calling this genocide, or at least caution against it. Christopher Wright believes this description "can be misleading."[6] He rightly notes that today, genocide is commonly associated with notions of racial superiority. Since Wright believes the divine command to kill Canaanites had nothing to do with their ethnicity and everything to do with their wickedness, he objects to using the term "genocide" to describe the events in Joshua 6–11. As Wright sees it: "The conquest was not human genocide. It was divine judgment."[7]

Still, Wright concedes that it is "technically . . . correct" to speak of this as genocide "inasmuch as the term literally means the killing of a nation, and that is what Israel was commanded to do to the Canaanites."[8]

Others have objected to the language of genocide because they believe the killing was not as widespread and indiscriminate as the text seems to suggest. Richard Hess, for example, claims that cities such as Jericho and Ai were more like forts that were rather sparsely populated by soldiers rather than civilians—Rahab and her family being a notable exception. Thus, Hess does not believe the Israelites killed noncombatants, such as women and children, when they destroyed the inhabitants of these cities.[9] While this would make these texts *somewhat* less offensive, though still problematic, Hess's proposal is unpersuasive. Other passages in the Old Testament make it clear that besieged cities were not just populated by soldiers.[10] They were filled with young and old, men and women, soldiers and civilians. Moreover, there is no indication in the book of Joshua that women, children, or other civilians were routinely spared when the Israelites engaged in battle. Every indication we have from Joshua 6–11 is that entire populations were decimated. It requires special pleading to argue that women and children were absent. Despite how uncomfortable we may be with the moral and theological implications of calling this "genocide," that term best describes what is envisioned here, and we should not shrink from using it.

Did the Conquest Happen and Does it Matter?

The majority of biblical scholars no longer regard the conquest narrative as a historically reliable account of how Israel came to possess the land of Canaan.[11] As John Collins recently observed: "All but conservative apologists have now abandoned the historicity of the Conquest story as found in Joshua."[12] One primary reason for this is the considerable amount of archaeological evidence that is impossible to correlate with the biblical description of the conquest recounted in the book of Joshua.[13] Many cities that were reportedly destroyed by the Israelites show no evidence of destruction during the supposed conquest, whereas other cities that were destroyed during this time period are never mentioned in the book of Joshua. It is especially striking to note that both Jericho and Ai were uninhabited when the Israelites supposedly conquered them. As William Dever puts it: "There is little that we can salvage from Joshua's stories of the rapid, wholesale destruction of Canaanite cities and the annihilation of the local population. *It simply did not happen; the archaeological evidence is indisputable.*"[14]

Though it is outside the scope of this study to discuss various theories about how Israel actually came to possess the land, many think that the people we now call the Israelites emerged in the land of Canaan toward the end of the thirteenth century BCE.[15] Most biblical scholars believe the conquest narrative was composed hundreds of years after this time.[16] Thus, while there is significant scholarly debate over the function of this narrative, this much seems clear: it is not a historically reliable account of how Israel came to possess the land. This should not be regarded as a threat to biblical authority or an embarrassment for people who regard the book of Joshua as Scripture. It simply means one must recognize that these chapters were never intended to report what actually happened. The function of this conquest narrative lies elsewhere.[17]

So does it matter? Could we solve the problem created by the presence of "virtuous" violence in this text—and others—if we could conclusively demonstrate that the events described there never actually happened? No. As James Barr astutely observes: "The problem is not whether the narratives are fact or fiction, the problem is that, whether fact or fiction, the ritual destruction is *commended*."[18] Precisely! Regardless of one's views about the historicity of the conquest narrative, what we have is a text containing a massive amount of "virtuous" violence—violence that was, ostensibly, divinely sanctioned. Unfortunately, the problems raised by the presence of "virtuous" violence in the Old Testament do not disappear if the passage is regarded as historically unreliable.

This is not meant to imply that how we answer the historical question is unimportant. On the contrary, I think it is exceedingly important for a number of reasons, most significantly for how it affects our view of God. If one accepts the historicity of the text in its fullest sense, including all its claims about what God said and did, the picture of God that emerges is extremely troubling, to say the least. We are left with a God who orders, sanctions, and participates in acts of genocide. On the other hand, if God did not actually say and do what the text claims, other possibilities emerge for dealing with this morally problematic portrayal of God. How one answers the historical question of whether God did what the text claims, has enormous theological ramifications, and we will need to return to it later in this chapter.

Critiquing Canaanite Genocide

Many of the reading strategies for critiquing "virtuous" violence described in the previous chapter can be effectively applied to our reading of Joshua 6–11. This critique is especially needed given the way this text has been used to harm others.

Finding Internal Critiques

To begin, we might ask whether there is any evidence of discomfort within the book of Joshua itself with all the killing and bloodshed it describes. While most interpreters assume the conquest narrative wholeheartedly embraces and sanctions Israel's violence, some beg to differ. Lawson Stone has cogently argued "that certain ethical dimensions of holy war did concern the tradents of Joshua, to the extent that the holy war traditions in their earliest form represented an unusable past."[19] Because of that, Stone believes "clear moves were made to guide the reader to a nonmilitaristic, nonterritorial actualization of the text."[20] Stone examines six texts (Josh. 2:9-11; 5:1; 9:1-2, 3-4a; 10:1-5; 11:1-5) that primarily focus on how the Canaanites respond to Yahweh's presence and action in the land. Those who assist Israelites, or make peace with them, are spared, while those who resist Yahweh are killed. On this reading, Canaanites are killed not because they are "morally decadent," as some texts *outside* the book of Joshua suggest, but because "they have resisted the action of Yahweh."[21] This leads Stone to conclude that these stories of conquest are "object lessons in responsiveness to Yahweh's action and warning against resistance."[22] He believes that those who reworked these stories "transformed the historical tradition of the conquest into a gigantic metaphor for the religious life."[23]

Daniel Hawk builds upon Stone's thesis and argues that there are clear signs of critique evident in the way these texts have been reworked (most scholars assume the book of Joshua went through a number of revisions, or redactions). Hawk contends that the "transitional comments" Stone identifies are "but one element of a comprehensive redactional program that defuses the ethnic antagonism of the conquest traditions."[24] Specifically, Hawk believes later editors revised some of these stories to recast the Canaanites in a more favorable light, making it far more difficult to dehumanize and demonize them. According to Hawk, this more positive portrayal of Canaanites stands as a critique of Israelite traditions that prescribed total annihilation without mercy.

One way in which Canaanites are portrayed more positively comes by assigning blame for Canaanite aggression to Canaanite kings and not to the Canaanite population at large. Hawk carefully demonstrates how the conquest narrative is constructed in a way that suggests Israel's real enemies are not Canaanites generally, but Canaanite kings specifically.[25] Canaanite kings consistently stand in opposition to Israel and the actions of Yahweh (Josh. 2:2-3; 8:14; 9:1-2; 10:1-5; 11:1-5). This opposition is not evident, however, when we meet "ordinary" Canaanites like Rahab and the Gibeonites. By portraying kings, rather than commoners, as the aggressors, Hawk believes the book of Joshua suggests that "the powers that threaten Israel . . . are not those of different ethnicity but those who wield political power."[26] This allows for a much more charitable reading of the Canaanites than would otherwise be possible.

A more favorable view of Canaanites also emerges from three stories in Joshua that destabilize boundaries and challenge conventional understandings about Israelites and Canaanites. These are the stories of Rahab (Joshua 2), Achan (Joshua 7), and the Gibeonites (Joshua 9). Rahab and the Gibeonites appear to be "good" Canaanites, while Achan is portrayed as a very "bad" Israelite. The way these stories are told subverts ethnic distinctions as indicators of morality by calling into question simplistic judgments about bad Canaanites and good Israelites. As Hawk puts it:

In the stories of Rahab and the Gibeonites (Josh 2:1-14; 9:3-15), the reader encounters "peoples of the land" who glorify Israel's God and display attributes of initiative, shrewdness, and perseverance that Israel prized as its own, while the story of Achan intimates that Israelites can be every bit as sinful as the Canaanites (Josh 7:16-23). With marvelous sophistication these anecdotes challenge the stereotypes that legitimize violence against the indigenous others, blur the boundaries between the people of God and the "nations," and undercut the theological claims of nationalist rhetoric.[27]

Hawk believes that the way these traditions were redacted "reveals a profound ambivalence about Israel's traditions of conquest" and contends that "the manner of their reworking reveals that the ethnic violence that infused them had become problematic."[28]

If Hawk is right, then the book of Joshua itself contains an early critique of some of the most violent traditions in ancient Israel. In contrast to the way Canaanites are portrayed in other Old Testament texts, such as Leviticus 18 and Deut. 9:1-5; 20:16-18, Canaanites are *not* portrayed as irredeemably wicked or inherently defiling in the book of Joshua. Rather, as the stories of Rahab and the Gibeonites suggest, some Canaanites embodied Israel's most cherished values and even acknowledge the power of Israel's God. It would appear that Canaanites were not so different from Israelites after all. Such a sympathetic portrayal of Canaanites effectively dismantles some common stereotypes and directly challenges the exceedingly negative portrayals of Canaanites found in other Old Testament texts. It also signals a measure of discomfort with the wholesale slaughter of Canaanites reported in the book of Joshua. Therefore, I think Hawk is right when he claims that "the critique of the conquest begins within the book of Joshua itself."[29]

While this kind of internal critique is certainly not able to solve all the problems raised by the presence of "virtuous" violence in Joshua 6–11, it is helpful nevertheless, and points us in the right direction. It reminds us to slow down and read carefully when encountering texts that appear to endorse the violence they contain. All is not necessarily as it seems.

Reading with the Canaanites

When most people read the conquest narrative, they do so from the perspective of the Israelites. They cheer when the walls of Jericho come crashing down, and they celebrate Israel's stunning victories over the inhabitants of the land. Those who read from this perspective believe Israel was acting appropriately under orders from God. Hence, they regard the slaughter of Canaanites as fully justified. But I believe reading this way is extremely dangerous. It makes violence a virtue and mercy a vice. Worse, it sanctions genocide.

To avoid this undesirable state of affairs, it helps to shift perspectives and read *with* the Canaanites.[30] Our perception of the story changes dramatically when we view it through their eyes. When we read from this perspective, and choose to sympathize with the Canaanites rather than rejoice with the Israelites, the story looks very different and our perception of it changes dramatically. Reading with the Canaanites problematizes the violence of this narrative and raises doubts about the legitimacy of Israelite aggression. From the Canaanites' perspective, the Israelites are hostile invaders who are intent on taking their land, unwilling to make peace, and determined to kill every last one of them. This perspective confronts the reader with a new set of questions and challenges that are not easily answered or dismissed. What right did the Israelites have to take their land? How could the Israelites possibly justify the slaughter of all Canaanites, including infants and toddlers as well as the elderly and infirm? Is it reasonable to believe God really required them to commit such moral atrocities? Questions like these force us to rethink how we read this story.

If we are to read with the Canaanites, we must first see them as human beings. As Hawk observes: "The critique of the conquest begins . . . with the humanizing of the Canaanites, whose deaths are reported elsewhere with cold detachment."[31] We must learn to see Canaanites as real people—moms and dads, aunts and uncles, brothers and sisters, nephews and nieces, grandmas and grandpas—who had hopes and dreams, strengths and weaknesses, virtues and vices, just like we do. They too were created in God's image. Since "genocide proceeds on the fiction that the victims are not humans,"[32] humanizing Canaanites is critical and undermines efforts to justify genocide.

One way to bring Canaanites out of the shadows, and to see them as unique individuals, is to retell biblical stories about them from their perspective. Since we do not typically hear their voices in the text, this retelling requires some imagination. It involves giving Canaanites a voice, and possibly a name, as we strain to hear what they have to say.[33] Telling the story this way shares certain similarities to Jewish midrash, a form of interpretation that starts with the biblical text but then adds additional characters, conversations, themes, and details not found in the text. When stories like these are told, they can help us develop compassion for the thousands of nameless, faceless Canaanites who die on the pages of the Old Testament. They remind us that Canaanites were people too, and they enable us to hear their side of the story—perhaps for the first time.

If we are serious about reading ethically, in a way that increases our love for others, promotes justice, and values all people, we must be willing to read with the Canaanites. Once we do, it becomes very difficult to regard killing Canaanites as an act of "virtuous" violence.

Reading from the Margins

Reading from the margins reinforces the importance of reading with the Canaanites. This is because those living on the margins today naturally identify with victimized Canaanites rather than with victorious Israelites for one simple reason: the plight of the Canaanites mirrors their own.[34] As Michael Prior asks: "Should the victims of oppression, such as Amerindians, black South Africans and Palestinians, not find themselves more naturally on the side of the Canaanites and others than on that of the Chosen People, mandated to cleanse the land of its indigenes, a fate to which their own experience corresponds?"[35]

Robert Allen Warrior, a member of the Osage Nation of American Indians, confirms this inclination in a classic essay titled "Canaanites, Cowboys, and Indians." He writes: "The obvious characters in the story [of the conquest] for Native Americans to identify with are the Canaanites, the people who already lived in the promised land."[36] Yet, according to this story, "the narrative tells us that Canaanites have status only as the people Yahweh removes from the land in order to bring the chosen people in. They are not to be trusted, nor are they to be allowed to enter into social relationships with the people of Israel. They are wicked, and their religion is to be avoided at all costs."[37] It is easy to see how a story like this, in which God sanctions the slaughter of indigenous people to make room for outsiders, is very unappealing to Native Americans.[38]

Palestinian Christians have also found the conquest narrative to be quite problematic. Like all those who have been colonized, forcibly relocated, and dispossessed, Palestinians most easily resonate with the Canaanites, who "stand in for all peoples whose lands have been conquered and expropriated."[39] This narrative becomes especially dangerous for Palestinians when it is read by those who embrace its violent ideology and then apply it to the current political situation in Israel-Palestine. As Naim Ateek puts it:

> This uncritical transposition . . . makes the Palestinians appear to represent the old Canaanites who were in the land at the time and who at God's command needed to be dispossessed. . . . To choose the motif of conquest of the promised land is to invite the need for the oppression, assimiliation, control, or dispossession of the indigenous population.[40]

It is not difficult to understand why Palestinians find little to celebrate in the conquest narrative.

When the exodus-conquest narrative is read from the margins, the violence of conquest becomes exceedingly problematic. "One's perspective on the Exodus story takes on a different complexion," writes Prior, "when read with the eyes of the 'Canaanites', that is, of any of several different cultures, which have been victims of a colonialism fired by religious imperialism, whether of the Indians in North or Latin America, the Maoris in New Zealand, the Aborigines in Australia, the Khoikhoi and San in southern Africa or the Palestinians in Palestine."[41] Asian theologian Kwok Pui-lan describes her experience of coming to this realization. She writes:

> I first became aware that other people might look at the Exodus story differently when I listened some years ago to C. S. Song, a Presbyterian theologian from Taiwan. From the perspective of the tribal people in Taiwan, Song explained, the Exodus story is oppressive because the Canaanites were treated badly. Later, as I had opportunities to visit the Maoris in New Zealand and the Aborigines in Australia, they shared similar insights. I had never read the story from the perspective of the Canaanites, and the experience was shocking to me.[42]

So it is. In the words of Laura Donaldson: "It is shocking and disorienting to be confronted with angles of vision that contest dominant assumptions, making it impossible to interpret a story in familiar ways."[43] Reading from the margins, with those who naturally identify with the Canaanites, casts this once familiar story in an entirely different light, one that invites a critique of the violence sanctioned by the text.

Deconstructing Divinely Sanctioned Violence

One reason the conquest narrative has done so much harm and has had such negative aftershocks is that killing Canaanites is portrayed as being divinely sanctioned. For some readers, this makes the act morally unassailable. Regardless of how we may feel about it, they say, Canaanite genocide must be right because God commanded it. Surely God would not command people to do what is wrong or sinful! While the logic seems valid, some have questioned the basic premise. Did God actually command the Israelites to kill Canaanites? Many think not.

In a recent article in the journal *Philosophia Christi*, Randal Rauser makes a compelling case that God never commanded Israelites to annihilate Canaanites, despite what the text claims.[44] Rauser advances four arguments that he believes demonstrate why God could not have issued such a terrible decree. Since his case does not depend on a particular theological tradition or set of religious beliefs, it has the advantage of being accepted by a broader audience.

His first argument is based on common sense and fundamental human decency. Rauser believes "the most compelling argument" supporting his claim that Yahweh did not command genocide "is rooted in an assertion that . . . every rational properly functioning person cannot help but know: *it is always wrong to bludgeon babies.*"[45] He believes there is no way to conceive of bashing babies as "a morally praiseworthy act."[46] It is a very persuasive point.

Second, Rauser believes that the problem with genocide is not confined to the harm it does to the "victims." It also harms the perpetrators. Genocide victimizes everyone, both those who are killed *and* those who do the killing. To put it another way, the problem with genocide is not just that people die, but that people kill—and killing messes people up, to put it colloquially. Rauser emphasizes this when he speaks of "the soul-destroying effect on the perpetrator."[47] He writes:

> If regular combat carried out under the modern world's relatively civilized rules of engagement is psychologically and spiritually shattering, what would be the impact of carrying out . . . genocide of women and children. Even after being declared *herem*, Canaanite children would still scream, beg for mercy, cry, and bleed just like Israelite children. . . . What type of effect would the bludgeoning of babies, children, women and the elderly have had upon the Israelites? Imagine the psychological agony of an Israelite soldier divinely commanded to hack up a Canaanite toddler one day only to bounce his Israelite toddler on his knee the next.[48]

Rauser believes the psychological trauma of engaging in this kind of warfare provides yet another reason why God would not—and did not—command Canaanite genocide.

Third, Rauser notes how the conquest narrative fits the typical pattern followed by those who wish to rationalize genocide. Rauser writes:

> There are commonly three elements in such justifications: (1) divide: first you distinguish between an in-group and out-group while attributing a superior authority or ontological status to the former; (2) demonize: next you accuse the out-group of promoting an injustice, inequality, or threat over against the in-group; (3) destroy: finally, you implore the in-group to redress the injustice, often with a divine or transcendent imprimatur.[49]

Rauser believes the narrative of Canaanite genocide fits this pattern. He writes: "We repudiate the justifying narratives of the Nazi or Hutu . . . because their rationalizations conform to the same old 'divide, demonize, destroy' typology that characterizes virtually all genocides. . . . The Canaanite genocide also conforms to this terrible pattern."[50] This similarity between the way Canaanite and modern genocides are justified undermines the claim that Canaanite genocide was *divinely* sanctioned, casting doubt on the assertion that killing Canaanites was an act of obedience to God.

Finally, Rauser emphasizes what he calls the "the cost of genocide." If God actually sanctioned Canaanite genocide, it stands to reason that over time some people would regard this as sufficient justification to perpetrate similar atrocities on others. Tragically, as we have seen, this is precisely what some people have done.

Because they believed God really commanded Israelites to kill Canaanites, they appropriated this narrative in lethal ways to justify their own acts of violence and killing. Since God would surely have known how people would use such an example of divinely sanctioned violence to harm others in the future, Rauser contends that God would not have sanctioned such indiscriminate slaughter in the first place. The cost of genocide would simply be too high, given all the violence it would be used to legitimate in years to come.

Using these four arguments, Rauser refutes the claim that God actually commanded Canaanite genocide. Despite what the text claims, he does not believe that God willed, ordered, or participated in the extermination of Canaanites. When the conquest narrative is read this way, without divine sanction or involvement, it becomes impossible to find any justification for the violence described in Joshua 6–11. Deconstructing divinely sanctioned violence in the Old Testament is one of the most effective ways to critique "virtuous" violence and, therefore, one of the most promising strategies for overcoming the Old Testament's troubling legacy. We will have more to say about this in the next chapter.

Questioning the Old Testament's Rationale for Canaanite Genocide

Another way to critique the violence of the conquest narrative is to question the Old Testament's rationale for killing Canaanites. In addition to fulfilling the divine promise to give the land of Canaan to Abraham and his descendants, the Old Testament supplies two primary reasons for the necessity of Canaanite genocide: (1) to punish Canaanite wickedness, and (2) to preserve Israel's religious purity. But are these compelling reasons for engaging in acts of genocide? Do they justify the slaughter of every Canaanite man, woman, and child?

There are a handful of Old Testament passages suggesting that the conquest of Canaan was an act of divine judgment upon wicked Canaanites (Lev. 18:24-28; 20:22-23; Deut. 9:4-5; see also Gen. 15:16). These texts draw a clear connection between Canaanite wickedness and their removal from the land. The Canaanites are accused of engaging in illicit practices and immoral behavior, and this is understood as the reason for God's judgment upon them.

The other reason given for the annihilation of the entire Canaanite population, the need to maintain Israel's religious purity, is clearly articulated in Deuteronomy 20:16-18:

> But as for the towns of these peoples that the LORD your God is giving you as an inheritance, you must not let anything that breathes remain alive. You shall annihilate them . . . so that they may not teach you to do all the abhorrent things that they do for their gods, and you thus sin against the LORD your God. (Deut. 20:16-18; see also Num. 33:55-56; Deut. 7:3-4)

According to this passage, allowing Canaanites to remain in the land would have catastrophic consequences for Israel's spiritual health and well-being. They would be a bad influence on Israelites and would lead them into religious apostasy. Therefore, they needed to be destroyed so that Israel could stay true to God and fulfill its mandate as a conduit of God's blessing for the world.[51]

This explanation, which thrives on what Walter Wink calls "the myth of redemptive violence," is regularly seized upon by Christians attempting to justify God's behavior in this story.[52] As Gleason Archer writes in his *Encyclopedia of Bible Difficulties*:

> Much as we regret the terrible loss of life, we must remember that far greater mischief would have resulted if they [the Canaanites] had been permitted to live on in the midst of the Hebrew nation. These incorrigible degenerates of the Canaanite civilization were a sinister threat to the spiritual survival of Abraham's race.[53]

Similarly, popular Christian writer John Ortberg argues that "the beliefs of the Canaanites were a cancer that had to be removed from the land before the people of God could live there with any hope of health. Thus, God ordered surgery for the long-term health and life of his people."[54]

Comments like these are dangerous since they reinforce and perpetuate the perspective of the text, namely, that violence can be "virtuous" and that killing others is sometimes necessary to achieve a greater good. Rather than adopting and defending this perspective, we ought to actively critique it.

Neither of the reasons given for Canaanite genocide strikes me as particularly persuasive. First, as noted above, when we actually encounter Canaanites in the book of Joshua, they do not appear to be exceedingly wicked. On the contrary, they display many character traits and values that Israelites themselves cherished. While some Canaanites presumably were wicked in certain ways, there is no evidence to suggest that the Canaanites were any more wicked than other people living at that time.[55] Even a conservative scholar like Tremper Longman recognizes this:

> Why the Canaanites? Why not some other people? Are the Canaanites really extraordinarily evil? While perhaps the case can be made from their own texts that the Canaanites were evil, *I do not think it can be shown that they were more evil than the Assyrians or the Israelites themselves.*[56]

Why order the extermination of Canaanites for their wickedness while letting others live who are were just as bad? This raises disturbing questions about divine justice.

Additionally, attempts to justify Canaanite genocide by appealing to the need to maintain Israel's spiritual purity are unconvincing. For example, as Daniel Hawk observes regarding one group of Canaanites:

The prominence given to the Gibeonites' story attests to the impact the indigenous inhabitants continued to have on the life of Israel, and it counters the assertion that their presence would contaminate Israel. Joshua, after all, had assigned them a place of service at the altar of God, hardly a location for those who might defile the nation.[57]

Moreover, if the only way to maintain one's faith requires killing others who believe differently, it is legitimate to wonder how desirable that faith really is. As C. S. Cowles observes:

> The "sanitized land theory" presents an unflattering view of Israel's God. It was a virtual admission that in free and open competition with Canaanite religion, Yahweh worship would lose out. So the only solution was to exterminate the competition. In any case, the . . . campaign utterly failed. The Canaanites were decimated but not destroyed, idolatry was not eradicated, and the Israelites were not preserved from moral and spiritual pollution. What could be more morally bankrupting and spiritually corrupting than slaughtering men, women, and children?[58]

In my mind, both explanations given in the Old Testament for Canaanite genocide are unsatisfying. Neither one really addresses the most pressing and obvious problem of all, namely, the immorality of genocide itself. We cannot lose sight of the fact that genocide involves killing everyone, including the weakest, the youngest and the most vulnerable. The Old Testament's rationale for genocide does not even begin to account for the slaughter of infants and toddlers—nor could it. Such acts are utterly unjustifiable. Despite what certain Old Testament texts suggest, genocide is never good, never moral, and never "virtuous."[59]

A Plea to Scholars: Stop Justifying Genocide!

In recent years, a number of scholars have addressed the morally problematic dimensions of Canaanite genocide directly.[60] This is a welcome change from the dearth of sustained attention this issue previously received. What is less welcome, and rather disconcerting, is how many of these scholars seem committed to *condoning* rather than condemning Canaanite genocide. It is disheartening to witness them trying so hard to persuade people that something as unquestionably evil as genocide is morally justifiable. Instead of helping people critique the violence sanctioned by the text, they add their voices in support of it. Allow me to cite a few examples.

In his provocatively titled book *God Behaving Badly*, David Lamb assures us that even though the conquest was "violent," it was "not unusual, harsh, cruel or unjustified."[61] Paul Copan, in his book *Is God a Moral Monster?*, contends that no civilians were harmed in the conquest of Canaan, making the invasion far less bloody than most people typically imagine. Moreover, even if infants had been killed, Copan does not regard this as a cause for alarm because "they aren't wronged . . . they will be compensated by God in the next life."[62] In *The God I Don't Understand*, Christopher Wright argues that the Canaanites were exceedingly wicked, as bad as the Bible makes them out to be, and therefore fully deserving of death. Wright believes God could not have saved the world without ordering their elimination. From his perspective, it was a necessary part of the divine master plan.[63] According to Wright:

> This is the way in which God in his sovereignty chose to work within human history to accomplish his saving purpose for humanity and for creation, including me. I may not understand why it had to be this way. I certainly do not like it. I may deplore the violence and suffering involved, even when I accept the Bible's verdict that it was an act of warranted judgment. I may wish there had been some other way.
>
> But at some point I have to stand back from my questions, criticisms, or complaint and receive the Bible's own word on the matter. What the Bible unequivocally tells me is that this was an act of God that took place within an overarching narrative through which the only hope for the world's salvation was constituted.[64]

While I respect Wright's efforts to wrestle with this issue and to acknowledge our human limitations, I do not agree that we must "accept the Bible's verdict that it was an act of warranted judgment." Nor do I believe that we should "stand back" from our "questions, criticisms, or complaint." To my way of thinking, doing so represents a failure to read these texts in an ethically responsible manner. When the Bible portrays God as one who commands genocide, and the text approves of the slaughter of men, women, children, and infants, we must step up and speak out. It is imperative to confront and critique the immorality of genocide lest people think God actually wills such atrocities.

To their credit, many scholars who defend the violence of Joshua 6–11 are quick to say that the conquest narrative should not be used to justify acts of genocide today. That is good, *but it is not enough.* The reality is that justifying genocide in the past inevitably opens the door for justifying it today. As Randal Rauser observes: "There is widespread agreement that the 'baptism' of violence in the past justifies use of violence in the present."[65]

The bottom line is simply this: there is no compelling reason to justify genocide in the Old Testament, and there are many compelling reasons not to.[66] Those who try to justify Canaanite genocide typically do so because of their preconceived ideas of what the Bible is and does. They are often committed to the belief that God actually said and did what the text claims. Therefore, they must find some way to explain God's behavior and to defend God against charges of wrongdoing. But this is a hermeneutical straitjacket of their own making. There is nothing that requires one to view the Bible this way, and there are many things that suggest otherwise.[67]

What is needed when reading the conquest narrative is not further justification *for* it but a robust critique *of* it. Yet, many interpreters fail to engage in this kind of ethical critique precisely where it is most sorely needed. This should not be! As Derek Flood observes:

> When the Bible helps us challenge and deepen our moral vision and character this is surely a good thing, but when it leads us to abandon our most basic notions of right and wrong, something has gone horribly wrong. The fact that so many biblical commentaries continue to attempt to justify the biblical genocide accounts reveals a profoundly disturbing disconnect between biblical scholarship and ethics.[68]

An ethically responsible reading of Canaanite genocide demands critique rather than justification. Those who wish to read responsibly should not try to convince people that something so obviously evil is somehow good. Doing so is not only misguided; it is dangerous.

What Is the Conquest Narrative Good For?

Though it is absolutely essential to engage in a critique of "virtuous" violence, those committed to reading the Old Testament as Scripture must also consider ways to redeem these violent texts. After critiquing the "virtuous" violence in the conquest narrative, how can it be read in ways that are theologically constructive? Or to put the question more crudely, What is the conquest narrative good for?

One of the most valuable functions of this narrative resides in its capacity to warn readers of the danger of religiously sanctioned violence. The conquest narrative provides a natural opportunity to talk about the way people justify moral atrocities in the name of God. As Charles Kimball observes: "More wars have been waged, more people killed, and more evil perpetrated in the name of religion than by any other institutional force in human history."[69] This is terribly disconcerting! In a day and age riddled by religiously motivated acts of violence and terror, it is important to be aware of the ways people use religion to justify acts of violence. The story of the conquest provides an entrée into this crucial conversation.

Second, and relatedly, the conquest narrative helps us reflect on the ways political leaders frequently use religion to serve their own agendas. If, as some scholars believe, portions of the book of Joshua were reshaped during the reign of King Josiah (640–609 BCE) and intended to function—at least partly—as a piece of political propaganda, it illustrates how violent religious rhetoric can be used for political ends.[70] Josiah clearly wanted to expand his borders, and some believe portions of the book of Joshua were intended to legitimate Josiah's expansionist policies.[71]

By portraying the territory in question as land given to Israel by God hundreds of years prior, the book of Joshua provided Josiah with all the religious justification he needed to engage in military action to retake it.

Like Josiah, political leaders today often use religion and religious language in very self-serving ways to give the impression that their initiatives have divine blessing and approval.[72] This is extraordinarily dangerous since the state often does things in God's name that God has neither willed nor sanctioned. Understanding this dimension of the conquest narrative reminds us of the danger of mixing religious rhetoric with political ambitions. As such, it serves as a helpful reminder to be extremely wary of those who do likewise.

Third, reading the conquest narrative nonviolently has the potential to facilitate constructive dialogue between the perpetrators and the victims of colonization. As Daniel Hawk sees it, "Joshua can play a key role in reconciling colonized and colonizing peoples."[73] He believes that "Joshua provokes colonizing peoples to confront their past" and regards this book as "a powerful biblical resource" that might lead them "to repentance."[74] This is especially true when the story is read from a Canaanite perspective. Reading from the side of the oppressed can sensitize oppressors to the suffering they have caused and can help them recognize the evil they have done. In this way, the book has the potential to "facilitate the peacemaking and ministry of reconciliation that lies at the heart of Christian mission in the world."[75] It also reminds us that even the most difficult parts of the Bible can be quite beneficial when read nonviolently.

Fourth, the two cameo appearances by Canaanites in the book of Joshua—Rahab (Joshua 2 and 6) and the Gibeonites (Joshua 9)—have some tantalizing possibilities for reflection and application. By portraying Canaanites positively, these passages invite readers to reconsider their view of Canaanites and, by extension, their view of others who are different from them. Referring to the story of Rahab, Hawk writes: "The biblical text . . . prods today's Christian readers to examine their own attitudes and perspectives. Who are the 'others' in our thinking? What stereotypes do we hold? What demeaning attitudes and perceptions should be exposed and discarded? Are we willing to make space for others in our hearts and in our churches?"[76] Using the story of Rahab, a good Canaanite, to raise and reflect on questions like these seems especially fruitful.

Should We Spiritualize the Conquest Narrative?

Finally, we need to consider one more way some interpreters believe this narrative can be used constructively, namely, by focusing on a less literal reading of it. This approach is favored by Douglas Earl in his recent book, *The Joshua Delusion?*[77] Taking his lead from ancient interpreters, Earl urges us to avoid a literal reading of the text in favor of looking for its spiritual significance.[78] When this is done, Earl believes the book of Joshua yields rich interpretive fruit. "Rather than being a troubling text of conquest," writes Earl, "Joshua emerges as a text that challenges the community of faith to respond wholeheartedly to God and to be willing to welcome those seemingly outside the community who display the 'signs of grace', perhaps signs that are shown in terms of justice, wisdom, love and goodness for example."[79]

While I do not deny the book of Joshua *can* be read in this way, I am nervous about this approach because it never *directly* challenges or critiques the violence sanctioned in the text.[80] While this is understandable given Earl's approach—he claims the point of the narrative is not about violence and killing—I believe it is still imperative to engage in an ethical critique of the violence in this text given the enormous potential it has to influence the way we think about, and behave toward, others. As Thom Stark observes, many of those who spiritualize or allegorize this text do so without "having confronted and condemned the literal meaning of the text. This fact leaves open the possibility (too frequently the reality) that literal readings of the morally problematic texts might creep in through the back door."[81] Throughout the history of the church, this is exactly what happened "with the emergence of the Crusades, the Inquisition, Manifest Destiny, and other Christian appropriations of the conquest ideology."[82]

It is problematic to spiritualize violent texts without first critiquing the violence contained in them. Still, this is quite typical of the way many people read the conquest narrative and other offensive passages in the Old Testament. As Peter Craigie observes:

> I have known many Christians who have for a long time been devoted and daily readers of the Bible. For many of them war is no longer a problem, if it ever was, for as they read, a process of "spiritualization" takes place. For example, they can read of the capture of Jericho by the forces of Joshua and rejoice in the whole chapter, for translated into spiritual terms it describes the victory of those totally committed to God. I do not want to dispute such spiritual meaning, but I simply want to stress that read at face value the chapter describes the literal slaughter of men and women, young and old, all in the name of obedience to God (Joshua 6). *A similar event in Vietnam was followed by a war crimes trial.* Thus before the spiritual implications are drawn from such a text, some serious thought must be given to what it actually says.[83]

Craigie makes an excellent point. Before we attempt to extract some spiritually edifying meaning from the text, we must come to grips with "what it actually says." And what it actually says, in this case and many others, is often terribly problematic at various levels. It distorts our view of God, celebrates acts of violence, and presents the slaughter of others as an expression of holy obedience. These literary realities must be addressed and critiqued before any "spiritual implications" are drawn.

Moreover, if we do spiritualize the text, we need to be very careful about what we affirm and what we do not. For example, while I recognize that the conquest narrative can be read positively, in ways that emphasize the importance of obeying God, I cannot affirm the violent *form* obedience takes in the book of Joshua. While there are many appropriate ways to express obedience to God, slaughtering others is not one of them! Obeying God and killing people are mutually exclusive. Those who spiritualize this text, and use it to summon others to obey God, should be very clear on this point. So while I am not opposed to this way of reading, and can see some real value in it, those who read violent texts this way must do so with extreme caution.

What I proposed in the previous chapter, and have tried to demonstrate in this one, is that overcoming the Old Testament's troubling legacy involves critiquing what is unusable without abandoning the text. When read nonviolently, all texts, even the most unsavory, have something constructive to offer us. After we have engaged in a robust critique of the violence at hand, we should consider how these texts might still speak to us today. To my mind, this represents an ethically responsible way to handle texts containing "virtuous" violence. It honestly acknowledges the very real problems these texts raise while recognizing the value they still have for those who regard them as Scripture.

While this chapter has focused more narrowly on the issue of Canaanite genocide, the next chapter considers the broader issue of war in the Old Testament. Many readers appeal to the presence of divinely sanctioned warfare in the Old Testament to support the legitimacy and morality of warfare today. If we are to overcome this aspect of the Old Testament's troubling legacy, we will need to find ways to read these texts nonviolently.

CHAPTER 8

Keeping the Old Testament from Being Used to Justify War

If killing was good enough for Joshua, then it's good enough for me!

—An undergraduate student[1]

It is default of duty for anyone to teach these stories of holy war without suitable correctives and warnings.

—Norman Gottwald[2]

Over three decades ago, Peter Craigie wrote a popular little book titled *The Problem of War in the Old Testament*.[3] It was his attempt to help Christians grapple with certain challenges raised by the overwhelming presence of martial material in the Old Testament. Early in the book, Craigie identifies "three principal areas of difficulty" occasioned by the presence of war in the Old Testament, one of which he describes as "the *problem of ethics*."[4] "If all the Bible has relevance for ethics," writes Craigie, "does it follow that war may be pursued legitimately?"[5] Or, to put the question more directly: Does the Old Testament support Christian participation in war?

For some people of faith, the answer is an unequivocal "Yes!" Hundreds of years ago, Martin Luther wrote: "If the waging of war and the military profession were in themselves wrong and displeasing to God, we should have to condemn Abraham,

Moses, Joshua, David and all the rest of the holy fathers, kings, and princes, who served God as soldiers and are highly praised in Scriptures because of this service."[6] More recently, professor George W. Knight III expressed a similar view:

> The God and Father of Abraham, Isaac, and Jacob, and of our Lord Jesus Christ, instructed his people of old to wage war when necessary and to slay the enemy. . . . These explicit instructions by God make it impossible to maintain that God prohibits the believer from engaging in war under any circumstances.[7]

Many Christians would agree with these sentiments. The presence of divinely sanctioned warfare in the Old Testament leads them to conclude that war is not always wrong. In fact, God's involvement in warfare and killing in the Old Testament is regarded as incontrovertible evidence that war is sometimes right because it is ordained by God.

Old Testament portrayals of God sanctioning war and participating in it have been used over and over again to justify subsequent acts of war and killing. Even today, many Christians continue to appeal to God's involvement in war in the Old Testament as evidence that war, in and of itself, cannot be categorically wrong. Since God ostensibly initiated, sanctioned, and sometimes even participated in acts of violence and war, they believe there are circumstances today in which war is not only permissible, but necessary. Just as God ordered Israelites to go to war in the past, they reason that God sometimes may want Christians to fight in the present. This is a familiar argument, routinely advanced during times of war.

In his book *When God Says War Is Right*, professor Darrell Cole emphasizes God's "warlike character" in the Old Testament and believes it has direct relevance for the question of Christian participation in war.[8] Since the Old Testament claims that God sometimes uses lethal force for the sake of justice, Cole believes Christians must do likewise in certain circumstances since they are to imitate God's behavior. Cole argues that God's expression of this warlike character through the "use of force" is to be understood as "a product of His justice, mercy, and love."[9] These are the principles Cole believes should also govern Christian participation in warfare.[10] As Cole sees it: "Christians fight for justice because God is like that—He uses force to check evil and to bring justice. Christians ought to use force to restrain evil because God is like that; God's order demands it."[11]

But can one legitimately draw such far-reaching conclusions about the appropriateness of a Christian's participation in war on the basis of Old Testament texts portraying God as warrior? I think not. While I agree with Cole's assertion that Christians—and others—should "fight for justice" and "restrain evil," I do not regard war as a morally acceptable option for doing so. Moreover, I strongly disagree with his contention that the Old Testament's portrayal of God's involvement in war serves as an example for Christians to follow. Such a claim makes the Bible an accessory to killing and results in using the Bible to harm others.

Since those who believe that the Old Testament legitimates Christian participation in war do so by emphasizing God's involvement in war in the Old Testament, this is where our effort to read war texts nonviolently needs to begin. If we hope to discourage people from using the Old Testament to justify war, we need to reconsider the Old Testament's claims about God's involvement in war.

The Theological Significance of War in Ancient Israel

In the ancient world, many things that happened were understood theologically. People perceived divine involvement and causality in events we would typically explain in other ways. Take, for example, natural disasters. Things like hailstorms, earthquakes, famines, and floods were thought to be caused by God and thus were fraught with theological significance. They were not viewed as mere "natural" disasters—and for good reason. People in the ancient world had no scientific explanation for why these kinds of things occurred. Therefore, they explained them the only way they knew how: theologically. Since they believed God was responsible for all these events—some of which were quite devastating—they understandably regarded them as acts of divine judgment.

Similarly, historical events carried theological meaning and significance in the ancient world, and this influenced the way people wrote about them. When rendering their version of the past, ancient historiographers often attached theological explanations and evaluations to the events they described. The "theologized history" that resulted was informed by their assumptions and presuppositions about God/the gods and the way they believed God worked in the world.[12] This is certainly evident in the way they wrote about war. For these writers, war had theological significance.[13]

People in the ancient world believed the gods were intimately involved in their experience of war. They routinely conceived of God as a warrior and were convinced that God/the gods commissioned war, participated in it, and determined the outcome of it. These assumptions about God's involvement in war are evident in *many* texts from the ancient world.[14] These texts, along with the witness of the Old Testament, make it unmistakably clear that divine involvement in war was a theological given in the ancient world. Everyone believed God/the gods was involved in the "business" of war. It was so much a part of the air they breathed that it went unquestioned and unchallenged.

In such a context, one would expect Israel's understanding of God's involvement in war to be similar to that of the surrounding nations—and it was.[15] Like other people in the ancient world, the Israelites believed God sanctioned their wars and fought for them and sometimes against them. They also shared the common belief that victory in battle was a sign of divine favor while defeat in battle reflected divine displeasure. These assumptions about the theological significance of war and God's role in it are evident in numerous Old Testament passages.[16] All this leads to a very important question: Given these similarities, how should we evaluate the Old Testament's claims about God's involvement in war?

Evaluating the Old Testament's Portrayal of God's Role in Warfare

Many Christians accept what the Old Testament says about God as warrior at face value. They believe that the Old Testament's description of God's involvement in war reflects God's actual involvement in warfare in history. This is largely due to their view of Scripture, which leads them to believe that the Bible faithfully narrates God's actions in the world. Therefore, when they read stories in the Old Testament that describe God sanctioning war, they naturally conclude that God has, at times, done so. Likewise, when they read about God commanding Israelites to slaughter others, they believe this is, in fact, precisely what God decreed. But is this an appropriate way to read and understand these texts? Are we to believe God actually sanctioned and participated in all the warfare and killing the Old Testament claims?

Many Christians think so. They work on the assumption that God did whatever the Old Testament claims. Yet, this assumption does not hold up well under scrutiny. For example, when one examines the archaeological record (which suggests that certain divinely sanctioned wars in the Old Testament never took place),[17] takes Israel's worldview and the nature of ancient Israelite historiography into account (which makes assumptions about divine causality many Christians today no longer believe),[18] considers the ubiquitous presence of the divine warrior motif in the ancient world (which explains why the Israelites, like everyone else around them, would conceive of God as a warrior),[19] and recognizes the mutually contradictory images of God in the Old Testament (about which we will say more in a moment), it is not difficult to conclude that some of the Old Testament's claims about God—particularly those related to God's involvement in war—are largely, if not completely, unrelated to what God actually said or did.

When assessing the Old Testament's portrayal of God as warrior, it is especially important to read conversantly rather than compliantly. Instead of passively accepting what the Old Testament says about God's involvement in war, we should evaluate these claims in light of their historical context, keeping in mind that Israelites understood God's involvement in war in much the same way as the nations around them did. Thus, while Old Testament portrayals of God as warrior make sense in light of the historical context from which they emerged, they do not necessarily serve as a reliable guide for understanding how God actually behaved in the past. Rather, they reveal more about what Israel believed to be true about God given their particular worldview.

While this conclusion may be disconcerting to some readers, it should not be all that surprising. Not every portrayal of God in the Old Testament helps us to see God clearly. While some portrayals certainly reveal God's character, others distort it.[20] For example, how many Christians or Jews really believe that God takes "delight" in bringing people "to ruin and destruction" (Deut. 28:63), would strike an innocent child with a terminal illness as punishment for his father's sin (2 Sam. 12:14-15), causes people to lie (1 Kgs. 22:23), commands people to kill babies (1 Sam. 15:3), commissions and sanctions genocide (Deut. 7:1-2; 20:16-18), sanctions adultery (2 Sam. 12:11), destroys people without compassion or "for no reason" (Jer. 13:14; Job 2:3), slaughters people without mercy (Lam. 2:21; see also 3:43), sends wild animals to kill people who do not worship God (2 Kgs. 17:25), or orders a woman to return and submit to an abuser (Gen. 16:1-9)? Is that the God people of faith love and worship? Yet, God is portrayed in all of these ways—and many others—in the Old Testament.

Therefore, if we want to use the Bible to help us know what God is really like, we must distinguish "between the textual God and the actual God," to borrow language from Terence Fretheim.[21] The textual God is a *literary* representation, whereas the actual God is a *living* reality. If we want to use the Bible to think about God as God really is, we must recognize this distinction and determine the degree of correspondence that exists between Old Testament portrayals of God and the true character of God.[22] The two should not be simplistically equated.

The need to make distinctions like this is exacerbated by the fact that the Old Testament contains many contrasting—and sometimes mutually exclusive—images of God within its pages. One passage claims that God is merciful (Exod. 34:6), while another depicts God commanding to kill without mercy (1 Sam. 15:2). One passage says God's mind can change (Jer. 18:7-10), while another passage says it cannot (1 Sam. 15:29). One passage claims God incited David to take a census (2 Sam. 24:1), while another claims it was Satan who did so (1 Chron. 21:1). If we want to use the Old Testament to help us think about what God is like, we obviously have some decisions to make. We must be discerning readers, able to adjudicate the competing claims the Old Testament makes about God in order to perceive what God is really like.[23] This task becomes especially urgent when dealing with Old Testament portrayals of God's involvement in war since these texts have had such a troubling legacy over the years.

If we hope to read Old Testament war texts in an ethically responsible manner, in ways that do not perpetuate the Old Testament's troubling legacy, we need to contextualize these warlike portrayals of God and be honest about their limitations for revealing God's character. The Old Testament image of a violent, war-making God reflects ancient assumptions about God's involvement in warfare and killing, assumptions that people of faith today should no longer accept. Victory in battle should not be interpreted as an indication of divine blessing any more than defeat in battle should be understood as the result of divine judgment. Nor should God be seen as one who initiates warfare or determines its outcome. Instead, we realize that wars are won or lost due to a whole host of factors, including troop size and strength, the number and technological sophistication of weapons, the skill of the commanding officers, and the ability to form powerful alliances.

Our worldview and our beliefs about God's involvement in war differ considerably from our ancient counterparts. In many respects, it makes no more sense for us to embrace Israel's culturally conditioned assumptions about God being a warrior than it does for us to accept their culturally conditioned assumptions about the afterlife (*Sheol*), the right to own slaves, or the value of sacrificing animals. Therefore, when Israel claims that God wills, ordains, sanctions, or otherwise blesses war, we must recognize this claim for what it is: a culturally conditioned explanation of divine involvement in warfare. While depictions of God sanctioning war, killing enemies, and determining the outcome of battles made perfect sense in their historical context, they should not be understood as reflecting what God actually said and did.

Recognizing this is exceedingly helpful for reading the Old Testament nonviolently. By challenging the notion that God actually sanctioned warfare, we effectively undermine efforts to use the Old Testament to legitimate war based on God's *supposed* approval of it and involvement in it. By properly contextualizing the image of God as warrior, we can read the Old Testament in ways that encourage life and peace rather than death and war.

What If I Am Not Convinced?

While *I* am convinced it is best to regard the Old Testament's description of God's involvement in war as reflective of how people thought about God in a particular historical context—rather than as descriptive of what God actually said and did—I realize that not everyone will agree. Some are equally convinced God really did participate in war in the past, and they believe the Old Testament basically tells it like it is (or was, as the case may be). Still, even those who believe what the Bible says about God's involvement in war sometimes caution modern readers against using the Old Testament as the basis for engaging in acts of war today.[24]

The reasons for offering this word of caution differ. Some, like Eugene Merrill, note the unique relationship God had with ancient Israel as a theocracy and emphasize that God no longer works primarily through one particular nation.[25] Since the church is transnational, the need to defend borders "in the name of God" no longer prevails. Others appeal to the notion of progressive revelation,[26] stressing that God had to meet people where they were in order to relate to them and to communicate effectively with them. That is why they believe God needed to get involved in the messiness of war and violence in the past but no longer needs to do so today, since we now have a better understanding of who God is and how God wants us to treat others.

These approaches are not without problems, and I have critiqued them elsewhere.[27] Still, I am always glad whenever adherents of these approaches try to dissuade people from simplistically using the Old Testament as justification for participating in war today. By doing so, they help us read the Old Testament less violently.

Reading War Texts with Eyes Wide Open

One of the challenges of reading the Old Testament nonviolently is the overwhelming approval it gives to the practice of war. In fact, according to John Goldingay, the Old Testament "does not critique peoples for going to war . . . it seems to accept that nations make war to defend themselves, to defend others, to enlarge their territory or power, and to take redress on others, and it makes little judgment on questions about war's propriety."[28] If we are unaware of this and/or take no steps to challenge the Old Testament's assumptions about war, we are likely to be unduly influenced by those assumptions. So what can we do to push back against this very accommodating attitude toward war? How can we read these texts in ways that at least give us pause and cause us to raise important questions about the morality of war?

In what follows, I will describe several strategies that can help us read Old Testament war texts in ways that accentuate and problematize the violence within them. While this will not convince everyone that war is always wrong, or that Christians must never participate in it, it will complicate readings that reinforce the "virtue" of war and should encourage reading these texts with greater care and ethical sensitivity.

Recognize the Bias of Israel's One-Sided War Stories

First, when reading Old Testament war narratives, we should remember that we are only hearing one side of the story. To state the obvious, these texts were written by Israelites who wrote about war from Israel's perspective.[29] They expected their readers to share this perspective and, presumably, many did—just like many people do today. A considerable number of modern readers are inclined to side with Israel before they even open the Bible. The reason for this is quite simple: the Israelites are regarded as "God's chosen people." Unless the text explicitly claims otherwise, many readers assume that Israel's wars against other nations were justified on the grounds that the Israelites were God's people and their opponents were not.

Our willingness to side with the Israelites is reinforced by the way Israel's opponents are routinely portrayed in these narratives. Israel's enemies are depicted as wrongdoers who deserve to be punished, and they are often demonized. They are characterized as being violent, oppressive, and unmerciful, and are despised for worshiping other gods. In short, they are portrayed as precisely the kind of people who deserve to die and need to be killed. Because of this, modern readers often develop negative stereotypes of Israel's enemies based solely on what the Old

Testament says about them. Unfortunately, these negative stereotypes are extremely difficult to overcome.

Take the Philistines, for example. As they are often—*but by no means always*—portrayed in the Old Testament, the Philistines are completely unlovable.[30] They are a constant thorn in Israel's proverbial side. Time and again, we find them engaged in acts of violence against the Israelites. The Philistines entrap and capture Samson, gouge out his eyes, and praise their god Dagon for delivering Israel's deliverer into their hands (Judg. 16:4-24). They kill thirty-four thousand Israelite soldiers *and* take the ark of the covenant, Israel's most sacred object, as a spoil of war (1 Sam. 4:1b-11). They capture Israelite cities and take Israelite territory (1 Sam. 7:14). They paralyze the army of Israel with fear by sending Goliath, an oversized Philistine warrior, to taunt them day after day (1 Sam. 17:1-11). And they inflict heavy casualties on Israelite forces on Mount Gilboa, where they mortally wound Saul, Israel's first king, and kill two of his sons (1 Samuel 31). So what is there to like about the Philistines? Not much, it would seem.

If you are like most readers of the Bible, you probably classify Philistines as the enemy. Since the Philistines consistently fought against the Israelites, and since they occupied land God ostensibly promised to Israel, you may be convinced they were on the wrong side of history. Therefore, you probably view Philistines with contempt and feel little, if any, compunction about seeing them killed in battle. In fact, I suspect many people feel no more regret over the death of a Philistine in the Bible than they do over the death of an orc in *The Lord of the Rings*.

This extremely negative view of Philistines is even reflected in the way we use the word today. In modern usage, the word *Philistine* has very negative connotations. After the obligatory "one of the people of ancient Philistia" entry in the dictionary I consulted, there were two additional definitions. Neither was complimentary: (1) "a smug, ignorant, esp. middle-class person who is held to be indifferent or antagonistic to artistic or cultural values," and (2) "one who lacks knowledge in a specific area." As an adjective, the word *philistine* means "boorish, barbarous."[31]

We have been conditioned to see Philistines as categorically bad and deserving of death. We are *not* encouraged to feel any degree of compassion for them, and most of us do not. It is a testimony to how well the biblical writers have done their work.

Yet, if we are to have any success reading the Old Testament nonviolently, we must read against the grain and resist these influences. We must recognize that we are hearing only one side of the story. Everything we read about the Philistines in the Old Testament was written by the Israelites, their enemies. It would be naive to think the Israelites left us with a fair and objective portrayal of the Philistines, the very people they were often trying to kill.[32] Think of it this way. If one of your worst enemies wrote the story of your life, how accurately do you think if would reflect who you really are? It would undoubtedly be skewed in ways that would reflect very badly on you. So, too, Israel's description of her enemies. We should assume that the Old Testament's portrayal of the Philistines is often quite biased.[33]

Don't misunderstand. I am sure the Israelites had plenty of legitimate grievances against the Philistines. But I am equally confident the Philistines had many legitimate grievances against the Israelites All of this cautions us against simplistically adopting the Old Testament's perspective when it comes to matters of war. There is always more than one side in any conflict, and part of reading nonviolently involves straining to hear that other side.

Develop Compassion for Israel's Enemies

As we just discussed, it is easy to buy into the Bible's prejudicial portrayal of Israel's enemies. We often demonize them, and approve of the violence done to them, especially when that violence is done in the name of God by "the people of God."

To illustrate this, consider how Goliath is depicted in the Old Testament. This formidable Philistine warrior is portrayed as an arrogant loudmouth whose sole aim in life is to terrorize Israelites. The picture we have of him in the Bible is completely negative and one-dimensional. We are never allowed to see Goliath as a human being with real feelings, needs, and vulnerabilities. Nor are we permitted to see him as someone's husband, father, son, or brother. Nor are we invited to watch him play with his children or to observe how tenderly he cares for his aging parents.

Consider how our perceptions might change and our feelings about Goliath might be altered if we were given even the smallest glimpse into his life *off* the battlefield. But we are never allowed to see him this way. We are only introduced to Goliath as a warrior who is a threat to Israel and therefore an enemy of God. He is portrayed as evil personified, as a menace who must be eliminated at all costs. But this portrayal of Goliath is extremely problematic, especially if we are committed to valuing all people. So what might help us see Goliath—and all Israel's enemies—in a different light? In a word, compassion.

If we are to read war texts responsibly, in ways that do not reinforce the notion of "virtuous" violence, we need to learn how to read compassionately. We need to develop compassion for those individuals who are shown none by the biblical writers. Since reading compassionately prevents us from reading violently, this way of reading is absolutely essential for overcoming the Old Testament's troubling legacy.

It is here that the work of Emmanuel Levinas is particularly helpful.[34] Carolyn Sharp highlights two Levinasian ideas she regards as "fruitful for biblical hermeneutics" in her recent book *Wrestling the Word*.[35] These include his "notion of attending to the Other and his suggestion that interrupting discourse is an ethical imperative."[36] Sharp illustrates the usefulness of these ideas by applying them to the battle between the Israelites and Canaanites in Judges 4–5, and more particularly to the death of the Canaanite commander Sisera at the hands of Jael. Sharp writes: "There is no doubt as to where the sympathies of the biblical narrator lie. Israel is meant to win; the Canaanites are meant to die in a bloodbath. But for the reader who hears Lévinas's call not to commodify the Other, matters may not be so simple. We may read resistantly."[37] Precisely! Reading nonviolently requires us to look compassionately into the eyes of those individuals whose deaths are sanctioned by the text.

Even though "this story tries to coerce us into reading with the Israelites," we can interrupt this discourse and read with Sisera and his Canaanite soldiers.[38] Rather than assuming that the Israelites have the moral high ground, we can consider what may have motivated Sisera to engage in this confrontation in the first place. As Sharp puts it: "We may read this story 'otherwise.' We may read that Sisera was the leader of the indigenous local Canaanite population who had been trying for twenty years to repel rapacious Israelite invaders who had fallen upon the Canaanites unprovoked, as Judges 1 makes clear."[39] While such a reading is not intended to justify Sisera's violence against Israel, it cautions us against simplistically adopting the text's perspective and assuming that Israelite violence was "virtuous." It should also cause us to look more compassionately upon the Canaanites slain in this story.

Reading Judges 4–5 nonviolently requires us to value everyone in the story, even Sisera. Sharp invites us to see Sisera in ways that complicate the text's celebration of Jael's violent act. She writes:

> This is not a military man in dress whites striding toward Jael's tent—we may picture a gasping, exhausted, terrified man staggering toward her, covered in blood, the sole survivor of a military massacre of his men. He whispers, with respect (the Hebrew there is polite and self-effacing), his request for a little water and for sanctuary.[40]

Seeing the face of Sisera enables us to develop some measure of compassion for him. As Sharp observes: "Sisera is the face of the Other. He is despised by the biblical narrator, who shows him no pity, narratologically speaking. But Lévinas's ethic requires that we see as inhuman not the Other, not the foreigner and the enemy, but the violence that dehumanizes all of us."[41]

I fear that many of us are rather *un*compassionate readers, especially where Israel's enemies are concerned. We are unmoved by their deaths and barely take note of them. But once we see their faces and hear their stories, everything changes. It is extremely difficult to sanction acts of violence against those for whom you feel compassion. That is one reason why developing compassion for Israel's enemies is such a valuable strategy for reading these texts nonviolently.

Put a Human Face on War

A third strategy for reading the violence of war in the Old Testament more critically, and one that also fits quite nicely with the Levinasian emphasis on seeing the face of the Other, involves what I call "putting a human face on war." This broadens the notion of reading compassionately to include all those who were adversely affected by war in the ancient world, including Israelites. Putting a human face on war involves trying to imagine what warfare in the ancient world was actually like. It requires us to slow down long enough to see and feel the devastating effects of war, and it forces us to move beyond statistics to stories of those affected by war. When we see war in this way, we are confronted by all its ugliness.

Warfare in the ancient world was an especially harrowing experience. Given the way wars were fought, you could see—and even smell—your opponents. You could hear weapons clashing, human flesh tearing, and wounded soldiers groaning. Because the fighting was done at close range, many died in hand-to-hand combat.[42]

Yet the casualties of war were not just soldiers engaged in battle. Civilians, including women and children, were also among the slain. Even pregnant women and their unborn babies were not safe from the ravages of war. Menahem, an eighth-century Israelite king, reportedly "ripped open all the pregnant women" of Tiphsah, a besieged city that refused to surrender (2 Kgs. 15:16). As shocking as that may be, his behavior was apparently not all that unusual. As T. R. Hobbs observes: "The brutality of Menahem's actions was, sadly enough, a very common feature of warfare in the ancient Near East."[43] Siege warfare was particularly nasty, especially when the walls were breached. As Hobbs describes it:

> At the moment when defenders were too weak to lift the sword, the attackers would break the walls and enter the city. The frustration of the besiegers, building up over weeks and months of waiting, would be let loose, and few commanders had the discipline, or even the inclination to hold back their troops. Now they came to claim the reward for waiting. Items of value that could be moved were taken, the rest were smashed or burned. Men still alive were slaughtered; children were cruelly butchered; pregnant women brutally murdered and other women raped and claimed by the intruder. The city itself would be razed to the ground.[44]

Ancient warfare—like its modern counterpart—was terrible and terrifying.

Many people who read accounts of war in the Old Testament are not inspired to reflect very deeply on the horror of war and its devastating consequences. This is due in part to the extreme brevity of most Old Testament battle reports. Many of these texts say very little about the actual battles themselves and even less about the human tragedy involved. They rarely acknowledge the enormous physical and psychological toll war took on soldiers and civilians alike. They do not describe in detail the gruesome slaughter of men, women, and children. We are not invited to see the mangled bodies, broken bones, severed limbs, decapitated heads, and disemboweled torsos littering the battlefield or strewn about the city.[45] Old Testament war narratives do not provide the kind of descriptions that enable us to hear the shrieks of the wounded or to smell the stench of battle. They do not linger over the agonizing fate of mortally wounded soliders, left to die on the battlefield.[46] Nor do these texts report the terrified screams of children who have just seen their parents slaughtered by strangers. Their agonizing cries are unrecorded. While the Old Testament provides glimpses of these terrible realities, we are largely shielded from the blood and gore of war in these accounts.

Rather than providing graphic descriptions of pain, suffering, and death, Old Testament war narratives include cursory references to casualties, such as "about three thousand of the people fell on that day" (Exod. 32:28), or Saul "utterly destroyed all the people with the edge of the sword" (1 Sam. 15:8). Such brief summary statements do not prompt most readers to reflect on the carnage of war and the amount of human suffering involved.

For example, although twenty-seven verses are devoted to the battle of Jericho, arguably the most well-known battle in the Old Testament, only two verses describe the battle itself.

> So the people shouted, and the trumpets were blown. As soon as the people heard the sound of the trumpets, they raised a great shout, and the wall fell down flat; so the people charged straight ahead into the city and captured it. Then they devoted to destruction by the edge of the sword all in the city, both men and women, young and old, oxen, sheep, and donkeys. (Josh. 6:20-21)

Regardless of whether or not you believe this particular event actually happened, the way it is told obscures the real horror of warfare. That is what concerns me here. This extremely brief description does not encourage readers to ponder the legitimacy of Israel's actions or to grieve the enormous loss of human life. Nothing is said about the terror the inhabitants of Jericho would have felt when the walls came tumbling down and the Israelites came charging in. Nor is there any mention of the chaos and carnage that ensued as armed Israelites terrorized and brutalized these unfortunate urbanites. Yet, all this, and much more, is implied by these two verses. But because these things are not spelled out, most readers never pause to consider them. What would happen if they did? How might it transform their reading of these texts?

Putting a human face on war broadens the nation of reading compassionately to include all those who are impacted by the violence of war, not just those slain in battle. Consider, for a moment, how putting a human face on war might affect one's reading of a story like the Moabite massacre in Judges 3. As the story goes, the Moabites had oppressed the Israelites for eighteen years (Judg. 3:14). When Israel cries for help, God appoints Ehud to deliver them (Judg. 3:15). After killing the king of Moab, Ehud says to the Israelites: "Follow after me; for the Lord has given your enemies the Moabites into your hand" (Judg. 3:28). What results is the slaughter of ten thousand "strong, able-bodied" Moabite men (Judg. 3:29). None escape.

Apart from the obvious tragedy of thousands of young men being killed, this text—like other Old Testament war texts—raises many troubling questions. How many Moabite women became widows as a result of this battle? How many were forced to resort to prostitution simply to earn enough money to stay alive? How many children died from malnutrition because their fathers or brothers were no longer alive to provide for them? What future acts of violence resulted from this massacre? How many Moabites sought to avenge the Israelites for killing their loved ones and changing their lives forever? And how did these hostilities eventually manifest themselves? Questions like these help us put a human face on war and caution us against uncritically embracing texts that bless war.

An additional dimension of putting a human face on war—and one that is less often addressed—involves considering the effect war has on those who kill. We should remember that the victims of war are not only those who get injured or killed in battle. Those who actually do the killing are also harmed in the process, even if they are fortunate enough to escape without physical injury. As we know all too well from the sadly familiar stories we hear today, soldiers returning from war often struggle with guilt, remorse, anxiety, depression, anger, nightmares, relational difficulties, and post-traumatic stress disorder (PTSD). Some resort to substance abuse, others to physical abuse, and tragically, some commit suicide. Presumably, things were not so different in antiquity. Yet, Old Testament war narratives rarely provide any insight into the devastating psychological effect killing others had on those who killed.[47] Putting a human face on war involves recognizing the debilitating effect warfare has on soldiers and allowing that knowledge to inform our reading and application of these Old Testament passages. When we do, it becomes much more difficult to view war positively despite the Old Testament's frequent approval of it.

Before leaving this point, I want to be clear that my comments here are *not* intended as a critique of ancient writers for presenting warfare as they have. Their perspectives on war were informed by their assumptions about the world, and their writing was influenced by standard literary conventions of the day. Had I been an Israelite scribe, I assume I would have written war narratives in much the same way. But as a Christian living in the modern world, I have a responsibility to raise questions about the way war is presented in these ancient texts. Putting a human face on war helps me read these texts more responsibly and encourages a critique of the Old Testament's accomodating attitude toward war.

Emphasize Old Testament Texts Critiquing Conventional Views of War

One final suggestion for how we might prevent the Old Testament from being used to justify war involves identifying and emphasizing texts that place constraints on warfare or that undermine conventional views of war. Such texts complicate the efforts of those who appeal to the Old Testament to legitimate war today. One of the most intriguing texts in this regard is Deut. 17:14-20. This passage, sometimes referred to as "the law of the king," forbids an Israelite king from behaving in certain ways. Verses 16–17 are the most relevant portion for our purposes:

> He [the king] must not acquire many horses for himself, or return the people to Egypt in order to acquire more horses, since the LORD has said to you, "You must never return that way again." And he must not acquire many wives for himself, or else his heart will turn away; also silver and gold he must not acquire in great quantity for himself.

According to these verses, the king is not to amass horses, acquire many wives, or accumulate lots of gold and silver. At least two of these three restrictions, and arguably all three, relate directly to the practice of warfare.[48] The restriction about horses was apparently intended to keep the king from seeking "military security" in the implements of war rather than in God.[49] Similarly, the prohibition against taking many wives had military ramifications since marriages were often a way of making foreign alliances. When a king married the daughter of another king, a political bond was forged between the two countries. Presumably, this made it less likely that these kings would fight against each other and more likely they would help each other in time of need. Yet, acquiring many wives was a form of "political security" that Israelite kings were instructed to avoid.[50]

But what was wrong with having military security in lots of horses, and political security in lots of foreign alliances? As the prophet Isaiah saw it, finding security in such things was antithetical to trusting in God.

> Alas for those who go down to Egypt for help and who rely on horses, who trust in chariots because they are many and in horsemen because they are very strong, but do not look to the Holy One of Israel or consult the LORD! (Isa. 31:1)

Trusting in such things was regarded as a sure recipe for disaster. As the prophet Hosea proclaimed:

> Because you have trusted in your power and in the multitude of your warriors, therefore the tumult of war shall rise against your people, and all your fortresses shall be destroyed. (Hos. 10:13b-14a)

Israel was expected to trust God for military deliverance. They were not to stockpile weapons, engage in political machinations, or rely on large numbers of soldiers for victory. Such behaviors were not extolled as acts of religious fidelity.

Interestingly, the Old Testament occasionally emphasizes the insignificance of the army's size in determining the outcome of battle as we see in the story of Gideon in Judges 7 (see also 2 Chron. 20:1-30). Although Gideon begins with an army of thirty-two thousand Israelite soldiers, God tells him: "The troops with you are too many for me to give the Midianites into their hand. Israel would only take the credit away from me, saying, 'My own hand has delivered me.'" (Judg. 7:2). To avoid that from happening, Gideon is ordered to reduce the number of troops who will go with him into battle. By day's end, only three hundred men were left, "armed" with nothing more than trumpets, torches, and pottery—definitely not standard-issue military equipment! According to this Old Testament story—and others like it—the size of the army and the sophistication of their weapons (or lack thereof) were ultimately irrelevant to the outcome of the battle.

Thus, while the Old Testament does not condemn war in principle, it does critique conventional understandings of war in numerous ways, and this has relevance for us today. It is difficult to see how standing armies, stockpiled weapons, and foreign alliances—the stuff of modern militarism—can be reconciled with texts like Deut. 17:16-17, Judg. 7:2, and Isa. 31:1.[51] The strong emphasis in these texts to ignore conventional military wisdom, and to trust God instead, has a corrosive effect on the business of war as usual. Amplifying these texts, and the perspectives they represent, can lead us toward less violent—and more responsible—readings of the Old Testament. Texts like these caution readers against trying to use the Old Testament to justify war since they stand at odds with the way warfare is conceive and waged in the modern world.

War causes enormous human suffering, trauma, and tragedy. Yet, the Old Testament is replete with stories about war, many of them ostensibly sanctioned by God who is often portrayed as a divine warrior. What should we do with such texts? While some have used them to justify further acts of war, I have tried to counter these efforts in various ways.

I find it particularly troubling—and dangerous—when people draw conclusions about the morality of warfare today by appealing to divinely sanctioned warfare in the Old Testament. To view God as the kind of being who sanctions the horrors of war is chilling indeed. The Old Testament's depiction of God as a warrior should always be contextualized. It represents a culturally conditioned understanding of Israel's views about God's role in war. There are no compelling reasons to view God—the actual God—as one who ordains war and commands people to kill others. On the contrary, there are many reasons to believe otherwise. By deconstructing divinely sanctioned warfare in the Old Testament, and by repudiating the notion that God sanctions war, people will be much less likely to turn to the Old Testament in support of war.

Likewise, when we invite people to recognize the bias of Israel's one-sided war stories, develop compassion for Israel's enemies, put a human face on war, and emphasize Old Testament texts that critique conventional views of war, we reduce the likelihood that they will use the Old Testament to justify modern acts of war. By encouraging these practices, we help people see war in the Old Testament from a different perspective, one that will hopefully discourage them from using these texts to justify further acts of warfare and killing. When this happens, we have taken another step forward in overcoming the Old Testament's troubling legacy.

CHAPTER 9

Preventing Violence against Women

In Western culture, the Bible has provided the single most important sustaining rationale for the oppression of women.

—PAMELA MILNE[1]

The Bible is not a safe space for women.

—NANCY BOWEN[2]

In her essay titled "Every Two Minutes," Susan Thistlethwaite briefly recounts an interchange she had with a battered wife. She writes: "A Maryland woman who was severely abused over many years told me that when she complained after some attacks that she had sustained injuries, her husband would retort that 'your bones are my bones—just like it says in the Bible.'"[3] While it is easy to fault this man for misquoting and misinterpreting Genesis 2:23, his assumption that the Bible authorizes the use of violence against women is not easily dismissed.

As much as we might wish it were not the case, an unmistakable gender bias *is* deeply embedded in the biblical texts. In countless ways, the Bible favors men over women. Old Testament laws, for example, privilege men and assume their "right" to control women in various ways, and many Old Testament narratives reveal a predominant emphasis on the concerns and perspectives of men. Tragically, this gender bias often manifests itself violently, both within the world of the text and beyond it.

Feminist readers are especially aware of this bias, and they recognize that the Bible contains dangerous terrain for women to traverse. As Linda Day and Carolyn Pressler observe: "The biblical tradition is far from a 'safe space' for women. Rather, it abounds with stories of physical and sexual violence perpetrated against women, laws that sanction such actions, and even prophecies that present God as acting in such ways."[4] As Nancy Bowen sees it, "Violence against women lies at the heart of 'sacred' Scripture."[5] Regardless of whether one agrees with this assessment, it is hard to deny that the Bible contains an enormous amount of violence against women. Sometimes this violence is explicitly condemned by the text. But often it is not. In fact, many biblical texts condone rather than critique the gendered violence they contain. When this happens, we are once again confronted by another manifestation of "virtuous" violence in the Old Testament.

These violent texts are problematic for women because of the very real and undeniable connection between textual violence and actual violence. As Bowen notes, "There *is* a causal connection between biblical views on the subordination of women and actual violence against women."[6] Negative views of women in the Bible have led to negative views of women more generally and have contributed to the mistreatment of women through various forms of discrimination, dehumanization, domestic violence, and sexual assault.

The Bible also has repeatedly been used *against* women striving for equal rights. As Pamela Milne notes: "There is certainly no lack of evidence to show that many people who oppose women in their struggle for equality appeal to the Bible for divine support of their views."[7] This is terribly distressing. One need not be a feminist biblical scholar to appreciate the troubling connection between biblical portrayals of women and contemporary views about what women can and cannot do. As one of my undergraduate students wrote after reading the book of Hosea:

> It really makes me angry that all the people who have major roles as either prophets or patriarchs or whatever are guys. And the women are always presented as property or as evil people who cheat on their husbands. Somehow men get all the glory; no wonder there is such discrepancy in the church today over who should be pastor and what roles women should play. Argh.[8]

As this student realized, the Bible's oppressive portrayal of women contributes to the oppression of women in the church (and the world) today; the two are not disconnected.[9] This is precisely what makes these texts so dangerous. We should be especially careful when handling biblical texts containing and condoning violence against women lest we read them in ways that perpetuate violent acts and attitudes toward them.

The primary purpose of this chapter is to examine how the Old Testament contributes to the problem of violence against women and to explore various ways to address it. But before we go too far down that road, it is important to emphasize that the Bible is not all bad for women.

The Old Testament as a Source of Both Oppression and Liberation

Despite the very negative consequences the Bible has had for women over the years, that is not the whole story. Although many women have found the Old Testament to be oppressive and demeaning, many have also experienced it as liberating and affirming.[10] This is an important point and one worth emphasizing, especially at the beginning of a chapter that will focus on parts of the Old Testament that have caused enormous problems for women.

From within the very same collection of texts that have been so troubling, many women have found invaluable resources for living faithfully, doing justice, and working to end all forms of violence and oppression. As Elisabeth Schüssler Fiorenza observes: "Christian women have found that the Bible has been used as a weapon against us but at the same time it has been a resource for courage, hope, and commitment in this struggle."[11] For all the trouble it has caused women, Schüssler Fiorenza realizes that "the Bible has inspired and continues to inspire countless women to speak out and to struggle against injustice, exploitation, and stereotyping. The biblical vision of freedom and wholeness still energizes women in all walks of life to struggle against poverty, unfreedom, and denigration."[12] Even though the Bible presents significant problems for women, it also offers a rich array of resources that women have found inspiring and liberating. Again, this is a point worth stressing.[13]

Perhaps here it may be helpful to say just a brief word about feminists and feminist biblical scholars. While some hold feminists in the highest regard, admiring them as courageous women who work for justice and equality, others view them as dangerous individuals who undermine religious values and morals.[14] Those who are suspicious of feminist causes and concerns often portray them as extremists who will stop at nothing to achieve their agenda. In my opinion, such negative views are extremely unfortunate and fail to recognize the good and important work feminists do.

According to one definition, "a feminist, broadly speaking, is one who seeks justice and equality for all people and who is especially concerned for the fate of women—all women—in the midst of all people."[15] Although one may not agree with everything done in the name of feminism, it is hard to see how anyone who cares about gender justice and the well-being of women could object to feminists' primary concerns. Anyone concerned about the dignity and equality of men and women, and about reading the Bible ethically and nonviolently, should be interested in feminist biblical scholarship. As we shall see, such scholarship has much to offer as we attempt to overcome the Old Testament's troubling legacy with respect to women.[16]

What Makes the Old Testament So Dangerous for Women?

There are many reasons why the Old Testament has been so problematic for women and has left such a troubling legacy in this regard. Part of the problem has to do with the way women are portrayed *in* the text, and part of it has to do with the way women's voices and concerns are excluded *from* the text. Other challenges arise from the ideological assumptions about women and "their place in the world" that are embedded in these texts and from the unfavorable way many Old Testament texts concerning women have been interpreted through the years.

In a recent essay exploring connections between the Old Testament and the feminist movement, Kathleen O'Connor helpfully identifies and discusses seven "Problems for Feminists Reading the Bible":

> 1) female characters are scarce in the Bible, 2) the Bible is androcentric, 3) sexist language for people and for God excludes women, 4) the texts encourage violence toward women, 5) the societies that produced the Bible were patriarchal and hierarchical, 6) the history of interpretation is biased against women, and 7) the question of how the Bible can be theologically and spiritually authoritative for women.[17]

In order to better understand the scope and severity of the problem the Old Testament creates for women—*and* for men, given the way these texts influence how men think about and behave toward women—I wish to elaborate on several of these points. This is important because the Old Testament's troubling legacy with respect to women is often not as widely recognized as some of its other harmful legacies. Many people do not realize how problematic the Old Testament's assumptions about women are, or how detrimental they can be—and have been!—to women's well-being. Even though these difficulties are less obvious to many readers, they are no less dangerous. Therefore, it is necessary to identify the problem as clearly as possible lest we fail to see how harmful some of these texts really are. To that end, I will focus on four issues that illustrate various ways the Old Testament is oppressive to women.

The Old Testament Is Androcentric

One part of the problem is that the Old Testament is thoroughly androcentric (male centered). These texts were primarily—and perhaps exclusively—written by men, for men, and from the perspective of men. As Schüssler Fiorenza writes: "Scripture [is] interpreted by a long line of men, written in androcentric language, reflective of religious male experience, [and] selected and transmitted by male religious leadership. Without question, the Bible is a male book."[18] Not surprisingly, most Old

Testament stories are primarily about men. There are very few stories about women in the Old Testament. Of these, none *ever* depicts a mother-daughter relationship, and only a handful say anything about how sisters related to one another. Moreover, when women do appear in the Old Testament, they seldom fare very well. They are often voiceless, nameless, and considerably less powerful than their male counterparts. It is not unusual for women in the Old Testament to be characterized quite negatively.

Given the androcentric nature of this literature, it is not surprising that we are almost never allowed to see things from a woman's perspective.[19] We rarely hear their voices, concerns, hopes, dreams, or desires. As Carole Fontaine observes with regard to the book of Psalms:

> I find no psalms that express despair over miscarriage, or seek vindication for the rape or incest survivor. My Psalter contains no thanksgiving psalms specifically aimed at the celebration of the survival of childbirth, no lyric praise for the miracle that takes place with menarche, no attention at all to the various phases of growth and biological change that mark a woman's life. . . . The Psalter I read is about the seasons and yearnings of men's lives.[20]

Whether in the Psalter or elsewhere, we know very little about the interior landscape of women or how they perceived their world.[21]

Even when women do feature prominently in Old Testament stories, these stories often serve androcentric interests. Women function to serve the "greater" story of men who are acting in the public world. Therefore, they speak and act in the interest of men. In fact, when we read the Old Testament, we often see women through the eyes of men, the way the male authors of these texts want us to see them. The women's voices we do hear in the Old Testament often support and reinforce patriarchal concerns.[22] Although some have argued that all traces of what might genuinely be called "women's concerns" have not been erased,[23] these concerns are not easy to discern. They are typically buried in the text or, more likely, in the gaps, silences, and fractures of the text. The androcentric nature of Old Testament texts results in a skewed picture of women at best.

The Old Testament Is Patriarchal

In addition to being androcentric, the Old Testament is also thoroughly patriarchal. Patriarchy is "a social system and . . . an ideology in which women are subordinated to men."[24] The Old Testament assumes patriarchy is normative and never questions it. As Linda Day and Carolyn Pressler observe: "The biblical texts themselves encode—and thus support—patriarchy."[25] This makes these texts very dangerous for women. In the words of Esther Fuchs:

There is nothing innocuous or quaint about biblical narratives. These narratives do not merely describe a male-dominated social order, but justify it as morally requisite and sanctioned by God. They do not merely tell us how women came to be inferior, they also tell us that this inferiority is necessary. In other words, though they often seem to be descriptive, they are more often than not prescriptive.[26]

Since patriarchy by its very nature is oppressive, domineering, and inherently violent, this creates a real dilemma, especially for readers who regard these texts as sacred *and* who care about the well-being of women.

Nancy Bowen spells out some of the violent implications of this troubling perspective. She writes:

Patriarchy constitutes *a form of structural or systemic violence against women* by using the force of ideology and social structures *in ways that harm women* by failing, for example, to consider that women have the right of autonomy, including the right to construct culture, to control property, to maintain bodily integrity, to make their own decisions, and to express their own views.[27]

This patriarchal ethos manifests itself in many ways throughout the Old Testament in texts that marginalize, silence, and oppress women time and again. These texts imply it is better to be a man than a woman. They assume that men have the "right" to dominate and control women in a wide variety of ways, from arranging marriages to things like punishing suspected infidelity and limiting their sphere of influence in the public realm. Numerous verses also reflect a fear of women's sexuality. This results in texts that are sexist (suggesting men are superior to—and more valuable than—women) and, in some cases, misogynistic (expressing hatred toward women). Of course, the Old Testament is no different in this regard from any other ancient literature of the time. As Fontaine reminds us: "The Bible is the *heir* of patriarchy, not its originator."[28]

Even though many of the views about women expressed in the Old Testament are understandable given the patriarchal context in which they emerged, they create serious problems when modern readers regard the Old Testament's patriarchal assumptions as normative. Texts like these can have very nasty consequences for women when people fail to make that all-important distinction between *de*scription and *pre*scription. Unfortunately, as Schüssler Fiorenza observes: "The Bible still functions today as a religious justification and ideological legitimization of patriarchy."[29] This is extremely troubling. Anyone who uses the Bible—Old or New Testament—to justify patriarchal practices today is misusing the Bible and reading it violently. Though patriarchal texts describe the way things were, they do not describe the way things should be.

One might think the problematic nature of these patriarchal assumptions would be self-evident to modern readers, yet this is not always the case. Many readers fail to notice the patriarchal nature of these texts for one simple reason: it does not conflict with their own patriarchal perspectives. As Julia O'Brien reports, based on teaching the book of Hosea for over twenty years: "In the classroom and in churches, the majority of readers cannot see the patriarchy in the text [of Hosea] until it is painstakingly pointed out to them."[30] According to O'Brien: "The most significant reason that women as well as men struggle to see Hosea as patriarchal is that all people internalize patriarchal ways of looking at the world."[31] She rightly recognizes that "the patriarchy of Hosea is not only in the *text*: it is often deeply embedded within *readers* as well."[32] In fact, O'Brien believes that "the patriarchal assumptions of Hosea's metaphor are so familiar to many of us that they remain invisible."[33] It is hard to critique what you "cannot see." If we hope to overcome the problem of patriarchy, patriarchal assumptions in the Bible must be exposed and problematized so they are not allowed to continue to harm women.

The Old Testament Condones Violence against Women

Rather than condemning violence against women, several Old Testament texts actually condone it. Various Old Testament laws sanctioned capital punishment for women who committed certain offenses. Women—as well as men—were to be put to death for things like bestiality (Lev. 20:16) and sorcery (Exod. 22:18; Lev. 20:27). For other offenses, women were subject to various forms of punishment that were quite severe, even if nonlethal. A married woman trying to help her husband in a fight faced the unpleasant prospect of having her hand chopped off if she grabbed the genitals of her husband's opponent (Deut. 25:11-12), and wives *suspected* of marital infidelity had to undergo a terrible ordeal to ascertain their guilt or innocence (Num. 5:11-22). While some might dismiss these laws as relics from the distant past, their violent ideology lingers on and continues to make itself felt even today.

Cheryl Anderson believes there is a correlation between these kinds of laws and the modern treatment of women. Specifically, she argues that the "male dominant/ female subordinate paradigm" found in the legal portions of Exodus and Deuteronomy is "directly related to actual violence against women today," particularly violence in the form "of rape and female battering."[34] Anderson writes:

> Reading these biblical laws today, it seems obvious that they contain problematic elements that do not provide direct and immutable guidance about how to treat in our own context the poor, females, or anyone who is of a different race, ethnicity, or religious affiliation. Whether we realize it or not, though, the same underlying attitudes can shape our own attitudes toward comparable groups in the contemporary context. *The interpretive impact of these laws does not remain locked away in the ancient Near East.*[35]

This is precisely what makes these Old Testament laws so dangerous.

In addition to troubling legal texts that *pre*scribe violence, some of the most disturbing passages in the Old Testament are those that actually *de*scribe acts of violence against women, the kind of passages Phyllis Trible has memorably called "texts of terror."[36] These passages recount physical—and often sexual—acts of violence against women.[37] Hagar is abused and told (by God!) to return to an abusive situation (Gen. 16:9), Dinah is raped (Gen. 34:1-2), as is Tamar (2 Sam. 13:1-14) and the Levite's concubine (Judg. 19:22-30), Jephthah's daughter is "sacrificed" (Judg. 11:34-40), the virgins of Jabesh-Gilead are taken as prisoners of war and forced to marry Benjaminites (Judg. 21:8-14), and the women of Shiloh are kidnapped and forced to do the same (Judg. 21:15-23).

Stories like these are especially detrimental to women when they are read uncritically, when the violence in them is passed over and left unchallenged. When this happens, harmful attitudes and actions toward women are tacitly endorsed. Reading texts compliantly rather than conversantly has all sorts of negative repercussions for women today. That is why we have an ethical obligation to read otherwise. Carol Hess illustrates the importance of this in her comments about the tragic story of Jephthah's daughter:

> The story, when read without struggle, leaves us with a dead girl and *the implicit message that the sacrifice of a girl is acceptable.* Whenever we interpret texts, we need to look at the "implicit" stories that are being told in the background of our "explicit" stories. The silences and "insignificant" details of a story convey meaning to readers and hearers; it is our task as preachers and teachers to notice these teachings going on in the background. Their consequences are far from incidental in women's lives.[38]

Whenever female victims of violence in the Old Testament are passed over in silence, or whenever their suffering is minimized or their abuse uncommented on, we may be left with the impression that what happened to them is insignificant or unimportant. In such cases, when we encounter biblical stories that could be construed as condoning violence against women, we have a moral obligation to interrupt the story and object. We must raise our voices in protest and critique these violent acts. Otherwise, those who read and hear these texts may be led to believe that such behavior is acceptable, or even appropriate.

The Old Testament Legitimates Sexual Abuse through Prophetic Metaphors

Some of the most problematic texts in the Old Testament for women—and some of the most offensive—are texts that describe God behaving in sexually violent ways. In a number of prophetic judgment oracles, God pronounces terrifying acts of sexual violence upon cities personified as women.[39] Although many of these are non-Israelite cities, Jerusalem itself is the target of God's wrath on more than one occasion. When these judgment oracles are directed against the people of God, God is portrayed as an abusive husband who sexually degrades and humiliates his wife (Israel). This is "sexual violence," writes Cheryl Exum, "where God appears as the subject and the object of his abuse is personified Israel/Judah/Jerusalem."[40]

In a particularly graphic passage in Ezekiel, God has this to say about Jerusalem, "his" unfaithful spouse:

> Therefore, O whore, hear the word of the LORD. . . . I will gather all your lovers . . . against you from all around, and will uncover your nakedness to them, so that they may see all your nakedness. I will judge you as women who commit adultery and shed blood are judged, and bring blood upon you in wrath and jealousy. I will deliver you into their hands. . . . They shall strip you of your clothes and take your beautiful objects and leave you naked and bare. They shall bring up a mob against you, and they shall stone you and cut you to pieces with their swords. They shall burn your houses and execute judgments on you in the sight of many women. . . . So I will satisfy my fury on you. (Ezek. 16:35-42)

Although this motif is sometimes referred to as the "marriage metaphor," that designation is unsuitable.[41] What is portrayed here is not a healthy picture of marriage but a horrifying depiction of spousal abuse, violence, and sexual degradation. Susanne Scholz comes nearer the mark when she refers to this as "the prophetic rape metaphor."[42] Scholz describes the relevant passages this way:

> The poems present God as decreeing sexual violence upon the women-cities, who are punished for their misbehaviors. Crude, brutal, and violent vocabulary prevails. In the case of Jerusalem, the charge is that she prostituted herself to other male nation-persons and disobeyed her husband/God; the charge in the case of the other ancient Near Eastern cities is that they destroyed Israel.[43]

Depicting sinful cities as faithless women who "deserve" to be punished in sexually violent ways creates all sorts of problems for modern readers. Some regard this image of God as irredeemable.[44] Others express significant discomfort with the ramifications of texts containing this imagery. As Katheryn Darr writes: "I become uneasy when Ezekiel employs female sexual imagery to depict the ostensible wickedness of sixth-century Judeans . . . because imagery, especially biblical imagery, that details the degradation and public humiliation of women . . . can have serious repercussions."[45]

What makes this metaphor particularly dangerous is not only that it distorts the character of God but that it encourages violence—sexual and otherwise—against women. In order for the metaphor to work the way the writer intended, we "are expected to sympathize with the divine perspective *against* the (personified) woman."[46] Yet, by doing so, as Scholz points out, we "justify rape as the proper form of punishment for idolatry and adultery."[47] This means that "the metaphor, read accordingly, can be used to excuse men who use sexual violence against women."[48] Such a reading is clearly inappropriate. As we have said, the Bible should never be used to harm others.

Numerous writers have commented on the negative impact biblical portrayals of God being abusive toward women—sexually or otherwise—have upon women. Gracia Ellwood believes that "the image of the outraged divine patriarch is unacceptable because it encourages tendencies to violence and domination in human husbands/fathers."[49] In her discussion of the book of Nahum, Judith Sanderson is particularly concerned about the real-world consequences of texts that portray God as being sexually violent. She writes: "In a society where violence against women is epidemic, it is extremely dangerous to image God as involved in it in any way. . . . To involve God in an image of sexual violence is, in a profound way, somehow to justify it and thereby to sanction it for human males who are for any reason angry with a woman."[50] More than we might care to acknowledge, biblical texts that portray God as being sexually abusive have contributed to problems of domestic violence, rape, and various other forms of violence against women. As Cheryl Exum reminds us: "A depressing body of evidence demonstrates how such texts oppress women by encouraging scapegoating and reinforcing the idea that physical abuse can be an appropriate measure for men to use against women."[51]

Those who may be tempted to think this image of God is not all that problematic because it is "just" a metaphor should think again. We should not underestimate the power of metaphor for shaping reality. As Athalya Brenner points out: "Metaphor is not just a matter of speech or discourse, a tool to elucidate a point to be made; it goes so much deeper into the fabric of our thought structures and conceptualization of the inner and outer world."[52] In other words, metaphors really matter! Texts condoning violence against women—prescriptively or descriptively, literally or metaphorically—reinforce dangerous patriarchal assumptions that men have a right to dominate women, control their bodies, and use physical violence against them if they get out of line. Therefore, we must be extremely careful how we read and interpret all such passages.

Although we have only looked at a handful of reasons why the Old Testament is so problematic for women (and for men who care about the well-being of women), enough has been said to demonstrate the seriousness of this problem. The Old Testament contains many views about women that are extremely harmful if left unchallenged. In light of that fact, it is difficult to overstate the importance of finding ways to mitigate the negative impact these texts have had on women.

Given the magnitude of the problems created by the Old Testament in this regard, one might wonder whether these texts are still even usable. Can Old Testament texts so thoroughly permeated by patriarchal assumptions and oppressive ideologies be salvaged? Or, as Mary Ann Tolbert phrases the question: "How does one deal with a biblical text that is so completely saturated in an unacceptable perspective?"[53] What should be done with laws, narratives, and prophetic oracles that are severely biased against women? Is there value in even reading texts that are androcentric, patriarchal, sexist, and misogynistic? I think there is.

As I have argued throughout this book, I believe even the most unpalatable and problematic passages have value when read nonviolently, in an ethically responsible manner. This is no less true for the kind of texts we are considering in this chapter.

Preventing Violent Readings against Women: Some Proposals

We are now ready to consider some specific suggestions for reading these texts in ethically responsible ways that do not devalue women or contribute to further abuse or oppression. As previously, this will involve elements of both critique and embrace.[54]

Critique and Condemn All Forms of Textual Violence against Women

In an effort to prevent textual violence from turning into actual violence, one of the first things we can do is to critique and condemn various expressions of violence against women in the Old Testament. We must constantly be on the alert, always ready to expose patriarchal ideologies, give voice to women silenced by the text, and critique the gender bias and violence embedded in these texts. This is especially needed when the text either sanctions the violence it contains or offers no significant critique of it.

Sometimes, even when the violence is not explicitly condemned, there may still be a measure of critique that can be discerned by engaging in a close reading of the narrative. Jacqueline Lapsley makes this case in her reading of Judges 19–21, three chapters that contain a considerable amount of violence against women. Lapsley writes: "Everyone in the story, except the women, I would argue, is in some way censured by the narrative. But this censure is deftly suggested rather than openly proclaimed. The narrator, while hoping to nudge the reader into deeper understanding, refuses to compromise the moral freedom of the reader by offering a plethora of obvious judgments."[55] We should certainly attend to these subtleties, since they can assist us in critiquing the violence we find in narratives like these. Yet, while this may help in some cases, it certainly will not in every case. For that reason, it is very important for us to be ready to interrupt what we are reading and to ask, "What's wrong with this picture?"[56]

This kind of questioning involves reading the Old Testament with a "hermeneutic of suspicion," something feminist biblical scholars routinely do. They realize there are things in the Bible that are not good for them. As Schüssler Fiorenza so colorfully puts it: "A feminist critical hermeneutics of suspicion places a warning label on all biblical texts: *Caution! Could be dangerous to your health and survival.*"[57]

We need to be fully aware of this danger if we hope to overcome the Old Testament's troubling legacy with respect to women. We must read with eyes wide open, alert "to the designs" these texts have on us.[58] "The first and never-ending task of a hermeneutics of suspicion," writes Schüssler Fiorenza, "is to elaborate as much as possible the patriarchal, destructive aspects and oppressive elements in the Bible."[59]

Since patriarchal ideology is often submerged in the deeper structures of the text—making it more difficult to detect but no less dangerous—readers may find it helpful to have some probing questions ready to assist them in ferreting out these problematic assumptions. The following set of questions, proposed by Exum, can help:

> What androcentric agenda does this text promote? Does it, for example, function to keep women in their place, under the control of men? Does it show male control of women as something necessary for society to function smoothly, or as something women desire? What buried and encoded messages does this text give to women?[60]

Since patriarchal ideology is *pervasive* throughout the Old Testament, it is not enough to isolate a few rogue passages, brand them as problematic, and declare "mission accomplished." Rather, we should be on the lookout for any Old Testament perspectives that devalue and demean women and should be ready to expose and critique them.

I realize some people may feel reluctant to engage in this kind of critique since it is tantamount to admitting there is something wrong with the Bible. Therefore, it is not surprising that some Christian scholars and apologists deny or minimize the patriarchal, sexist, and misogynistic tendencies of the Old Testament.[61] But I believe such efforts are misguided and fail to recognize how prevalent and problematic these assumptions are throughout the Old Testament. The violent ideologies embedded in these texts constitute a *serious* problem that cannot be easily dismissed.

These Old Testament texts—and various interpretations of them—have done enormous harm to women over the years. If we are committed to reading nonviolently, we must not shrink from critiquing texts that condone violence against women and that contain harmful and oppressive views. Instead, we should confront them, taking great care that our own interpretations do not reinforce or reinscribe these violent perspectives.

Challenge Sexist and Misogynistic Interpretations of Old Testament Texts

As we have seen, the Old Testament's troubling legacy with respect to women is not just a matter of interpretation. The texts themselves are deeply problematic in many respects. Still, some individuals have exacerbated the problem by offering interpretations that are even *more* sexist and misogynistic than the texts themselves appear to be. This has made things worse and resulted in even greater harm to women. When this happens, we have an obligation to set the record straight.

Carol Hess, who offers ten helpful strategies for dealing with difficult texts, believes "the most obvious strategy when dealing with texts that are oppressive to women is to question the history of interpretation."[62] Hess cites two stories of women in the Old Testament that she believes have often suffered from distorted interpretations: the story of Eve (Genesis 3) and the story of Jephthah's daughter (Judges 11).[63] Earlier, we noted how terribly problematic Genesis 3 has been for women. People have historically viewed Eve very negatively. Unfortunately, people have projected this negative view onto women generally since Eve is sometimes regarded as representative of all women.

To illustrate, consider these words about women from Tertullian, a prominent third-century Christian leader:

> And do you not know that you are each an Eve? The sentence of God on this sex of yours lives in this age: the guilt, of necessity, must live too. You are the devil's gateway; you are the unsealer of that forbidden tree; you are the first deserter of the divine law; you are she who persuaded him whom the devil was not valiant enough to attack. You destroyed so easily God's image, man.[64]

Although Tertullian lays all the blame at the feet of Eve, portraying her as a temptress, the text does not warrant such an interpretation. Eve simply hands the fruit to Adam, and he eats it. There is no hint of her actively trying to persuade him to eat the forbidden fruit. Ascribing such behavior to Eve makes an already problematic text even more difficult. "We do well to correct distortions," writes Hess, "by returning to the text and reading with new eyes, and consulting feminist literary critics can aid us in doing so."[65]

When dealing with particular texts, like Genesis 3, that have had a long and uneasy history of interpretation vis-à-vis women's concerns, we should be honest about the way the church has misinterpreted them over the years and should renounce interpretations that are oppressive and harmful to women. Feminist biblical scholarship can help us immensely in this regard, and we do well to pay attention to what they have to say about these matters. If we are serious about confronting the Old Testament's troubling legacy of violence against women, we need to be intentional about critiquing and challenging sexist and misogynistic interpretations of these texts.

Use Problematic Texts to Begin Conversations about Violence against Women Today

One way to use these difficult texts constructively is to utilize them as starting points for conversations about the violence and abuse so many women experience today. Conversations like these are sorely needed. Over the years, the church has not done enough to confront the problem of violence against women. It is a subject that is rarely discussed, if acknowledged at all, in many churches. This is unhealthy. Old Testament stories containing violence against women provide natural opportunities to talk about the overwhelming amount of violence women face on a regular basis. As Fontaine recognizes: "Denial of the widespread abuse experienced by women, children and others is still a feature of the religious communities' day-to-day existence. A Bible filled with abuse offers us a legitimate tool for foregrounding these issues that are so readily repressed by leaders and laypeople alike."[66] Focusing on some of the more violent and problematic aspects of these texts provides us with a convenient point of entry into some of these very difficult conversations.

There are a number of Old Testament texts that would be quite useful in generating conversations around the issue of sexual violence against women, for example. In her recent study on rape texts in the Hebrew Bible, Susanne Scholz contends that one of the benefits of having these stories in the Bible is that we can use them to speak up—and speak out—about rape. This kind of advocacy is, at least partly, the motivation behind her work. Scholz writes: "The hope of this study . . . is that the naming of biblical rape texts and the expression of discontent with the violent status quo . . . will eventually make it less likely that readers, religious or secular, will remain silent about the 'unmentionable sin.'"[67] Since "silence keeps the violent status quo alive and enables it," speaking about rape is extremely important.[68] When we use rape texts in the Old Testament to talk about the problem of rape in our world today, we break the silence. Using these texts to confront the problem of sexual violence represents a constructive way of using them to address a severe form of violence against women.

Numerous Old Testament texts also lend themselves quite naturally to discussions about domestic violence. In her study of Ezekiel 16, Linda Day discusses the typical pattern of abuse that battered women experience (tension building, acute violence, and contrite behavior) and then demonstrates that this is precisely how God behaves toward Jerusalem in this chapter of Ezekiel.[69] Similar observations have also been made about the way God treats Gomer in the book of Hosea.[70] Even though these texts do not censure the abuser (God!), when read critically they can be used to demonstrate the damaging patterns of abuse that are all too common in our world today. This is helpful because it raises our awareness of the problematic nature of these patterns and provides opportunities for conversation, storytelling, and healing. "As the 'tough stuff' stories of the Bible are read, exegeted and reflected upon," writes Keree Casey, "members of our communities of faith are not only made aware of the issue of sexual abuse and domestic violence, victims are also encouraged to tell their own stories of abuse."[71] This can begin a process of healing for those who have suffered from physical, sexual, or psychological abuse.

One way the church can model an openness and willingness to talk about these issues is to preach from passages containing violence against women. Doing so has the potential to be really helpful and healing to women (and men) who have experienced sexual violence and abuse. This is what Professor John Thompson discovered when he took a risk and decided to preach from one of these texts. Thompson had been invited to preach the baccalaureate sermon at Fuller Theological Seminary and says he was given the freedom to pick "any text I thought appropriate."[72] Thompson eventually chose to preach on the story of the sacrifice of Jephthah's daughter in Judges 11, though only after a severe struggle over the wisdom of choosing such a troubling text. The response he received surprised him. "I was stunned at the reports that filtered back," writes Thompson. "Apparently, there were some in attendance who were at that moment struggling with the effects of past abuse, but who found encouragement and even some closure in my remarks."[73]

We should be more intentional about preaching and teaching from these difficult texts. We should also work more diligently to create opportunities to use the Old Testament as a springboard to have meaningful conversations around issues related to violence against women. This would represent a very tangible way to use these troubling texts constructively.

Tell Old Testament Stories of Violence against Women "in Memory of" Them

Another way to overcome the Old Testament's troubling legacy—and this is closely related to the point just made—involves telling Old Testament stories of violence against women to remember them and the wrongs committed against them. We remember stories of violence, injustice, and oppression in order to learn from them and to do everything in our power to keep them from happening again. That is why it is essential for us to tell biblical stories of violence against women.

This approach is the one taken by Phyllis Trible in her now classic book *Texts of Terror*. In this book, Trible tells the stories of four Old Testament women: Hagar (Genesis 16), Tamar (2 Samuel 13), the Levite's concubine (Judges 19), and Jephthah's daughter (Judges 11). These women experienced tremendous pain and suffering and, in the latter two cases, death. Trible describes her approach as one that "recounts tales of terror *in memoriam* to offer sympathetic readings of abused women. . . . It interprets stories of outrage on behalf of their female victims in order to recover a neglected history, to remember a past that the present embodies, and to pray that these terrors shall not come to pass again."[74]

Tikva Frymer-Kensky accents this point in her review of Trible's book. She writes: "Trible retells these stories in order to make them meaningful to us today. We cannot ignore what it is perilous to forget, and therefore *Texts of Terror* is, metaphorically, a book of holocaust studies, told so that we should remember and in remembering say, 'never again.'"[75] Telling these stories in a way that elicits a sympathetic and compassionate hearing can go a long way toward overcoming the Old Testament's violent legacy as it relates to women.

Imaginatively Retell Old Testament Stories of Women from Their Perspective

As discussed earlier, the Old Testament says very little about the unique interests and concerns of women. We rarely hear *her* story or see things from a woman's perspective. Instead, women in the Old Testament are routinely marginalized, suppressed, and silenced. Many of the women who do appear are portrayed negatively or only allowed roles that serve patriarchal purposes. *Her* concerns revolve around *his*. Unfortunately, all this leaves readers with the impression that women are inferior to men and that their particular struggles and concerns, their hopes and dreams, are secondary at best.

One way to address this problem is to imaginatively (re)tell these Old Testament stories from a woman's perspective. What would Jephthah's daughter say about her father's lethal vow? How would Michal talk about the way she was treated by David? What would Tamar have to say about being raped by her half-brother Amnon? Hearing these stories in the first person, from the perspective of these women, would cast them in a very different light.

Hess advocates this approach and believes that a "particularly creative" way to resist oppressive parts of the Bible "is to rewrite or interact with a text or narrative to give voice to silenced players."[76] Giving biblical women a voice involves starting with the text and then going beyond it. New details and dialogues can be added to the basic storyline, along with new perspectives and plot developments that are not currently present. By filling in the gaps, reading between the lines, and allowing these women to tell their own stories, readers can begin to mitigate some of the harmful effects of these one-sided, patriarchal presentations.

Schüssler Fiorenza describes this approach as "a hermeneutics of creative actualization."[77] She writes:

> A hermeneutics of creative actualization seeks to retell biblical stories from a feminist perspective, to reformulate biblical visions and injunctions in the perspective of the discipleship of equals, to create narrative amplifications of the feminist remnants that have survived in patriarchal texts. In this process of creative re-vision it utilizes all available means of artistic imagination—literary creativity, music, and dance.[78]

Bowen also recognizes the value of using such an approach with biblical stories in which women have been victimized by violence. "We can retell biblical stories of women and violence," writes Bowen, "In ways that critique the violence and promote egalitarian, nonhierarchical paradigms for how to live."[79] As Bowen emphasizes, such retellings not only criticize violence but also enable the reader to imagine the story differently, in ways that can give new dignity and worth to the victims. Bowen's own version of Tamar's story, based on 2 Samuel 13, is one such example of this imaginative act.[80]

Retelling Old Testament stories in this way has much in common with Jewish midrash, and can be used with great advantage for the sake of women. As Hess notes: "There is a long tradition in Judaism of 'making midrash,' playing with and wrestling with the biblical text to discover meaning between the lines and in the silent gaps."[81] This is valuable because, as Hess points out, "the women's sides of biblical stories are often screaming from the silent gaps."[82] By filling these gaps, we hear a different side of the story, one that is not determined by patriarchal priorities. This subverts the text's violent ideology and opens up new ways of reading these texts that are more favorable toward women.

There are a number of resources available to help us imaginatively retell these stories. In addition to numerous retellings that have been written by modern authors,[83] we can read what some of the earlier, precritical commentators had to say about texts describing various acts of violence against women. In his book *Writing the Wrongs*, John Thompson argues that early interpreters often felt quite uneasy about certain things that happened to women in biblical texts. He writes:

> Christian interpreters through the centuries have regularly wrestled with the texts of terror, sometimes writing volumes "between the lines" of Scripture out of an apparent concern for the women in these stories. Indeed, many struggled with these texts in ways that seem to subordinate their patriarchal instincts to a far more existential concern with issues of justice, humanity, and women's dignity.[84]

We would do well to take these ancient voices into account.

We can also read stories of contemporary women who have experienced tragedies similar to those recounted in the Bible. Such stories can help us imagine what their ancient counterparts might have said, thought, and felt. Alice Bach uses an excerpt from *The Bridge Betrayed: Religion and Genocide in Bosnia* to help readers imagine the horror of rape experienced by the young women forced to be wives of the nearly decimated tribe of Benjamin in Judges 21. Bach believes that "after reading rape accounts . . . from the recent genocide in Bosnia, the reader will fill the gaps and silences in Judges 21 with the cries of the victims of ethnic/religious rape of massive proportions."[85]

In addition to *reading* accounts like these, we can *listen* carefully to women who have experienced violence against them and are willing to share their story. They, too, can help us fill in what is missing from the biblical text. Whatever combination of resources we use, imaginatively retelling the stories of Old Testament women from their perspective is a powerful tool in overcoming the Old Testament's troubling legacy against women. It provides yet another way to mitigate the dangers of these texts as we attempt to use them more constructively.

Using the strategies proposed here to read these Old Testament texts nonviolently moves us in more ethical directions. It allows us to critique aspects of the text that are oppressive *and* to embrace ways of reading these texts that are constructive and redemptive. Though I have emphasized this point throughout the book, it bears repeating once again: reading texts nonviolently involves both critique and embrace. As O'Connor so helpfully reminds us: "Because the text is patriarchal, sexist, and androcentric does not mean that it cannot be a word of God for us when studied from other angles."[86] Despite their difficulties, when these texts are read responsibly, they can become significant resources for reflection, conversation, and spiritual insight.

If we desire to prevent textual violence against women from turning into actual violence, it is critical to develop and utilize strategies for reading the Old Testament that help, rather than harm, women. As Bowen recognizes: "In the current culture of violence against women, for anyone who advocates liberation for women, including liberation from violence, biblical interpretation becomes an *urgent* ethical issue."[87] Yet, unfortunately, in many quarters, there seems to be a distinct *lack* of urgency surrounding this issue. Most churches seem exceedingly uncomfortable with texts depicting violence against women and avoid them like the plague in preaching and teaching. A great number of Christian colleges and seminaries devote little class time or attention to the problems of patriarchy, sexism, and misogyny in the biblical text.[88] Even many biblical scholars (especially those who are men) often fail to adequately address these issues in books, articles, and commentaries that would quite naturally lend themselves to a discussion of such matters.[89] Clearly, there is still very much work to be done in this regard.

If we are genuinely concerned about the dignity and well-being of women, we should be honest about the problems the Old Testament raises for them and work to find ways to confront these problems directly. Otherwise, we run the risk of perpetuating negative attitudes toward women and encouraging further acts of violence against them.

The presence of androcentric, patriarchal, sexist, and misogynistic texts in the Old Testament represents a problem that can only be managed, never cured. What I have offered in this chapter are several ways of managing the problem. While none of the nonviolent reading strategies explored here solves the problem of patriarchy or ensures that these texts will never again be used to legitimate violence against women, they do help us read these texts more responsibly. This takes us a long way toward overcoming this especially egregious aspect of the Old Testament's troubling legacy.

CHAPTER 10

The Necessity and Urgency of Reading the Old Testament Nonviolently: Some Conclusions

Ignoring violent texts is like camping on the bank of a crocodile-infested river. It is dangerous. It is naive in the extreme. These Leviathan-like texts should be treated with the utmost respect and caution. They can erupt with violent force when it is least expected.

—WILLIAM W. EMILSEN AND JOHN T. SQUIRES[1]

I believe it is important, even ethically mandatory, to recognize and resist dangerous thinking wherever it occurs, including and perhaps especially in the Bible.

—JULIA O'BRIEN[2]

Throughout this book, I have argued that the key to overcoming the Old Testament's troubling legacy involves reading nonviolently. In this chapter, I would like to make a final plea for reading the Old Testament this way by emphasizing the necessity and urgency of the task at hand. Although this book has focused on the Old Testament, I would make the same plea in regard to the New Testament since it too has a troubling legacy. Far too often, New Testament texts also have been read violently, causing significant harm to women, slaves, Jews, gays and lesbians, and many others. We need to read New Testament texts nonviolently as well, and more sustained attention is needed in this regard.[3]

Why Is It Imperative to Read the Bible Nonviolently?

By now, I hope that enough has been said about *how* to read nonviolently that readers have a good sense of the basic mechanics of this approach. In what follows, I want to discuss several reasons why I think this way of reading the Bible is a matter of great urgency, one we ought to make a top priority. Since much of what I am about to say applies equally well to both testaments, I will sometimes refer to the Bible generally rather than just the Old Testament.

To Overcome the Old Testament's Troubling Legacy of Being Used to Harm Others

One of the primary reasons we need to read nonviolently is to help us avoid using the Bible oppressively. As we have seen, the Bible has been used to harm others over and over again.[4] The church has a truly awful track record in this regard, and has used Scripture to exploit, subjugate, oppress, and sometimes even kill others. Unfortunately, this is not just a thing of the past. The Bible continues to be used in hurtful and damaging ways even today. It is used to demonize gays and lesbians, support capital punishment, oppress women, endorse nationalism, abuse children, promote war, and engage in domestic violence—to name just some of the ways it is used to harm others. This must stop! As I stated at the outset, this book is based on the fairly simple premise that the Bible should never be used to inspire, promote, or justify acts of violence. Using the Bible for such destructive ends is not only inappropriate, it is unethical and has no place in the life of the church. By reading nonviolently, we can avoid perpetuating the Old Testament's troubling legacy in these ways.

In addition to being personally committed to reading the Old Testament nonviolently, we should be equally zealous about confronting violent readings of the Bible wherever we find them. We should critique any interpretation of Scripture that harms others and should speak out against any attempt to use the Bible to justify, legitimate, or otherwise sanction acts of violence. Given the many ways the Bible has been used—and continues to be used—to do harm, we need to be very vigilant in this regard.

As I have argued, overcoming the Old Testament's troubling legacy requires paying close attention to the violent texts that are the source of the problem. We simply cannot afford to ignore them. Doing so is extremely dangerous, "like camping on the bank of a crocodile-infested river," as Emilsen and Squires so vividly express it.[5] The danger is intensified with respect to texts containing "virtuous" violence. When the church ignores these texts, or fails to critique the "virtuous" violence contained in them, it allows harmful perspectives about violence to go unchallenged. It also leaves these texts open to the kind of harmful interpretations that have been given to them in the past, and that will undoubtedly be given to them in the future. As Philip Jenkins remarks: "The last Christian who will seek to exterminate another nation on the pretense of killing Amalekites has not yet been born."[6] But if the church is intentional about helping people know how to handle these texts responsibly, then violent and unethical readings can be recognized more easily and confronted more quickly and effectively.

Since violent texts are the source of many problematic readings and applications of the Bible, critiquing these texts and the "virtuous" violence they contain becomes a powerful deterrent against using them to harm others. When the Bible is used in an ethically responsible way it will not be used to justify violence against women, children, ethnic minorities, gays and lesbians, Muslims, or anyone else. Reading nonviolently severs the link between textual and actual violence and thereby effectively neutralizes all such troubled readings. In a world riddled with religiously sanctioned and religiously motivated violence, reading the Bible this way seems an especially urgent task.

To Be Honest about the Bible's Moral and Theological Limitations

As discussed earlier, while there is obviously a great deal we can embrace and celebrate when reading the Old Testament, not everything we encounter there is good for us. The Old (and New) Testament sometimes endorses values and viewpoints most people of faith today find objectionable. This is certainly the case when it sanctions genocide, promotes intolerance, legitimates killing, and endorses all sorts of violence against women, children, and others. One of the real advantages of reading nonviolently is that it allows us to be completely honest about these morally problematic parts of the Bible. We can freely acknowledge these difficulties without feeling pressure to pretend the Bible is something it is not.

For all the profound wisdom, spiritual insight, and moral guidance it offers, the Old Testament is not—and was never intended to be—a perfect guide for ethics, morality, or theology. This is difficult for many people of faith to acknowledge. Many Christians are disinclined to recognize the Bible's limitations. Fewer still are willing to admit there are serious problems with it or to acknowledge that the Bible might contain ideas that are not only wrong, but downright dangerous. In many Christian contexts, the clear expectation is to say only "nice" things about the Bible: how wonderful it is, how useful it is to draw us closer to God, how helpful it is for our spiritual growth, and so forth. While all this is certainly true—*and I do not for a moment wish to minimize the significance of these things*—it does not give us the full picture.

Some people want the Bible to be good so badly they are willing to do whatever it takes make that happen. Julia O'Brien has seen this happen time and time again. She writes:

> Countless experiences of watching students and congregation members encounter Hos. 1-2 and other prophetic images of violence against women have convinced me that *most Christian readers will go to great lengths to protect their views about the Bible.* They marginalize Hosea as a "problem passage" or "an example of Old Testament thinking." No matter how many "problem passages" they encounter—biblical celebrations of war, the slaughter of innocents, even the violence of Hosea 2—many believers continue to insist that these texts are occasional blips in an otherwise steady heartbeat of a good-hearted Bible.[7]

O'Brien's comments illustrate how extremely difficult it is for some people to admit that the Bible is not the entirely good book they thought it was or might like it to be.

While the efforts of Christians who "defend" the Bible or insist there is nothing wrong with it may seem noble, they are actually quite unhelpful and counterproductive. They perpetuate an erroneous view of the Bible that sets up unrealistic expectations. Worse still, they lead readers to believe that everything they encounter in the Bible is good for them without alerting them to the potential dangers involved in reading it. Portraying the Bible as an unblemished book of "pure goodness" will cause some readers to accept what they ought to reject, and embrace what they ought to critique.

To avoid this undesirable state of affairs, the church needs to change the way it talks about the Bible. It needs to do a better job of helping people appreciate what is genuinely good in Scripture without preventing them from seeing what is terribly problematic. In short, the church needs to stop defending the Bible and start reading it more responsibly. Among other things, this means being honest about the Old Testament's moral and theological limitations. Reading nonviolently is one of the best ways to accomplish this since it encourages people to acknowledge various kinds of problems raised by the Bible's troublesome texts.

To Avoid Being Negatively Influenced by Harmful Ideologies in These Texts

To extend the previous point a bit further, reading nonviolently is extremely important since it can prevent us from being negatively influenced by the violent assumptions embedded in this texts. This approach to Scripture reminds us of the need to be *very* careful how we read. Competing ideologies in the Bible clamor for our attention and acceptance. While many of these are worthy of our embrace, others should be directly challenged or even flatly renounced. This is why we must be *conversant* readers who engage the biblical text in a very active way.

Whether or not we realize it, biblical texts do their work on us in ways that are sometimes barely perceptible but that are very significant.[8] They shape some of our deepest convictions about such things as our view of women, the propriety of violence, and the nature of God. While this is not necessarily a bad thing, it can be. As Carolyn Sharp reminds us: "Reading is powerful—and not only for good."[9] Individuals who read violent texts uncritically, and embrace the views and perspectives reflected in them, will inevitably conclude that violence is sometimes both acceptable and appropriate. They will believe that there are times when people can—and should—behave violently, and they will believe this because "the Bible says so." This is dangerous.

When we read texts that endorse and encourage favorable attitudes toward violence, we need to read on high alert lest we be led astray. Reading nonviolently is essential to this task. It provides us with a way to read the Bible with our eyes wide open, fully aware that not everything we read is beneficial. While there are many ideas and perspectives in the Bible that we can embrace wholeheartedly and unreservedly, there are others we cannot and should not. Adopting a reading strategy like this—one that is willing to question, challenge, and critique various aspects of the biblical text—can prevent us from being negatively influenced by some of the harmful ideologies we encounter there.

To Remove Obstacles That Hinder People from Reading the Old Testament and from Coming to Faith

The interpretive approach advocated in this book holds special promise for those who may feel alienated from the Bible and Christianity. Some people—religious or otherwise—find it difficult to read the Bible because of how much violence it contains. For some people of faith, violent texts are among the most troublesome parts of the Old Testament. As William Bellinger observes: "In my work with churches, I find three issues that bother contemporary believers in their attempts to read the Hebrew Scriptures. The first is that the Old Testament seems so violent. The second is that the God described in the Old Testament is a harsh and judgmental God. . . . The third is that this book seems so foreign."[10] Likewise, Julia O'Brien writes:

> In my experience the one thing that most troubles people about the Old Testament is its violence. People regularly plead with me to say something positive about the violence of the conquest of the land in the book of Joshua, the violence of God's smiting of the people with a plague in the book of Numbers, and of course, the violence of God's angry tirades in the Prophetic Books.[11]

The violence of Scripture is a real stumbling block for many readers who cannot get past all the killing and bloodshed and, for that reason, read it reluctantly if at all.

The reading strategy I have proposed has the distinct advantage of allowing people to acknowledge the difficulties they have with the Old Testament without suggesting they ought to avoid it on that account. Helping people realize there are others ways of reading these texts, ways that are actually quite beneficial, may be all the encouragement some need to pick up the Bible and read it once again. Without the benefit of such an approach, many people will continue to neglect this wonderfully rich collection of texts simply because they cannot find a way past its apparent bloodlust.

Additionally, reading the Old Testament nonviolently provides a path to (or back to) faith for individuals who have been wounded by people who have used the Bible against them. These individuals know firsthand how dangerous biblical texts can be. If they are to have any hope of ever reading these texts for spiritual edification, or of becoming part of a faith community that affirms such texts as sacred Scripture, they will need to know there are ways to read the Bible that are not harmful. They will need to regard the Bible as their ally, rather than their enemy. And they will need to see the church as an institution that stands against violence rather than one that sponsors it. This is what makes reading nonviolently so incredibly important. With its emphasis on promoting justice, valuing *all* people, and doing no harm, this approach offers those on the outside a point of entry—or reentry—into communities of faith by helping them experience the positive side of the Bible and Christianity.

Reading nonviolently also offers hope to those who are really struggling with their faith because they simply cannot accept some of what the Bible sanctions. It throws them a lifeline and encourages them to read in new ways. Helping such individuals realize they need not accept everything the Bible says can have a very positive impact on them. It can pull them back from the brink and allow new possibilities to emerge. As they come to understand that an ethically responsible reading actually *requires* them to raise questions, enter into a spirited dialogue with the Bible, and genuinely converse with these texts, they may find their faith strengthened. For some, realizing they can (and should!) read the Bible nonviolently may be just enough to save their faith, or at least to encourage them to give it a second chance. For others, it might be just the word they need to hear to consider exploring questions of faith seriously for the very first time.

To Help Children Develop Good Morals and Christian Values

Anyone who is concerned about how the Bible shapes and forms the morals and values of children will want to pay careful attention to the way biblical texts—especially violent ones—are taught to them. Here is where reading the Bible nonviolently takes on special urgency. Since young children think very concretely, and do not have the same capacity to spiritualize violent texts the way adults do, it is very important to be cautious about how we handle these texts in their presence. For example, children are *not* going to think of the story of David and Goliath as a story about the way God helps us overcome the metaphorical giants in our life. Rather, they will see the story for what it literally is: a story about a boy who throws a rock at a man and kills him. What will they learn from this? That throwing stones is an effective way to deal with bullies? That God is pleased when we kill someone? That fighting is the only way to resolve conflicts? We need to take great care how these stories are told lest we convey messages we have no interest in communicating.

How we talk about violent biblical texts with children will depend on a number of factors, including the age of the child, the story under discussion, and the context in which it is being discussed. Some violent stories are simply unsuitable for young children and should not be taught to them. The gang rape and dismemberment of the Levite's concubine in Judges 19 would be one obvious example. The content is just too graphic. Any value a young child might possible derive from such a story would be far outweighed by the negative impact of hearing it.

To be clear, I am not opposed to children reading or hearing *certain* biblical stories that contain some violence. Violence is part and parcel of our world, and we can use biblical texts to help them reflect on violence in age-appropriate ways over time. But I am *very* concerned about what happens to children when they read and hear Old Testament stories containing "virtuous" violence, especially in the absence of any critique. How do stories that sanction certain acts of violence and portray them as being commanded by God, influence a child's view of violence, not to mention their view of God? And how can we help children learn to read the Old Testament in ways that challenge the violence these texts so often condone?

Considering how impressionable children can be, at the very least it seems we should take great care *not* to reinforce any positive assessments of violence found in these texts. Instead, we should help children understand that violence is always wrong, even though certain biblical texts suggest otherwise. This means we will need to be very careful about which biblical characters we exalt as heroes and heroines and what actions we honor as praiseworthy. If we hope to teach our children that violence and killing are wrong, it makes little sense to celebrate biblical characters who behave in precisely these ways.

We should help children think of heroes are people who *save* lives rather than destroy them. They are brave individuals who resolve conflict without resorting to violence, and who take significant risks to help people without harming others in the process. We should be on the lookout for people who behave in these ways since their stories can be quite useful for promoting the kinds of values and virtues we wish to encourage in children (and adults!). Thus, rather than celebrating the violence of Jael, who kills a man by driving a tent peg through his skull, we ought to praise the nonviolence of Abigail, who prevents a massacre through her courageous words and deeds. Or rather than praising David for killing a giant, we ought to praise Joseph for forgiving his brothers.[12]

If we want to instill positive values in our children, we will need to redefine some of our ideas about who is great and what is praiseworthy in many of these biblical texts. Otherwise, we send terribly confusing mixed messages. What are children to think if one week we tell them to love their enemies, and the next week praise David for killing his?[13] And why should they believe our bold proclamation that God loves all people when, in the same breath, we also insist that God wanted the Israelites to kill every last Canaanite? If we are really serious about inculcating Christian values in children and enhancing their moral development, it is absolutely essential to read these texts in ways that do not reinforce positive portrayals of violence.

One way to do this way with very young children would be to tell modified versions of these stories. These modified versions should exclude parts of the story that explicitly sanction violence or that present violence favorably in some way. Once the story is retold without these evaluative statements, children could be asked questions designed to help them exercise their own moral judgment. For example, if we were to use the story of David and Goliath this way with children, we would surely want to leave out David's bold proclamations that God would help him overcome Goliath (1 Sam. 17:37, 45-47). Then, after telling this modified version, children could be asked questions like these: How do you feel about the way Goliath treated David, and about what David did to Goliath? How do you think God felt about the way David and Goliath behaved? What are some other ways they might have tried to work out their differences? What would you have done if you were David? How do you think God would have liked this story to end? Rather than engaging in simplistic moralizing that tends to reinforce "virtuous" violence, exploring questions like these is much more likely to develop an ethical sensitivity in children and to help them come to their own realization that violence is harmful and displeasing to God.[14]

Additionally, at certain ages, I think it is appropriate to introduce children to some of the Bible's more violent stories by engaging in a selective retelling of them that avoids the most troubling parts of the stories while emphasizing other aspects that are less objectionable. When talking to young children about the flood in Genesis, for instance, it makes sense to focus on the salvation of Noah, his family, and the boatload of animals while ignoring the deadly ramifications of the flood for the rest of humanity. For children who are six or seven years old, that way of reading the story is fine. But, this kind of selectively sanitized reading is no longer adequate when they become teenagers. At that age, they need to realize the story of Noah's ark is more than a colorful tale about a floating zoo with smiling animals. They also need to consider the view from *outside* the ark, and we should help them find responsible ways to process some of the more troublesome dimensions of the narrative.

A Special Appeal to Biblical Scholars and Interpreters

Many people look to biblical scholars, clergy, and other religious professionals as the "experts" when it comes to matters of biblical interpretation. They expect these individuals, above all others, to help them make sense of the many questions and challenges they face when reading the Bible. Therefore, it is incumbent upon those of us who make our living from the Bible, so to speak, to be extremely careful about how we handle troublesome texts, especially violent ones. People are watching! We of all people have a special obligation to read and interpret the Old Testament in an ethically responsible manner. As Eryl Davies admonishes: "The biblical exegete should be prepared to tackle what may perhaps be *the most important task of the biblical interpreter*, namely, that of interacting with the text and reflecting consciously and critically upon the validity or otherwise of its claims."[15]

Perhaps our mantra as biblical scholars should be "No explanation without evaluation!" To explain the text without evaluating its values, assumptions, and perspectives is to leave our job unfinished and to fail to do a significant part of our work.[16] It is not enough just to help people understand what a text may mean; we must also help them understand how a text should be read: ethically, responsibly, and nonviolently. Among other things, this means we need to start talking about the problem of "virtuous" violence in the Old Testament, something many religious professionals are hesitant to do. Rather than shying away from these violent texts, pastors and professors should use them for preaching and teaching. They should be given special attention in college and seminary classes, especially in classes that cover biblical books in which some of the most notoriously problematic texts reside, and scholars should address the problems they raise in the books and commentaries they write.[17]

We simply cannot afford to ignore these texts or to pass over them with nary a word about the problematic nature of their positive portrayals of violence. If those of us with specialized training in biblical studies fail to speak, our silence may give people the impression that we do not object to the violence these texts condone. As Davies puts it: "Failure to critique the Hebrew Bible may be construed as tacit approval of the values it promotes."[18] Yet, there are many values the Bible "promotes" that we should certainly dispute. Whenever we encounter biblical texts that sanction violence, oppression, and killing, we should raise our voices in protest. Keeping quiet about such things is like hearing an offensive joke or racial slur and pretending it does not really matter—when it really does!

As religious professionals, we have a moral obligation to read the Bible in ethically responsible ways, to alert people to the dangers of "virtuous" violence, and to offer guidance about how to deal with these violent verses. We should routinely critique biblical texts that sanction violence and suggest ways these texts can still function constructively. In short, we should read nonviolently, demonstrating our commitment to use the Bible in ways that do not harm others.

Since those of us with specialized training are uniquely positioned to help people overcome the Old Testament's troubling legacy, I would make a special appeal to fellow biblical scholars, ministers, and teachers to take up this cause in earnest and to make it a real priority. I would urge you to read the Old Testament nonviolently and to do all you can to help those in your care to do likewise. Lives are at stake!

Augmenting Nonviolent Readings with Nonviolent Alternatives for Resolving Conflict

Before concluding, I briefly want to make one additional suggestion that complements and adds credibility to the reading strategy I have been advocating in this book. As we have seen, reading the Old Testament nonviolently involves critiquing violence at every turn and at all levels. But when violence is taken off the table, so to speak, how is one to confront evil and resolve conflict? Some people are convinced that certain kinds of conflict can be resolved *only* by using violent force, and not everyone believes all forms of violence are wrong. Before such individuals may be ready to read nonviolently, they may first need to gain a greater understanding of the many effective ways of responding to injustice and oppression that do not require the use of violence.[19] Otherwise, a nonviolent reading strategy may seem idealistic and out of touch with the harsh realities of the modern world. To encourage such readers this is not the case, it is important to have some awareness of the history and success of nonviolent movements.

In the past one hundred years, many nonviolent strategies have been used with great effect to change laws, stop oppression, and confront evil *without* harming others.[20] Stories abound of people who have worked together to do justice, overthrow dictators, and bring about real and lasting change without recourse to violence.[21] Introducing people to this rich history of nonviolent struggle demonstrates that violence is certainly not the only—or even the most effective—way of dealing with conflict. Although people will continue to debate the "virtue" of certain forms of violence, raising awareness of various alternatives can go a long way toward making a nonviolent reading strategy more viable to those who might otherwise be hesitant to accept it.[22]

For too long, Christians (and others) have read the Old Testament violently, in ways that have caused significant harm to others. Old Testament texts have been used to justify an astonishing array of moral atrocities, oppressive practices, and violent acts. The church needs to take a hard look in the historical mirror and admit how Christians have often contributed to this troubling legacy by failing to read these texts responsibly. As someone who is deeply committed to the church, I wish there was no "troubling legacy" to speak of, but there is. And though we might prefer to ignore it, this will not help us overcome it.

Since the Old Testament's troubling legacy has been a long time in the making, it will not vanish overnight. But we can make real progress if we commit ourselves to reading in ways that do no harm. This will involve intentionality, hard work, and determination, but it is worth our very best efforts. People of all ages and walks of life can choose to read nonviolently. It can be done by Sunday school teachers in the local church and by biblical scholars in peer-reviewed journals. It can be something as simple as looking at a story or text from the perspective of the victim, or it can be much more complex, and may involve exposing violent ideologies embedded in the text by drawing on postmodern literary theory. Although there is no foolproof way to ensure the Bible will not be used to harm others when it is read and interpreted, utilizing the approach offered in this book—and encouraging others to do the same—should certainly help us avoid some of the most egregious forms of abuse.

While reading nonviolently is more about reading from a certain perspective than following a particular methodology, having that perspective makes all the difference. I sincerely hope this book has provided both the inspiration to read from this perspective and the practical tools for doing so. There is much work to be done here and a lot at stake. Although overcoming the Old Testament's troubling legacy will not be an easy task, it is well worth our time and energy. People *are* significantly affected by these texts and our reading of them. With that in mind, we should strive to read in ways that are life-affirming and liberating and that express our love for God and others. When we do, we can be sure we are reading in the right direction.

A Brief Word about Biblical Authority

The issue of biblical authority is bound . . . to remain endlessly unsettled and . . . perpetually disputatious.

—WALTER BRUEGGEMANN[1]

My proposal to read the Old Testament nonviolently will inevitably raise questions about biblical authority in the minds of some people. Therefore, a few comments about the nature of biblical authority are in order at this point. Since I have discussed my views on the inspiration and authority of Scripture more extensively elsewhere, my treatment here will be relatively brief.[2]

While most Christians affirm the authority of Scripture, what they mean by that theological affirmation varies greatly.[3] Part of what is at issue here is a significant difference of opinion about what *makes* the Bible authoritative. For example, is the Bible intrinsically authoritative and, if so, in what way? Or is its authority extrinsic, based on what the Church says about it? Then again, perhaps the authority of Scripture is a combination of both, or maybe it is something altogether different. While it is not my intention to wade very deep into these waters in this short appendix, I would like to offer some thoughts on the value of describing the authority of Scripture *functionally*, based on what it does.

For many Christians, affirming the authority of Scripture is a way of asserting their confidence in the truthfulness and the trustworthiness of the Bible. They believe that what the Bible says—or what they think it says—is true. They see the Bible as an essential guide—some would say *the* essential guide—for determining

Christian values, morals, and beliefs. It is viewed as the ultimate standard for determining right and wrong, one that governs all of our beliefs and behaviors.

To be more specific, for some Christians, especially those from conservative theological traditions, affirming the authority of Scripture involves embracing certain views about its historical accuracy and its theological veracity. For them, claiming the Bible is authoritative means believing that it more or less describes things the way they actually happened—what you see on the pages of the Bible is essentially what you would have seen had you lived in ancient times. They also believe the Bible is theologically trustworthy and true—what it says about God, sin, and salvation, for example, is regarded as being completely reliable. While I understand the desire to describe biblical authority in this way, I think all such attempts to tether the authority of Scripture to its presumed historical accuracy and theological reliability are misguided and, ultimately, untenable.[4]

While the Old Testament obviously describes many historical people and events, to regard everything (or mostly everything) it says as a reliable record of the past fundamentally misunderstands the nature and function of the Old Testament. Many reasons could be given to demonstrate this point. For our purposes, suffice it to say that ancient historiographers had different goals and methods than their modern counterparts, not to mention a considerably different worldview. They were far more concerned about using "the past" for the sake of the present, to communicate to people in their day and time, than they were about describing what actually happened.[5]

Likewise, it is problematic to contend that the Bible's authority rests upon its complete and absolute theological reliability. Such an assertion claims too much. While there is much that is true about the Bible, the Bible is not always a dependable guide ethically, morally, or theologically. For example, the Old Testament sometimes makes theological claims most people of faith today would deny such as the belief that God causes natural disasters to punish sinners and that all people go to Sheol when they die. The Old Testament also sometimes portrays God in ways that do not correspond very well—if at all—to the way most Christians actually view God. Tying the authority of the Bible to its theological "correctness" creates problems that are difficult to overcome.

But if this is true, why do so many people make such broad and sweeping claims about the authority of Scripture based upon its supposed historical accuracy and theological reliability? They do so, in large part, because of their belief about the Bible's divine origins. They typically subscribe to a view of divine inspiration that attributes a very high degree of divine involvement to the formation of Scripture. They are convinced that the *content* of the Bible is accurate and dependable because they believe God put it there, albeit through human writers.

While I have no doubt that God was involved in the formation of Scripture in various ways, I think these individuals *overemphasize* God's involvement and *underestimate* the very real and significant role human beings played in the process. This leads them to develop unrealistic views of Scripture and its authority. They end up claiming more for the Bible than the Bible claims for itself, and they expect the Bible to be something it is not.[6] Although they claim to believe what the Bible says, the Bible "says" innumerable things, many of which are quite incompatible and sometimes even mutually contradictory.[7] This creates enormous difficulties for those who make sweeping pronouncements about the authority of Scripture based upon its presumed God-given content.

What is especially troubling about this way of viewing biblical authority is that it has all too often led to violent and oppressive ways of reading and appropriating the Bible. As Carole Fontaine sees it: "It is precisely because religious communities have held a privileged view of the Bible's 'nature' as some sort of divine product with divine content and purpose that it has been so difficult to analyze the ways in which the Bible might be contributing to the various oppressions visited upon different groups."[8] This view of biblical authority has also complicated efforts to critique the "virtuous" violence contained within its pages.[9] People who believe the content of the Bible was determined by God feel hesitant to critique the Bible because they regard it as sacrosanct. Their view of Scripture compels them to embrace its violent views of God and its justification of violence against others. Obviously, this creates serious challenges for those wanting to engage in an ethically responsible reading of Scripture. But this is a problem of their own making—one that I believe is based upon an inappropriate understanding of biblical authority.

Rather than arguing that the Bible is authoritative because it is divinely inspired, I believe it is more appropriate—and accurate—to describe biblical authority *functionally*.[10] Defined functionally, the authority of the Bible resides less in what it *is* and more in what it *does*. In other words, what makes the Bible authoritative is not its divine inspiration nor its alleged historical reliability or unassailable theological veracity. Rather, the Bible is authoritative—or, perhaps better said, functions authoritatively—when people take it seriously and allow their lives to be transformed by it in faith-affirming and God-honoring ways. To put it another way, we might say that affirming the authority of Scripture has less to do with what we *say* about it and more to do with how we *live* in light of it. Affirming the authority of Scripture is not primarily about giving cognitive assent to comprehensive statements about the Bible's trustworthiness and reliability. Rather, it is about giving ourselves to the God who speaks through its pages and calls us to live lives of faithfulness and obedience. We affirm the authority of Scripture by demonstrating our willingness to be shaped by these texts even as we enter into a critical dialogue with them.

Therefore, if you want to know whether someone *really* believes in the authority of Scripture, consider how they might answer questions like these: Does your reading of the Bible increase your love of God and neighbor? Does it inspire you to trust God wholeheartedly and to seek God unreservedly? Does it compel you to act justly, love mercy, and walk humbly with God (Mic. 6:8)? Does it move you to behave compassionately toward the most vulnerable members in your community? Does it prompt you to love your enemy and reconcile with your adversary? Does it create in you a desire to do all you can to see God's reign of peace and justice realized in the world? Those who answer "Yes" to such questions embrace the authority of Scripture in a profound way regardless of whether they believe everything in it actually happened or regard all of it as theologically "true." Those who cannot answer questions like these affirmatively, on the other hand, can claim whatever they wish about biblical authority, but their lives ultimately belie their words. The Bible is only truly authoritative in our lives when it functions in ways that transform us into God's image and align our priorities with God's.

The approach to Scripture I have advocated in this book corresponds well with a functional understanding of biblical authority. I have argued that we should read Scripture in ways that increase our love for God and others, that promote justice, and that value all people. All these things emphasize the importance Scripture has upon our attitudes and actions. Reading nonviolently, in an ethically responsible manner, should profoundly influence how we order our lives and how we live in relation to God and neighbor. When this happens, it will be clear that we affirm the authority of Scripture in our lives in the most radical way possible.

Notes

Chapter 1: Introduction: The Bible Should Never Be Used to Harm Others

1. Esther Epp-Tiessen, "Conquering the Land," in *Under Vine and Fig Tree: Biblical Theologies of Land and the Palestinian-Israeli Conflict*, ed. Alain Epp Weaver (Telford, PA: Cascadia, 2007), 70, emphasis mine.

2. Laura E. Donaldson, "Postcolonialism and Biblical Reading: An Introduction," *Semeia* 75 (1996): 9. Estimates of Pequot casualties are said to range from three hundred to seven hundred, according to Charles M. Segal and David C. Stineback, *Puritans, Indians, and Manifest Destiny* (New York: G. P. Putnam's Sons, 1977), 137.

3. Donaldson, "Postcolonialism and Biblical Reading," 8.

4. I am indebted to Matthew Kruer, "Red Albion: Genocide and English Colonialism, 1622–1646," (master's thesis, Graduate School of the University of Oregon, 2009), 109–10, for noting this connection. Although Underhill never mentions the specific war in question, Kruer argues that "Puritan chroniclers . . . clearly connected the two events [the Pequot War and David's war with the Ammonites] in their histories of New England" (110).

5. Segal and Stineback, *Puritans, Indians, and Manifest Destiny*, 136–37.

6. Kruer, "Red Albion," 110.

7. Examples include Jim Hill and Rand Cheadle, *The Bible Tells Me So: Uses and Abuses of Holy Scripture* (New York: Doubleday, 1996); John Shelby Spong, *The Sins of Scripture: Exposing the Bible's Texts of Hate to Reveal the God of Love* (San Francisco: HarperSanFrancisco, 2005); Adrian Thatcher, *The Savage Text: The Use and Abuse of the Bible* (Malden, MA: Wiley-Blackwell, 2008); and Philip Jenkins, *Laying Down the Sword: Why We Can't Ignore the Bible's Violent Verses* (New York: HarperOne, 2011).

8. Thatcher (*Savage Text*) uses the phrase "savage text" to describe the Bible "when its use results in the marginalization, or persecution, or victimization, of any of the people or creatures for whom . . . Christ died" (4). He regards it as an appropriate designation for "what Christians have made of the Bible when they have used its pages to endorse cruelty, hatred, murder, oppression, and condemnation, often of other Christians" (5).

9. For some orientation to the issue of violence in the New Testament, see Michel Desjardins, *Peace, Violence and the New Testament* (Sheffield: Sheffield Academic, 1997); Philip

L. Tite, *Conceiving Peace and Violence: A New Testament Legacy* (Dallas: University Press of America, 2004); Shelly Matthews and E. Leigh Gibson, eds., *Violence in the New Testament* (New York: T & T Clark, 2005); and Thomas R. Yoder Neufeld, *Killing Enmity: Violence and the New Testament* (Grand Rapids, MI: Baker, 2011).

10. The household codes (Eph. 5:21—6:9; Col. 3:18—4:1) are particularly problematic in this regard. For a critique of these codes, see Elisabeth Schüssler Fiorenza, *Bread Not Stone: The Challenge of Feminist Biblical Interpretation* (Boston: Beacon, 1984), 65–92, who regards these as "patriarchal texts that must be critically evaluated rather than justified" (xxi).

11. See Spong, *Sins of Scripture*, 181–210. Spong (181) cites three "terrible texts": Matt. 27:24-25; John 8:39, 44; Rom. 11:7-8.

12. For some of the difficulties associated with the penal substitution view of the atonement, see Brad Jersak, "Nonviolent Identification and the Victory of Christ," in *Stricken by God? Nonviolent Identification and the Victory of Christ*, ed. Brad Jersak and Michael Hardin (Grand Rapids, MI: Eerdmans, 2007), 23–24; Gregory Anderson Love, *Love, Violence, and the Cross: How the Nonviolent God Saves Us through the Cross of Christ* (Eugene, OR: Cascade, 2010), 27–51. For difficulties with traditional views of hell, see Sharon L. Baker, *Razing Hell: Rethinking Everything You've Been Taught about God's Wrath and Judgment* (Louisville, KY: Westminster John Knox, 2010), 3–18.

13. Philip Jenkins, *Laying down the Sword: Why We Can't Ignore the Bible's Violent Verses* (New York: HarperOne, 2011).

14. Cheryl A. Kirk-Duggan, *Violence and Theology* (Nashville: Abingdon, 2006), 25.

15. For a brief discussion about the authority of Scripture, see the appendix.

16. Walter Wink, *Engaging the Powers: Discernment and Resistance in a World of Domination* (Minneapolis: Fortress Press, 1992), esp. 12–31.

17. See chapter 10 for a very brief discussion of this and for some resources in the notes there for further reading.

18. For a brief discussion of how the Bible was formed, see John Barton, *How the Bible Came to Be* (Louisville, KY: Westminster John Knox, 1997).

19. See, for example, the discussion of the book of Joshua in chapter 7.

20. See the end of chapter 5.

21. See Glen H. Stassen and Michael L. Westmoreland-White, "Defining Violence and Nonviolence" in *Teaching Peace: Nonviolence and the Liberal Arts*, ed. J. Denny Weaver and Gerald Biesecker-Mast (Lanham, MD: Rowman and Littlefield, 2003), 17–21. They define violence as "destruction to a victim or victims by means that overpoer [sic] the victim's consent" (21).

22. This definition does not include a component about intent. Although a great deal of violence is done intentionally (someone wants to harm someone else), that is not always the case. Violence can sometimes happen unintentionally, especially within complex structures.

23. John J. Collins, *Does the Bible Justify Violence?* (Minneapolis: Fortress Press, 2004), 3.

24. See chapter 4.

25. Eric A. Seibert, *Disturbing Divine Behavior: Troubling Old Testament Images of God* (Minneapolis: Fortress Press, 2009), 3–4.

26. For a popular treatment of why the Old Testament matters, see Philip Yancey, *The Bible Jesus Read* (Grand Rapids, MI: Zondervan, 1999). For a more scholarly, though very readable, book encouraging people to read and value the Old Testament, see Ellen F. Davis, *Getting Involved with God: Rediscovering the Old Testament* (Cambridge, MA: Cowley, 2001).

Chapter 2: The Old Testament's Troubling Legacy

1. John Shelby Spong, *The Sins of Scripture: Exposing the Bible's Texts of Hate to Reveal the God of Love* (San Francisco: HarperSanFrancisco, 2005), 4.

2. David M. Gunn and Danna Nolan Fewell, *Narrative in the Hebrew Bible* (Oxford: Oxford University Press, 1993), 205, emphasis in original.

3. For a modern feature film depicting something of the horror of the Crusades, see *Kingdom of Heaven*, starring Orlando Bloom.

4. Roland H. Bainton, *Christian Attitudes toward War and Peace: A Historical Survey and Critical Re-evaluation* (Nashville: Abingdon, 1960), 112–13.

5. Obviously, the Crusades were justified in many ways, not just by appealing to the Bible. Moreover, when the Bible was cited, both Old and New Testament texts were used to legitimate these ill-conceived military campaigns. Interestingly, some Old Testament texts one might have expected to play a more prominent role in this regard, such as those found in the book of Joshua, apparently did not. As Douglas S. Earl (*The Joshua Delusion? Rethinking Genocide in the Bible* [Eugene, OR: Cascade, 2010], 7) notes: "The gospels played a far more prominent role in justifying the Crusades than the book of Joshua, which is conspicuous by its absence." See also Earl, *Joshua Delusion?*, 158–59, note 14.

6. Joseph H. Lynch, "The First Crusade: Some Theological and Historical Context," in *Must Christianity Be Violent? Reflections on History, Practice, and Theology*, ed. Kenneth R. Chase and Alan Jacobs (Grand Rapids, MI: Brazos, 2003), 28. Lynch identifies four specific "connections" between the crusaders and the Old Testament.

7. Lynch, "First Crusade," 31.

8. Christopher Tyerman, *God's War: A New History of the Crusades* (Cambridge, MA: Harvard University Press, 2008), 47. This translation of Jer. 48:10 is supplied in Tyerman's book.

9. Tyerman, *God's War*, 482.

10. Louise and Jonathan Riley-Smith, *The Crusades: Idea and Reality, 1095–1274* (London: Edward Arnold, 1981), 134. I am indebted to Tyerman (*God's War*, 477) for this reference.

11. Peter C. Craigie, *The Problem of War in the Old Testament* (Grand Rapids, MI: Eerdmans, 1978), 28. On the Bible's enormous importance for soldiers during the Civil War, see, for example, Robert J. Miller, *Both Prayed to the Same God: Religion and Faith in the American Civil War* (Lanham, MD: Lexington, 2007), 41–49.

12. William Klassen, "Love Your Enemy: A Study of New Testament Teaching on Coping with an Enemy," in *Biblical Realism Confronts the Nation: Ten Christian Scholars Summon the Church to the Discipleship of Peace*, ed. Paul Peachey (Scottdale, PA: Herald, 1963), 153. See also William Klassen, "The Authenticity of the Command: 'Love Your Enemies,'" in *Authenticating the Words of Jesus*, ed. Bruce Chilton and Craig A. Evans (Boston: Brill, 2002), 392; and Ben C. Ollenburger, "Introduction: Gerhard von Rad's Theory of Holy War," in Gerhard von Rad, *Holy War in Ancient Israel*, trans. and ed. Marva J. Dawn (Grand Rapids, MI: Eerdmans, 1991), 9–10.

13. The first three hundred years are a notable exception. See John Driver, *How Christians Made Peace with War: Early Christian Understandings of War* (Scottdale, PA: Herald, 1988).

14. Richard B. Hays, *The Moral Vision of the New Testament: Community, Cross, New Creation: A Contemporary Introduction to New Testament Ethics* (San Francisco: HarperSanFrancisco, 1996), 336.

15. Hays, *Moral Vision*, 336.

16. Hays, *Moral Vision*, 336.

17. Regardless of one's views about Christian participation in war, all of us ought to be extremely concerned when sacred texts are read in ways that encourage and sanction the use of violence against others.

18. For an extensive study exploring the relationship between biblical texts and colonialism, see Michael Prior, *The Bible and Colonialism: A Moral Critique* (Sheffield: Sheffield Academic, 1997). See also David M. Gunn, "Colonialism and the Vagaries of Scripture: Te Kooti in Canaan: (A Story of Bible and Dispossession in Aotearoa/New Zealand)," in *God in the Fray: A Tribute to Walter Brueggemann*, ed. Tod Linafelt and Timothy K. Beal (Minneapolis: Fortress Press, 1998), 127–42.

19. John J. Collins, *The Bible after Babel: Historical Criticism in a Postmodern Age* (Grand Rapids, MI: Eerdmans, 2005), 62–63, emphasis mine. See further Sylvester Johnson, "New Israel, New Canaan: The Bible, the People of God, and the American Holocaust," *Union Seminary Quarterly Review* 59 (2005): 25–39.

20. Esther Epp-Tiessen, "Conquering the Land," in *Under Vine and Fig Tree: Biblical Theologies of Land and the Palestinian-Israeli Conflict*, ed. Alain Epp Weaver (Telford, PA: Cascadia, 2007), 72.

21. Prior, *Bible and Colonialism*, 292.

22. Naim Stifan Ateek, *Justice and Only Justice: A Palestinian Theology of Liberation* (Maryknoll, NY: Orbis, 1989), 77.

23. For a convenient discussion of the evidence both for and against slavery in the Bible, see Willard W. Swartley, *Slavery, Sabbath, War, and Women* (Scottdale, PA: Herald, 1983), 31–64. For a very helpful discussion of the way prominent individuals used the Bible in the debate over slavery, see Mark A. Noll, *The Civil War as a Theological Crisis* (Chapel Hill: University of North Carolina Press, 2006), 31–50. For a list of numerous additional secondary sources on this question, see Noll, *Civil War*, 169–70, note 4.

24. Of course, New Testament texts such as 1 Cor. 7:20-21; Eph. 6:6-8, Col. 3:22, 1 Pet. 2:18-21, and the book of Philemon were also marshaled in support of slavery.

25. All Scripture quotations are from the New Revised Standard Version unless otherwise noted.

26. Stephen R. Haynes, *Noah's Curse: The Biblical Justification of American Slavery* (New York: Oxford, 2002), 65–104.

27. Haynes, *Noah's Curse*, 67.

28. James H. Evans Jr., *We Have Been Believers: An African American Systematic Theology* (Minneapolis: Fortress Press, 1992), 39.

29. Kathleen M. O'Connor, "The Feminist Movement Meets the Old Testament: One Woman's Perspective," in *Engaging the Bible in a Gendered World: An Introduction to Feminist Biblical Interpretation in Honor of Katharine Doob Sakenfeld*, ed. Linda Day and Carolyn Pressler (Louisville, KY: Westminster John Knox, 2006), 13. This is one of seven problems O'Connor identifies for feminist biblical scholars.

30. Pamela J. Milne, "Eve and Adam: A Feminist Reading," in *Approaches to the Bible: The Best of Bible Review*, vol. 2, *A Multitude of Perspectives*, ed. Harvey Minkoff (Washington, DC: Biblical Archaeology Society, 1995), 261. See also Danna Nolan Fewell, "Reading the Bible Ideologically: Feminist Criticism," in *To Each Its Own Meaning: An Introduction to Biblical Criticisms and Their Application*, ed. Steven L. McKenzie and Stephen R. Haynes, rev. and exp. ed. (Louisville, KY: Westminster John Knox, 1999), 270–78. Fewell (270) writes: "Genesis 2–3, perhaps more than any other biblical text, has been the biggest influence on

the way men and women relate to one another in the Western world. Cited most often as 'proof' that women are inferior to men and as support for male dominance over women, Genesis 2–3 has hardly been a liberating text."

31. Alice Ogden Bellis, *Helpmates, Harlots, and Heroes: Women's Stories in the Hebrew Bible*, 2nd ed. (Louisville, KY: Westminster John Knox, 2007), 37.

32. Milne, "Eve and Adam," 262. For further discussion on the church's complicity in witch hunts, see Helen Ellerbe, *The Dark Side of Christian History* (Windermere, FL: Morningstar and Lark, 1995), 114–38.

33. Pamela J. Milne, "Labouring with Abusive Biblical Texts: Tracing Trajectories of Misogyny," in *The Labour of Reading: Desire, Alienation, and Biblical Interpretation*, Semeia Studies 36, ed. Fiona C. Black, Roland Boer, and Erin Runions (Atlanta: Society of Biblical Literature, 1999), 270.

34. For a recent collection of essays related to children in the Bible, see Marcia J. Bunge, Terence E. Fretheim, and Beverly Roberts Gaventa, eds., *The Child in the Bible* (Grand Rapids, MI: Eerdmans, 2008).

35. Deut. 13:6-11; 21:18-21; Prov. 13:24; 22:15; 23:13-14; 29:15.

36. For more on the way the Bible has been harmful to children, see Spong, *Sins of Scripture*, 143–80, and Adrian Thatcher, *The Savage Text: The Use and Abuse of the Bible* (Malden, MA: Wiley-Blackwell, 2008), 78–94.

37. Andreas Michel, "Sexual Violence against Children in the Bible," in *The Structural Betrayal of Trust*, Concilium 2004/3, ed. Regina Ammicht-Quinn, Hille Haker, and Maureen Junker-Kenny (London: SCM, 2004), 56.

38. See Terence E. Fretheim, "'God Was with the Boy' (Genesis 21:20): Children in the Book of Genesis," in Bunge et al., eds., *The Child in the Bible*, 16–17, and the references cited there.

39. Tedd Tripp, *Shepherding a Child's Heart*, 2nd ed. (Wapwallopen, PA: Shepherd, 2005), 104–5.

40. Tripp, *Shepherding*, 103.

41. Tripp, *Shepherding*, 103.

42. Tripp, *Shepherding*, 105–6.

43. For a recent treatment of this issue, see William J. Webb, *Corporal Punishment in the Bible: A Redemptive Movement Hermeneutic for Troubling Texts* (Downers Grove, IL: InterVarsity, 2011).

44. For a helpful guide designed for pastors and others, see David K. Switzer, *Pastoral Care of Gays, Lesbians and Their Families* (Minneapolis: Fortress Press, 1999).

45. For an excellent discussion of the problem with labels and the categories we use, see Jenell Williams Paris, *The End of Sexual Identity: Why Sex Is Too Important to Define Who We Are* (Downers Grove, IL: InterVarsity, 2011).

46. For a discussion of different Christian perspectives on the issue, see L. R. Holben, *What Christians Think about Homosexuality: Six Representative Viewpoints* (North Richland Hills, TX: BIBAL, 1999).

47. Gary David Comstock, *Violence against Lesbians and Gay Men* (New York: Columbia University Press, 1991), 122.

48. Comstock, *Violence against Lesbians and Gay Men*, 122.

49. Comstock, *Violence against Lesbians and Gay Men*, 122. He provides two examples from 1986, one from the Catholic Church and one from the United States Supreme Court, both of which made reference to Leviticus in condemning homosexual behavior. Comstock offers three additional examples in note 19, pp. 258–59.

50. Linda J. Patterson, *Hate Thy Neighbor: How the Bible Is Misused to Condemn Homosexuality* (West Conshohocken, PA: Infinity, 2009), 9–22.

51. Patterson, *Hate Thy Neighbor*, 22.

52. The following texts are among those often used in debates about the morality of homosexuality: Gen. 19:1-11; Lev. 18:22, 20:13; Judges 19; Rom. 1:18-32. For an interesting discussion of how specialty Bibles sometimes use their explanatory notes to condemn *all* forms of homosexual behavior despite the fact that this goes well beyond what the Bible actually says, see Timothy Beal, *The Rise and Fall of the Bible: The Unexpected History of an Accidental Book* (Boston: Houghton Mifflin Harcourt, 2011), 54–58.

53. Some would challenge the very notion that the Bible provides unambiguous guidelines for sexual ethics. See, for example, Jennifer Wright Knust, *Unprotected Texts: The Bible's Surprising Contradictions about Sex and Desire* (New York: HarperOne, 2011). According to Knust: "When read as a whole, the Bible provides neither clear nor consistent advice about sex and bodies" (244). Therefore, she believes "it is up to readers to decide what a biblically informed and faithful sexual morality might look like" (245).

54. For more on how the Bible has been used to oppress members of the LGBTQ community, see Thatcher, *Savage Text*, 15–35, and Spong, *Sins of Scripture*, 111–42.

55. For various Christian perspectives affirming gay and lesbian individuals, see Walter Wink, ed., *Homosexuality and Christian Faith: Questions of Conscience for the Churches* (Minneapolis: Fortress Press, 1999); Dale B. Martin, *Sex and the Single Savior: Gender and Sexuality in Biblical Interpretation* (Louisville, KY: Westminster John Knox, 2006); and Jack Rogers, *Jesus, the Bible, and Homosexuality: Explode the Myths, Heal the Church*, rev. and exp. ed. (Louisville, KY: Westminster John Knox, 2009).

56. David Plotz, *Good Book: The Bizarre, Hilarious, Disturbing, Marvelous, and Inspiring Things I Learned When I Read Every Single Word of the Bible* (New York: Harper, 2009), 302.

57. For a brief sampling of comments new atheists have made in this regard, see Paul Copan, "Is Yahweh a Moral Monster? The New Atheists and Old Testament Ethics," *Philosophia Christi* 10 (2008): 7–9.

58. Richard Dawkins, *The God Delusion* (Boston: Houghton Mifflin, 2006), 31.

59. For an extensive critique of the way the new atheists have spoken about God in the Old Testament, see Copan, "Is Yahweh a Moral Monster?", 9–37. Copan accuses the new atheists of unfairly focusing on the most troubling aspects of God's behavior without taking into account the historical context in which the Old Testament was written or considering alternative views of God elsewhere in the Bible. When these things are done, Copan believes their very negative statements about God in the Old Testament are not sustainable.

60. See Eric A. Seibert, *Disturbing Divine Behavior: Troubling Old Testament Images of God* (Minneapolis: Fortress Press, 2009). I argue that many Old Testament portrayals of God distort God's character and do not reflect what God actually said and did. In addition to offering an extensive rationale for this approach, I propose an interpretive method designed to help readers determine which Old Testament portrayals of God are reliable and to encourage them to find value in all Old Testament passages, even those containing troubling images of God.

61. On the latter point, see, for example, Richard Kelly Hoskins, *Vigilantes of Christendom: The Story of the Phineas Priesthood* (Lynchburg, VA: Virginia, 1990), and Hector Avalos, *Fighting Words: The Origins of Religious Violence* (Amherst, NY: Prometheus, 2005), 303–24.

62. For further examples of the Old Testament's troubling legacy, see John J. Collins, *Does the Bible Justify Violence?* (Minneapolis: Fortress Press, 2004), 17–20.

63. Terence E. Fretheim and Karlfried Froehlich, *The Bible as Word of God: In a Postmodern Age* (Minneapolis: Fortress Press, 1998), 99–100, emphasis in original.

64. As Prior (*Bible and Colonialism*, 45–46) recognizes: "Several traditions within the Bible lend themselves to oppressive interpretations and applications precisely because of *their inherently oppressive nature*" (emphasis mine).

65. Those who regard the Bible as inerrant or infallible will obviously take issue with this statement. For my views on the inspiration and authority of Scripture, see my *Disturbing Divine Behavior*, appendix B. For a recent, devastating critique of inerrancy, see Thom Stark, *The Human Faces of God: What Scripture Reveals When It Gets God Wrong (and Why Inerrancy Tries to Hide It)* (Eugene, OR: Wipf & Stock, 2011).

66. Compare Carole E. Fontaine, "The Abusive Bible: On the Use of Feminist Method in Pastoral Contexts," in *A Feminist Companion to Reading the Bible: Approaches, Methods and Strategies*, ed. Athalya Brenner and Carole Fontaine (Sheffield: Sheffield Academic, 1997), 89. When reflecting on the way the Bible is used to justify violence against women, Fontaine opines: "I only wish that it were so simple as a case of misinterpretation that could be solved with better translations and more thorough historical-critical research. Unfortunately, the problem goes deeper than that, into the core of the Bible itself."

Chapter 3: The Pervasive Presence of "Virtuous" Violence in the Old Testament

1. Michael Prior, *The Bible and Colonialism: A Moral Critique* (Sheffield: Sheffield Academic, 1997), 261.

2. Mark McEntire, *The Blood of Abel: The Violent Plot in the Hebrew Bible* (Macon, GA: Mercer University Press, 1999), 6.

3. Raymund Schwager, *Must There Be Scapegoats?: Violence and Redemption in the Bible*, trans. Maria L. Assad (New York: Crossroad, 2000), 47, emphasis in original.

4. Schwager, *Must There Be Scapegoats?*, 47.

5. Schwager, *Must There Be Scapegoats?*, 55. Additionally, Schwager notes that "aside from the approximately one thousand verses in which Yahweh himself appears as the direct executioner of violent punishments, and the many texts in which the Lord delivers the criminal to the punisher's sword, in over one hundred other passages Yahweh expressly gives the command to kill people" (60).

6. Athalya Brenner, "Some Reflections on Violence against Women and the Image of God in the Hebrew Bible," in *On the Cutting Edge: The Study of Women in Biblical Worlds: Essays in Honor of Elisabeth Schüssler Fiorenza*, ed. Jane Schaberg, Alice Bach, and Esther Fuchs (New York: Continuum, 2003), 74.

7. Compare the use of the phrase "constructive violence" in Caryn A. Reeder, *The Enemy in the Household: Family Violence in Deuteronomy and Beyond* (Grand Rapids, MI: Baker, 2012), 8–9, et passim.

8. For a history of the interpretation of this text, see John Byron, *Cain and Abel in Text and Tradition: Jewish and Christian Interpretations of the First Sibling Rivalry* (Leiden: Brill, 2011). For a creative proposal about why God rejected Cain's offering, see Gary A. Herion, "Why God Rejected Cain's Offering: The Obvious Answer," in *Fortunate the Eyes That See: Essays in Honor of David Noel Freedman in Celebration of His Seventieth Birthday*, ed. Astrid B. Beck et al. (Grand Rapids, MI: Eerdmans, 1995), 52–65.

9. Given the patriarchal nature of this text, David is explicitly condemned for the wrong he committed against Uriah rather than the harm done to Bathsheba. This patriarchal bias

constitutes another layer of violence in the Old Testament, albeit one that is *not* condemned here. The problem of patriarchy will be addressed later, in chapter 9.

10. A number of proverbs regard violence as something undesirable. See, for example, Prov. 3:31; 10:11; 16:29.

11. For a brief, but helpful, discussion of the complex compositional history of this passage and other issues related to this text, see conveniently Steven L. McKenzie, *King David: A Biography* (New York: Oxford University Press, 2000), 70–77.

12. For one exception, see Robert F. Shedinger, "Who Killed Goliath? History and Legend in Biblical Narrative," in *Who Killed Goliath? Reading the Bible with Heart and Mind*, ed. Robert F. Shedinger and Deborah J. Spink (Valley Forge, PA: Judson, 2001), 27–38.

13. For a similar example from the Apocrypha, see Jth. 13:18-20.

14. James L. Kugel (*Traditions of the Bible: A Guide to the Bible As It Was at the Beginning of the Common Era* [Cambridge, MA: Harvard University Press, 1998], 609) cites a fascinating Talmudic tradition (b. *Megillah* 10b) in which God expresses incredulity that angels would be singing at such a time, suggesting that God felt compassion for the drowning Egyptians.

15. See, for example, Deut. 2:16—3:7; 1 Sam. 7:7-14; 1 Sam. 14:1-23; 2 Sam. 23:11-12; and 2 Chron. 26:3-7.

16. The oracles against the nations also envision war as divine judgment. See, for example, Isa. 13–23; Jer. 46–51; and Ezek. 25–35.

17. Judg. 3:9, 15; 4:6; 6:11-14; 11:29. In Judges, Samson also partially delivers Israel, but he alone does all the fighting and killing. He never leads others in battle.

18. See chapter 7.

19. I say, "the text seems to suggest God also approved of this massacre" because it is not entirely clear whether 2 Kgs. 10:30 refers only to Jehu's destruction of Ahab's descendants or also to what he did to the worshippers of Baal. Both Terence E. Fretheim, *First and Second Kings* (Louisville: Westminster John Knox, 1999), 172, and Gwilym H. Jones, *1 and 2 Kings* vol. 2 (Grand Rapids: Eerdmans, 1984), 472–73, read this verse as including divine approval for what Jehu did to the worshippers of Baal.

20. See Rob Barrett, *Disloyalty and Destruction: Religion and Politics in Deuteronomy and the Modern World*, LHBOTS 511 (New York: T & T Clark, 2009), 128–59, for an insightful discussion of Deuteronomy 13, a chapter he identifies as "a lightning rod for modern condemnation of Old Testament ethics" (129). See also Jeffries Hamilton, "How to Read an Abhorrent Text: Deuteronomy 13 and the Nature of Authority," *HBT* 20 (1998): 12–32, esp. p. 15, where Hamilton questions the usefulness of this text for contemporary readers.

21. Some doubt Jephthah actually kills his daughter since the text never explicitly says he does, but this certainly seems to be what is implied in Judg. 11:39.

22. John L. Thompson, *Reading the Bible with the Dead: What You Can Learn from the History of Exegesis That You Can't Learn from Exegesis Alone* (Grand Rapids, MI: Eerdmans, 2007), 1–2.

23. David J. A. Clines, *Interested Parties: The Ideology of Writers and Readers of the Hebrew Bible*, JSOTSup 205 (Sheffield: Sheffield Academic, 1995), 217.

24. Even the Chronicler, who whitewashes David's life by excluding any reference to the Bathsheba-Uriah debacle, still acknowledges David's violent legacy and uses it to explain why David did not build a temple for Yahweh (1 Chron. 22:7-8).

25. Peter J. Gomes, *The Good Book: Reading the Bible with Mind and Heart* (New York, Avon, 1996), 25.

26. As Jonathan Kirsch observes in *The Harlot by the Side of the Road: Forbidden Tales of the Bible* (New York: Ballantine, 1997), "Casual readers rarely find their way to the 'forbidden' stories of the Bible because they simply do not know such stories exist and do not bother to look for them" (9).

27. On the general disuse of the Old Testament in the Church, see Ellen F. Davis, "Losing a Friend: The Loss of the Old Testament to the Church," in *Jews, Christians, and the Theology of the Hebrew Scriptures*, ed. Alice Ogden Bellis and Joel S. Kaminsky, SBL Symposium Series 8 (Atlanta: Society of Biblical Literature, 2000), 83–94.

28. See Philip Jenkins, *Laying Down the Sword: Why We Can't Ignore the Bible's Violent Verses* (New York: HarperOne, 2011), 201–8.

29. This tendency to omit violent parts of the Old Testament is also prevalent in the Roman Catholic Mass and the Liturgy of the Hours. See Prior, *Bible and Colonialism*, 273–78. Gordon Matties (*Joshua*, BCBC [Harrisonburg, VA: Herald, 2012], 27) refers to the process of omitting something objectionable from the Bible as a "textectomy," citing Eugene Petersen, who memorably refers to the removal of difficult parts of Psalms as "psalmectomies."

30. Thompson, *Reading the Bible with the Dead*, 2.

31. Barbara Brown Taylor, "Hard Words," *ChrCent* 118 (May 2001): 24.

32. As the text portrays it, there really was no battle in the traditional sense of two sides locked in armed combat. After the walls fell, Israelites simply slaughtered Canaanites.

33. As we will see, this same tendency expresses itself in biblical scholarship as well.

Chapter 4: The Danger of Reading the Bible

1. Eugene H. Peterson, *Eat This Book: A Conversation in the Art of Spiritual Reading* (Grand Rapids, MI: Eerdmans, 2006), 82, emphasis in original.

2. Carolyn J. Sharp, *Wrestling the Word: The Hebrew Scriptures and the Christian Believer* (Louisville, KY: Westminster John Knox, 2010), 2.

3. Dr. Seuss, *Fox in Socks* (New York: Beginner, 1965), unnumbered page at the beginning.

4. Mieke Bal, *On Story-Telling: Essays in Narratology*, ed. David Jobling (Sonoma, CA: Polebridge, 1981), 14, emphasis mine. Quoted in John J. Collins, *Does the Bible Justify Violence?* (Minneapolis: Fortress Press, 2004), 1.

5. John Barton, *Understanding Old Testament Ethics: Approaches and Explorations* (Louisville, KY: Westminster John Knox, 2003), 73–74.

6. For an alternate perspective, see Stephen Fowl, "Texts Don't Have Ideologies," *BibInt* 3 (1995): 15–34.

7. M. M. Bakhtin, *The Dialogic Imagination: Four Essays*, ed. Michael Holquist, trans. Caryl Emerson and Michael Holquist (Austin: University of Texas Press, 1981), 8. Quoted in Tina Pippin, "Ideology, Ideological Criticism, and the Bible, *CurBs*, 4 (1996): 54.

8. Julia M. O'Brien, *Challenging Prophetic Metaphor: Theology and Ideology in the Prophets* (Louisville, KY: Westminster John Knox, 2008), xvii.

9. David J. A. Clines, *Interested Parties: The Ideology of Writers and Readers of the Hebrew Bible*, JSOTSup 205, (Sheffield: Sheffield Academic, 1995), 21.

10. This distinction between what texts "mean" and "do" is from Stanley E. Fish, *Self-Consuming Artifacts: The Experience of Seventeenth Century Literature* (Berkeley: University of California Press, 1972), 387–88. Cited in Eryl W. Davies, *The Immoral Bible: Approaches to Biblical Ethics* (London: T & T Clark, 2010), 122.

11. Davies, *Immoral Bible*, 122, referring to the view of reader-response critics.

12. Davies, *Immoral Bible*, 122.

13. There are clear commands that limit violence and that suggest life is sacred to God (for example, Exod. 20:13, the sixth commandment), and the prophets regularly tell people to stop doing violence.

14. Clines, *Interested Parties*, 21.

15. See Jack Nelson-Pallmeyer, *Is Religion Killing Us? Violence in the Bible and the Quran* (Harrisburg, PA: Trinity Press International, 2003), 45, who speaks of the exodus-conquest narrative having "a dangerous afterlife."

16. Adrian Thatcher, *The Savage Text: The Use and Abuse of the Bible* (Malden, MA: Wiley-Blackwell, 2008), 63.

17. This is precisely what Thatcher (*Savage Text*, 57) believes may have happened to many Christians across the centuries. He argues that both "the level, and the persistence, of violence throughout the Bible, but especially in the Old Testament, may have desensitized Christians throughout the history of Christianity to the horror of it."

18. See Charles H. Cosgrove, *Appealing to Scripture in Moral Debate: Five Hermeneutical Rules* (Grand Rapids, MI: Eerdmans, 2002).

19. One looks long and hard to find very much emphasis in the Old Testament on the value of interpersonal forgiveness or the need for reconciliation. See David J. Reimer, "Stories of Forgiveness: Narrative Ethics and the Old Testament," in *Reflection and Refraction: Studies in Biblical Historiography in Honour of A. Graeme Auld*, ed. Robert Rezetko, Timothy H. Lim, and W. Brian Aucker, VTSup 113 (Leiden: Brill, 2007), 362. According to Reimer, only three narratives really address the theme of "interpersonal forgiveness": the story of Jacob and Esau (Genesis 32–33), the story of Joseph and his brothers (Genesis 50), and the story of David and Abigail (1 Samuel 25).

20. David M. Gunn and Danna Nolan Fewell, *Narrative in the Hebrew Bible* (Oxford: Oxford University Press, 1993), 197.

21. For an extensive discussion of how to handle problematic portrayals of God in the Old Testament, see Eric A. Seibert, *Disturbing Divine Behavior: Troubling Old Testament Images of God* (Minneapolis: Fortress Press, 2009).

22. See, for example, Hector Avalos, "The Letter Killeth," *Journal of Religion, Conflict, and Peace* 1 (2007), http://www.plowsharesproject.org/journal/php/archive/archive.php?issu_list_id=8.

23. For a general discussion of this, see Jonathan Klawans (with contributions by David A. Bernat), "Introduction: Religion, Violence, and the Bible," in *Religion and Violence: The Biblical Heritage*, ed. David A. Bernat and Jonathan Klawans (Sheffield: Sheffield Phoenix, 2007), 1–15. For a look at this question from a psychological perspective, though one I think somewhat underestimates how influential these texts are in shaping our opinions about violence, see D. Andrew Kille, "'The Bible Made Me Do It': Text, Interpretation, and Violence," in *The Destructive Power of Religion: Violence in Judaism, Christianity, and Islam*, ed. J. Harold Ellens, condensed and updated ed. (Westport, CT: Praeger, 2007), 8–24.

24. See, for example, Brad J. Bushman and Craig A. Anderson, "Media Violence and the American Public: Scientific Facts versus Media Misinformation," *American Psychologist* 56 (2001): 477–89; Craig A. Anderson and Brad J. Bushman, "The Effects of Media Violence on Society," *Science* 295 (2002): 2377, 2379; and Christopher R. Engelhardt et al., "This Is Your Brain on Violent Video Games: Neural Desensitization to Violence Predicts Increased Aggression Following Violent Video Game Exposure," *Journal of Experimental Social Psychology* 47 (2011): 1033–36.

25. Brad J. Bushman et al. "When God Sanctions Killing: Effect of Scriptural Violence on Aggression," *Psychological Science* 18 (2007): 204–7.

26. Bushman, "When God Sanctions Killing," 206. It should be noted that, for this study, participants read just one passage of Scripture (Judges 19–21) in isolation from its context (p. 207).

27. John Goldingay, *Israel's Life*, vol. 3 of *Old Testament Theology* (Downers Grove, IL: InterVarsity, 2009), 555.

28. Though I would again emphasize that numerous people who have committed acts of violence throughout history have drawn inspiration from—and made connections to—various Old Testament texts. See chapter 2.

29. Pippin, "Ideology," 51, emphasis mine.

30. For a very brief discussion of Weber's "ideal types" and an application of this concept to scribal activity in the ancient world, see Eric A. Seibert, *Subversive Scribes and the Solomonic Narrative: A Rereading of 1 Kings 1–11*, LHBOTS 436 (New York: T & T Clark, 2006), 61–65.

31. Compare Mary E. Shields, "An Abusive God? Identity and Power/Gender and Violence in Ezekiel 23," in *Postmodern Interpretations of the Bible: A Reader*, ed. A. K. M. Adam (St. Louis: Chalice, 2001), 130–31. Shields identifies a number of "male scholars" she regards as "compliant readers who accept the gender characterization with little or no discussion" (p. 130).

32. For a discussion of various views of inspiration, see Seibert, *Disturbing Divine Behavior*, appendix B.

33. Cheryl B. Anderson, *Ancient Laws and Contemporary Controversies: The Need for Inclusive Biblical Interpretation* (Oxford: Oxford University Press, 2009), 3.

34. For example, they would have no difficulty accepting the command to love God and neighbor, to care for the poor and needy, and to refrain from harmful behaviors such as stealing and adultery.

35. Clines, *Interested Parties*, 19. See also Eryl W. Davies, "The Morally Dubious Passages of the Hebrew Bible: An Examination of Some Proposed Solutions," *Currents in Biblical Research* 3 (2005): 220. Davies writes: "It is a curious truism that biblical scholars have generally been quite prepared to question the historical accuracy or reliability of the biblical traditions but have shied away from questioning the validity of its moral norms and underlying assumptions. They have usually proceeded from an examination of the text to an explanation of its meaning without pausing for a moment to pass judgment on its content. As a result, the task of evaluation has all but been evacuated from the realm of biblical criticism. But there must be a place in biblical scholarship—and a respectable and honourable place—for moral critique and appraisal of the biblical tradition." I heartily concur.

36. Clines, *Interested Parties*, 19.

37. Clines, *Interested Parties*, 21.

38. Clines, *Interested Parties*, 21.

Chapter 5: Developing Good Reading Habits

1. Eryl W. Davies, *The Immoral Bible: Approaches to Biblical Ethics* (London: T & T Clark, 2010), 145–46.

2. Carol Lakey Hess, *Caretakers of Our Common House: Women's Development in Communities of Faith* (Nashville: Abingdon, 1997), 202.

3. The assigned passages are Numbers 31; Joshua 6–11; 1 Samuel 15; and 2 Kings 18–19.

4. This comes from a student's journal submitted for my 2009 January term course, Issues of War, Peace and Social Justice in Biblical Texts.

5. Danna Nolan Fewell, *The Children of Israel: Reading the Bible for the Sake of Our Children* (Nashville: Abingdon, 2003), 37. Fewell borrows the phrase "fighting to find what they must in the holy text" from Daniel Boyarin, *Intertextuality and the Reading of Midrash* (Bloomington: Indiana University Press, 1990), 16.

6. Thomas Merton, *Opening the Bible* (Collegeville: Liturgical, 1986), 37.

7. Davies, *The Immoral Bible*, 121.

8. Renita J. Weems, *Battered Love: Marriage, Sex, and Violence in the Hebrew Prophets* (Minneapolis: Fortress Press, 1995), 101.

9. Hess, *Caretakers of Our Common House*, 193, emphasis mine.

10. Hess, *Caretakers of Our Common House*, 194.

11. Hess, *Caretakers of Our Common House*, 194.

12. The phrase "morally dubious" is from Eryl W. Davies, "The Morally Dubious Passages of the Hebrew Bible: An Examination of Some Proposed Solutions," *Currents in Biblical Research* 3 (2005).

13. Fewell, *Children of Israel*, 33. Fewell cites the flood narrative and the destruction of Sodom as "stories that . . . invite *interruption*" (32), emphasis in original. Though Fewell uses this strategy to focus on the plight of children in the Old Testament who are often the invisible victims of horrific acts of violence and killing, it is equally applicable to any stories that are ethically or morally problematic.

14. William L. Holladay, *Long Ago God Spoke: How Christians May Hear the Old Testament Today* (Minneapolis: Fortress Press, 1995), 117. For a similar experience, see Regina M. Schwartz, *The Curse of Cain: The Violent Legacy of Monotheism* (Chicago: University of Chicago Press, 1997), ix–x. Once, when promoting a liberationist reading of the Exodus account in an undergraduate class Schwartz was teaching, a student asked, "What about the Canaanites?" That simple question, Schwartz claims, compelled her to write the book.

15. Weems, *Battered Love*, 103.

16. David J. A. Clines, *Interested Parties: The Ideology of Writers and Readers of the Hebrew Bible*, JSOTSup 205 (Sheffield: Sheffield Academic, 1995), 20, emphasis mine.

17. Clines, *Interested Parties*, 21.

18. Davies, "Morally Dubious Passages," 219.

19. See Davies, *Immoral Bible*, 120–38, for an excellent discussion of an "ethical critique" of Scripture.

20. Davies, *Immoral Bible*, 124.

21. Judith Fetterley, *The Resisting Reader: A Feminist Approach to American Fiction* (Bloomington: Indiana University Press, 1978).

22. Davies, *Immoral Bible*, 120–21.

23. Elisabeth Schüssler Fiorenza, "The Ethics of Biblical Interpretation: Decentering Biblical Scholarship," *JBL* 107 (1988): 15, emphasis in original.

24. Cheryl B. Anderson, *Ancient Laws and Contemporary Controversies: The Need for Inclusive Biblical Interpretation* (Oxford: Oxford University Press, 2009), 147.

25. Others fear it undermines the authority of Scripture by setting the reader above the Bible as one who is able to pass judgment upon it. For a brief discussion of biblical authority, see the appendix.

26. Matt. 22:34-40; Mark 12:28-34.

27. *On Christian Doctrine* 1.36. For this quotation, I am indebted to Kenton L. Sparks, *God's Word in Human Words: An Evangelical Appropriation of Critical Biblical Scholarship* (Grand Rapids, MI: Baker, 2008), 324. Sparks briefly discusses how this principle led Augustine to allegorize things he found in Scripture that were out of line with it. As an example, Sparks cites Augustine's allegorization of Psalm 137, a text that joyfully anticipates bashing babies against rocks.

28. *Presbyterian Understanding and Use of Holy Scripture* (Louisville, KY: Office of the General Assembly, 1992), 20. Cited by Patrick D. Miller, "What I Have Learned from My Sisters," in *Engaging the Bible in a Gendered World: An Introduction to Feminist Biblical Interpretation in Honor of Katharine Doob Sakenfeld*, ed. Linda Day and Carolyn Pressler (Louisville, KY: Westminster John Knox, 2006), 249, note 24.

29. Christopher J. H. Wright, *Old Testament Ethics for the People of God* (Downers Grove, IL: InterVarsity, 2004), 256.

30. See Perry B. Yoder, *Shalom: The Bible's Word for Salvation, Justice, and Peace* (Nappanee, IN: Evangel, 1987).

31. See Anderson, *Ancient Laws*, 28–29. The teaching of Jesus further supports reading the Bible in ways that promote justice. Jesus' central message, the topic he returned to time and again, was the kingdom of God. Jesus used kingdom language to describe God's reign of justice and peace over all creation. The new community that Jesus was forming, the community we now call the church, was to participate in—and advance—the kingdom of God.

32. Rosemary Radford Ruether, *Sexism and God-Talk: Toward a Feminist Theology* (Boston: Beacon, 1983), 23.

33. Ruether, *Sexism and God-Talk*, 23.

34. Ruether, *Sexism and God-Talk*, 23.

35. Ruether, *Sexism and God-Talk*, 23.

36. I realize that there are some limitations of using language of "justice." As Julia M. O'Brien observes (*Challenging Prophetic Metaphor: Theology and Ideology in the Prophets* [Louisville, KY: Westminster John Knox, 2008], xxi): "If 'justice' means 'what is fair and right,' then humans are not likely to reach consensus on when justice has been achieved because they do not share a common definition of the 'right.'"

37. As Ruether (*Sexism and God-Talk*, 27) writes: "It is important to see that the prophetic-liberating tradition is not and cannot be made into a static set of 'ideas.' Rather it is a plumb line of truth and untruth, justice and injustice that has to be constantly adapted to changing social contexts and circumstances."

38. As Elisabeth Schüssler Fiorenza puts it (*Bread Not Stone: The Challenge of Feminist Biblical Interpretation* [Boston: Beacon, 1984], xiii): "*The* litmus test for invoking Scripture as the Word of God must be whether or not biblical texts and traditions seek to end relations of domination and exploitation."

39. See Joseph Cardinal Bernardin, "A Consistent Ethic of Life: An American-Catholic Dialogue" (Gannon Lecture; Fordham University, New York, December 6, 1983), 1-6, and Jim Wallis, *God's Politics: Why the Right Gets It Wrong and the Left Doesn't Get It* (San Francisco: HarperSanFrancisco, 2005), 297–306.

40. For a wonderful discussion on treating people with reverence, see Richard J. Mouw, *Uncommon Decency: Christian Civility in an Uncivil World* (Downers Grove, IL: InterVarsity, 1992), 22–29.

41. Harriet Sider Bicksler, "Pursuing Peace," in *Focusing Our Faith: Brethren in Christ Core Values*, ed. Terry L. Brensinger (Nappanee, IN: Evangel, 2000), 133–34.

42. For a very helpful discussion of this issue from a New Testament perspective, see Richard B. Hays, *The Moral Vision of the New Testament: Community, Cross, New Creation: A Contemporary Introduction to New Testament Ethics* (San Francisco: HarperSanFrancisco, 1996), 317–46.

43. For an extensive discussion of the disputatious nature of the Old Testament generally, see Walter Brueggemann, *Theology of the Old Testament: Testimony, Dispute, Advocacy* (Minneapolis: Fortress Press, 1997).

44. Davies, *Immoral Bible*, 133.

45. Davies, *Immoral Bible*, 135. See pp. 132–36.

46. Clines, *Interested Parties*, 192.

47. Weems, *Battered Love*, 111.

48. Thom Stark, *The Human Faces of God: What Scripture Reveals When It Gets God Wrong (and Why Inerrancy Tries to Hide It)* (Eugene, OR: Wipf & Stock, 2011), 233.

49. Jacqueline E. Lapsley, *Whispering the Word: Hearing Women's Stories in the Old Testament* (Louisville, KY: Westminster John Knox, 2005), 12.

50. Davies, *Immoral Bible*, 136.

51. Davies, *Immoral Bible*, 136.

52. David J. A. Clines, *Interested Parties*, 19–20. As Bruce C. Birch (*Let Justice Roll Down: The Old Testament, Ethics, and Christian Life* [Louisville, KY: Westminster John Knox, 1991], 43) puts it: "Any adequate approach to the Old Testament as moral resource must seek not only to *retrieve* moral perspectives that inform our ethics but in some instances to *reclaim* the biblical text from elements that distort or limit its moral witness." Quoted in Anderson, *Ancient Laws*, 9.

Chapter 6: Reading the Old Testament Nonviolently

1. J. Cheryl Exum, "Feminist Criticism: Whose Interests Are Being Served?", in *Judges and Method: New Approaches in Biblical Studies*, ed. Gale A. Yee, 2nd ed. (Minneapolis: Fortress Press, 2007), 68.

2. Alastair G. Hunter, "(De)nominating Amalek: Racist Stereotyping in the Bible and the Justification of Discrimination," in *Sanctified Aggression: Legacies of Biblical and Post Biblical Vocabularies of Violence*, ed. Jonneke Bekkenkamp and Yvonne Sherwood (London: T & T Clark, 2003), 107.

3. For some orientation, see A. K. M. Adam, *Handbook of Postmodern Biblical Interpretation* (St. Louis: Chalice, 2000).

4. For helpful discussions of these (and other) methods with application to specific biblical texts, see Gale A. Yee, ed., *Judges and Method. New Approaches in Biblical Studies*, 2nd ed. (Minneapolis: Fortress Press, 2007), and Steven L. McKenzie and Stephen R. Haynes, eds., *To Each Its Own Meaning: An Introduction to Biblical Criticisms and Their Application*, rev. and exp. ed. (Louisville, KY: Westminster John Knox, 1999), 183–306.

5. Nancy R. Bowen, "Women, Violence, and the Bible," in *Engaging the Bible in a Gendered World: An Introduction to Feminist Biblical Interpretation in Honor of Katharine Doob Sakenfeld*, ed. Linda Day and Carolyn Pressler (Louisville, KY: Westminster John Knox, 2006), 187.

6. Don Everts, *God in the Flesh: What Speechless Lawyers, Kneeling Soldiers, and Shocked Crowds Teach Us about Jesus* (Downers Grove, IL: InterVarsity, 2005), 27.

7. Everts, *God in the Flesh*, 27.

8. The phrase "internal critique" comes from Frances Flannery, "'Go Back by the Way You Came': An Internal Textual Critique of Elijah's Violence in 1 Kings 18–19," in *Writing and Reading War: Rhetoric, Gender, and Ethics in Biblical and Modern Contexts*, ed. Brad E. Kelle and Frank Ritchel Ames, SBLSymS 42 (Atlanta: Society of Biblical Literature, 2008), 173.

9. See Eric A. Seibert, *Subversive Scribes and the Solomonic Narrative: A Rereading of 1 Kings 1–11*, LHBOTS 436 (New York: T & T Clark, 2006), 138–54.

10. According to Frances Flannery ("Go Back by the Way You Came," 162), "most commentators assume that in the text God sanctions Elijah's violence, although they do find the scene ethically problematic."

11. Flannery, "Go Back by the Way You Came," 162.

12. Flannery, "Go Back by the Way You Came," 161.

13. Flannery, "Go Back by the Way You Came," 173.

14. Carolyn J. Sharp, *Irony and Meaning in the Hebrew Bible* (Bloomington: Indiana University Press, 2009), 68–69.

15. Sharp, *Irony and Meaning*, 65.

16. Sharp, *Irony and Meaning*, 65.

17. Sharp, *Irony and Meaning*, 74.

18. Sharp, *Irony and Meaning*, 74.

19. Sharp, *Irony and Meaning*, 69, emphasis mine.

20. David M. Gunn and Danna Nolan Fewell, *Narrative in the Hebrew Bible* (Oxford: Oxford University Press, 1993), 204, emphasis mine.

21. Gunn and Fewell, *Narrative in the Hebrew Bible*, 204.

22. John J. Collins, *Does the Bible Justify Violence?* (Minneapolis: Fortress Press, 2004), 30.

23. Collins, *Does the Bible Justify Violence?*, 30.

24. For a discussion of intertextuality, see, conveniently, Danna Nolan Fewell, ed., *Reading between Texts: Intertextuality and the Hebrew Bible* (Louisville, KY: Westminster John Knox, 1992). The essay by Tod Linafelt, "Taking Women in Samuel: Readers/Responses/Responsibility," 99–113, is especially relevant to some of the concerns in this book.

25. For an excellent discussion and incisive critique of reading the Bible this way, see Eryl W. Davies, *The Immoral Bible: Approaches to Biblical Ethics* (London: T & T Clark, 2010), 63–100, 141–44.

26. A related strategy, though one I have not developed here, would be to consider how Jesus and parts of the New Testament might be used to challenge the presence of "virtuous" violence in the Old Testament. Elsewhere, I have argued for using a Christocentric hermeneutic to evaluate problematic portrayals of God in the Old Testament. See Eric A. Seibert, *Disturbing Divine Behavior: Troubling Old Testament Images of God* (Minneapolis: Fortress Press, 2009), 183–207. For a very interesting article dealing with the way Paul handled certain violent Old Testament texts and the implications this has for us as readers today, see Derek Flood, "The Way of Peace and Grace: How Paul Wrestled with Violent Passages in the Hebrew Bible," *Sojourners* 41 (January 2012): 34–37, 46.

27. Cheryl B. Anderson, *Ancient Laws and Contemporary Controversies: The Need for Inclusive Biblical Interpretation* (Oxford: Oxford University Press, 2009), 73.

28. In the next chapter, we will consider the impact of reading the conquest of Canaan in Joshua 6–11 from the perspective of the Canaanites.

29. Andreas Michel, "Sexual Violence against Children in the Bible," in *The Structural Betrayal of Trust*, ed. Regina Ammicht-Quinn, Hille Haker, and Maureen Junker-Kenny, Concilium 2004/3 (London: SCM, 2004), 51. Michel notes that there are additional texts

like these, "another 50 from the deutero-canonical writings of the Old Testament, and a few from the New Testament."

30. See Gustave Doré, *The Doré Bible Illustrations* (Mineola, NY: Dover, 1974), 6–8. Two of these are conveniently reproduced in Danna Nolan Fewell, *The Children of Israel: Reading the Bible for the Sake of Our Children* (Nashville: Abingdon, 2003), 30–31.

31. See, for example, Deut. 2:30-33, 36; 3:2-3.

32. Fewell, *The Children of Israel*, 27.

33. Fewell, *The Children of Israel*, 27.

34. Gary A. Phillips, "The Killing Fields of Matthew's Gospel," in *The Labour of Reading: Desire, Alienation, and Biblical Interpretation*, ed. Fiona C. Black, Roland Boer, and Erin Runions, Semeia Studies 36 (Atlanta: Society of Biblical Literature, 1999), 254.

35. Phillips, "Killing Fields," 264.

36. Chris Heard, "Hearing the Children's Cries: Commentary, Deconstruction, Ethics, and the Book of Habakkuk," in *Bible and Ethics of Reading*, ed. Danna Nolan Fewell and Gary A. Phillips, *Semeia* 77 (1997): 75-89. For a helpful introduction to deconstruction as it relates to biblical studies, see Danna Nolan Fewell, "Deconstructive Criticism: Achsah and the (E)razed City of Writing," in *Judges and Method: New Approaches in Biblical Studies*, ed. Gale A. Yee, 2nd ed. (Minneapolis: Fortress Press, 2007), 115–37.

37. Heard, "Hearing the Children's Cries," 81.

38. Heard, "Hearing the Children's Cries," 84.

39. Heard, "Hearing the Children's Cries," 85–86.

40. Heard, "Hearing the Children's Cries," 75, from the abstract.

41. Heard, "Hearing the Children's Cries," 88.

42. One of the best examples is R. S. Sugirtharajah, *Voices from the Margin: Interpreting the Bible in the Third World*, 3rd ed. (Maryknoll, NY: Orbis, 2006). See also Daniel Patte et al., eds., *Global Bible Commentary* (Nashville: Abingdon, 2004); Fernando F. Segovia and Mary Ann Tolbert, *Reading from This Place*, vol. 2, *Social Location and Biblical Interpretation in Global Perspective* (Minneapolis: Fortress Press, 1995); and Gerald O. West, *The Academy of the Poor: Towards a Dialogical Reading of the Bible* (Sheffield: Sheffield Academic, 1999).

43. Miguel A. De La Torre, *Reading the Bible from the Margins* (Maryknoll, NY: Orbis, 2002), 4–5.

44. Anderson, *Ancient Laws*, 57.

45. Anderson, *Ancient Laws*, 135.

46. Esther Epp-Tiessen, "Conquering the Land," in *Under Vine and Fig Tree: Biblical Theologies of Land and the Palestinian-Israeli Conflict*, ed. Alain Epp Weaver (Telford, PA: Cascadia, 2007), 71.

47. Epp-Tiessen, "Conquering the Land," 72.

48. See Naim Stifan Ateek, *Justice and Only Justice: A Palestinian Theology of Liberation* (Maryknoll, NY: Orbis, 1989), and also his essay titled "A Palestinian Perspective: The Bible and Liberation," in *Biblical Studies Alternatively: An Introductory Reader*, ed. Susanne Scholz (Upper Saddle River, NJ: Prentice Hall, 2003).

49. Renita J. Weems, *Battered Love: Marriage, Sex, and Violence in the Hebrew Prophets* (Minneapolis: Fortress Press, 1995), 8.

50. See chapter 9 for a discussion of the troubling nature of the Old Testament as it relates to women and what can be done about it.

51. Emerson B. Powery, "Reading the Bible as a Minority," in *Brethren in Christ History and Life* 33 (April 2010): 178.

52. Powery, "Reading the Bible," 181.

53. Powery, "Reading the Bible," 185.

54. Renita J. Weems, "Reading Her Way through the Struggle: African American Women and the Bible," in *Stony the Road We Trod: African American Biblical Interpretation*, ed. Cain Hope Felder (Minneapolis: Fortress Press, 1991), 63. Cited in Powery, "Reading the Bible," 193, note 24.

55. This phrase is from the title of Michael Prior's article "The Bible as Instrument of Oppression," *ScrB* 25 (1995): 2–14.

56. See Randal Rauser, "'Let Nothing That Breathes Remain Alive': On the Problem of Divinely Commanded Genocide," *Philosophia Christi* 11 (2009): 33–35.

57. Jacqueline E. Lapsley, *Whispering the Word: Hearing Women's Stories in the Old Testament* (Louisville, KY: Westminster John Knox, 2005), 9.

58. Julia M. O'Brien, *Challenging Prophetic Metaphor: Theology and Ideology in the Prophets* (Louisville, KY: Westminster John Knox, 2008), 69.

59. This direct quote is from my wife, Elisa Joy Seibert.

60. Bowen, "Women, Violence, and the Bible," 194.

61. Thom Stark, *The Human Faces of God: What Scripture Reveals When It Gets God Wrong (and Why Inerrancy Tries to Hide It)* (Eugene, OR: Wipf & Stock, 2011), 218, emphasis in original. See also pp. 223, 230–31.

62. Stark, *Human Faces of God*, 230.

63. Stark, *Human Faces of God*, 218.

64. Stark, *Human Faces of God*, 223.

65. Anderson, *Ancient Laws*, 67.

66. Anderson, *Ancient Laws*, 67.

67. Lapsley, *Whispering the Word*, 7, emphasis in original.

68. Lapsley, *Whispering the Word*, 5.

69. Lapsley, *Whispering the Word*, 8. Lapsley pursues these "other interpretations" by exploring Rachel's words in Genesis 31, the evaluation of violence in Judges 19–21, the women in Exodus 1–4, and the book of Ruth.

70. O'Brien, *Challenging Prophetic Metaphor*, xiii, emphasis mine.

71. O'Brien, *Challenging Prophetic Metaphor*, 110–24.

72. O'Brien, *Challenging Prophetic Metaphor*, 116. O'Brien argues similarly for the prophet Hosea, 40–43.

73. O'Brien, *Challenging Prophetic Metaphor*, 117.

74. O'Brien, *Challenging Prophetic Metaphor*, 117–23.

75. O'Brien, *Challenging Prophetic Metaphor*, 122–23.

76. Katharine Doob Sakenfeld, *Just Wives? Stories of Power and Survival in the Old Testament and Today* (Louisville, KY: Westminster John Knox, 2003), 106. See her discussion on pp. 99–106.

77. Weems, *Battered Love*, 9–10.

78. Weems, *Battered Love*, 100.

79. For further discussion, see Seibert, *Disturbing Divine Behavior*, 212–22.

80. O'Brien demonstrates this convincingly in *Challenging Prophetic Metaphor*.

Chapter 7: Confronting Canaanite Genocide and Its Toxic Afterlife

1. L. Daniel Hawk, *Joshua in 3-D: A Commentary on Biblical Conquest and Manifest Destiny* (Eugene, OR: Cascade, 2010), xi.

2. See chapter 2 for a brief discussion of this.

3. Eryl W. Davies, *The Immoral Bible: Approaches to Biblical Ethics* (London: T & T Clark, 2010), 131.

4. For a somewhat different tradition regarding how the Israelites would come to possess the land, see Exod. 23:20-33. According to this text, God will drive the Canaanites out of the land over time. Nothing is said about Israelites slaughtering them.

5. Compare Deut. 20:16, which summons Israelites to refuse to allow "anything that breathes [to] remain alive."

6. Christopher J. H. Wright, *The God I Don't Understand: Reflections on Tough Questions of Faith* (Grand Rapids, MI: Zondervan, 2008), 92.

7. Wright, *The God I Don't Understand*, 93.

8. Wright, *The God I Don't Understand*, 92.

9. Richard S. Hess, "The Jericho and Ai of the Book of Joshua," in *Critical Issues in Early Israelite History*, ed. Richard S. Hess, Gerald A. Klingbeil, and Paul J. Ray Jr., BBRSup 3 (Winona Lake, IN: Eisenbrauns, 2008), 33–46. Hess is followed by Paul Copan, *Is God a Moral Monster? Making Sense of the Old Testament God* (Grand Rapids, MI: Baker, 2011), 175–77. For a searing critique, see Thom Stark, *Is God a Moral Compromiser? A Critical Review of Paul Copan's "Is God a Moral Monster,"* 2nd ed. (2011): 280–94, http://thomstark. net/copan/stark_copan-review.pdf.

10. For a discussion of this point, see Stark, *Is God a Moral Compromiser?*, 278–94.

11. For a discussion that argues for the essential historicity of the biblical account, see Iain Provan, V. Philips Long, and Tremper Longman III, *A Biblical History of Israel* (Louisville, KY: Westminster John Knox, 2003), 138–92

12. John J. Collins, *The Bible after Babel: Historical Criticism in a Postmodern Age* (Grand Rapids, MI: Eerdmans, 2005), 61.

13. For a convenient discussion of various points of views, see Collins, *Bible after Babel*, 34–46. For an excellent treatment of the archaeological evidence along with a helpful table considering the biblical and archaeological evidence side by side, see William G. Dever, *Who Were the Early Israelites and Where Did They Come From?* (Grand Rapids, MI: Eerdmans, 2003), 37–74.

14. Dever, *Who Were the Early Israelites*, 227–28, emphasis mine.

15. For a brief discussion of the various theories, see William H. Stiebing Jr., *Out of the Desert? Archaeology and the Exodus/Conquest Narratives* (Amherst, NY: Prometheus, 1989), 149–65. For an attempt to provide an explanation that best accords with recent archaeological evidence, see Dever, *Who Were the Early Israelites*, 71–74, 167–89.

16. For a discussion of various conquest accounts from the ancient Near East and a comparison with Joshua 9–12, see K. Lawson Younger Jr., *Ancient Conquest Accounts: A Study in Ancient Near Eastern and Biblical History Writing*, JSOTSup 98 (Sheffield: JSOT Press, 1990).

17. For a brief discussion of some potential functions of this narrative, see Eric A. Seibert, *Disturbing Divine Behavior: Troubling Old Testament Images of God* (Minneapolis: Fortress Press, 2009), 140–43.

18. James Barr, *Biblical Faith and Natural Theology: The Gifford Lectures for 1991* (Oxford: Clarendon, 1993), 209.

19. Lawson G. Stone, "Ethical and Apologetic Tendencies in the Redaction of the Book of Joshua," *CBQ* 53 (1991): 36.

20. Stone, "Ethical and Apologetic Tendencies," 36.

21. Stone, "Ethical and Apologetic Tendencies," 34.

22. Stone, "Ethical and Apologetic Tendencies," 34.

23. Stone, "Ethical and Apologetic Tendencies," 36.

24. L. Daniel Hawk, "Conquest Reconfigured: Recasting Warfare in the Redaction of Joshua," in *Writing and Reading War: Rhetoric, Gender, and Ethics in Biblical and Modern Contexts*, ed. Brad E. Kelle and Frank Ritchel Ames, SBLSymS 42 (Atlanta: Society of Biblical Literature, 2008), 147.

25. See, conveniently, Hawk, "Conquest Reconfigured," 147–52.

26. L. Daniel Hawk, "The God of the Conquest: The Theological Problem of the Book of Joshua," *TBT* 46 (2008): 145.

27. Hawk, "God of Conquest," 145.

28. Hawk, "Conquest Reconfigured," 159. Hawk views this happening in the postexilic period in an effort to counter Ezra's efforts to maintain strict ethnic separation and to blame foreign women for Israel's problems.

29. Hawk, "God of Conquest," 147.

30. Collins (*Bible after Babel*, 64) cites Edward Said as the first scholar to read Exodus through the eyes of Canaanites. Many others have followed.

31. Hawk, *Joshua in 3-D*, 138.

32. Hawk, *Joshua in 3-D*, 76.

33. For an example of this, see the story by Ulrike Bechmann, "The Jericho Women," in Esther Epp-Tiessen, "Conquering the Land," in *Under Vine and Fig Tree: Biblical Theologies of Land and the Palestinian-Israeli Conflict*, ed. Alain Epp Weaver (Telford, PA: Cascadia, 2007), 64–65. See also the various contributions in Philip R. Davies, ed., *First Person: Essays in Biblical Autobiography* (Sheffield: Sheffield Academic, 2002). One by Athalya Brenner gives voice to Rahab (pp. 47–58).

34. As Laura E. Donaldson ("Postcolonialism and Biblical Reading: An Introduction," *Semeia* 75, ed. Laura E. Donaldson and R. S. Sugirtharajah [1996]: 11) points out, postcolonial criticism "teaches us . . . to read like Canaanites."

35. Michael Prior, *The Bible and Colonialism: A Moral Critique* (Sheffield: Sheffield Academic, 1997), 281–82.

36. Robert Allen Warrior, "Canaanites, Cowboys, and Indians: Deliverance, Conquest, and Liberation Theology Today," *Christianity and Crisis* 49 (1989): 262.

37. Warrior, "Canaanites, Cowboys, and Indians," 263.

38. Warrior, "Canaanites, Cowboys, and Indians," 264.

39. Donaldson, "Postcolonialism and Biblical Reading," 11.

40. Naim Stifan Ateek, *Justice and Only Justice: A Palestinian Theology of Liberation* (Maryknoll, NY: Orbis, 1989), 86–87.

41. Prior, *Bible and Colonialism*, 39.

42. Kwok Pui-lan, *Discovering the Bible in the Non-Biblical World* (Maryknoll, NY: Orbis, 1995), 98.

43. Donaldson, "Postcolonialism and Biblical Reading," 12.

44. Randal Rauser, "'Let Nothing That Breathes Remain Alive': On the Problem of Divinely Commanded Genocide," *Philosophia Christi* 11 (2009): 27–41. For another interesting essay written from a philosophical point of view, and one that also concludes God did not command Canaanite or Amalekite genocide, see Dwight Van Winkle, "Canaanite Genocide and Amalekite Genocide and the God of Love" (1989 Winifred E. Weter Faculty Award Lecture; Seattle Pacific University, Washington, April 6, 1989), 1–45.

45. Rauser, "Let Nothing That Breathes Remain Alive," 33, emphasis in original.

46. Rauser, "Let Nothing That Breathes Remain Alive," 34.

47. Rauser, "Let Nothing That Breathes Remain Alive," 37.

48. Rauser, "Let Nothing That Breathes Remain Alive," 36.

49. Rauser, "Let Nothing That Breathes Remain Alive," 37.

50. Rauser, "Let Nothing That Breathes Remain Alive," 39.

51. For a discussion of this point, see Wright, *The God I Don't Understand*, 98–107.

52. Walter Wink, *Engaging the Powers: Discernment and Resistance in a World of Domination* (Minneapolis: Fortress Press, 1992), 13–31.

53. Gleason L. Archer, *New International Encyclopedia of Bible Difficulties* (Grand Rapids, MI: Zondervan, 1982), 158.

54. John Ortberg, *Stepping Out in Faith: Life-Changing Examples from the History of Israel* (Grand Rapids, MI: Zondervan, 2003), 36.

55. For an introduction to the Canaanites, see Niels Peter Lemche, *The Canaanites and Their Land: The Tradition of the Canaanites*, JSOTSup 110 (Sheffield: JSOT, 1991).

56. Tremper Longman III, "The Case for Spiritual Continuity," in C. S. Cowles et al., *Show Them No Mercy: Four Views on God and Canaanite Genocide* (Grand Rapids, MI: Zondervan, 2003), 185–86, emphasis mine.

57. Hawk, *Joshua in 3-D*, 118. See Josh. 9:22-27.

58. C. S. Cowles, "A Response to Eugene H. Merrill," in C. S. Cowles et al., *Show Them No Mercy: Four Views on God and Canaanite Genocide* (Grand Rapids, MI: Zondervan, 2003), 98.

59. Winkle, "Canaanite Genocide and Amalekite Genocide," argues that genocide is justifiable under certain conditions, though he does not believe these are met for either Canaanite or Amalakite genocide in the Bible.

60. Some examples include C. S. Cowles et al., *Show Them No Mercy*; Copan, *Is God a Moral Monster*, 158–97; Wright, *The God I Don't Understand*, 76–108; and David T. Lamb, *God Behaving Badly: Is the God of the Old Testament Angry, Sexist, and Racist?* (Downers Grove, IL: InterVarsity, 2011), 39–41, 76–81, 100–101.

61. Lamb, *God Behaving Badly*, 101.

62. Copan, *Is God a Moral Monster?*, 170, 175–76, 194.

63. Wright, *The God I Don't Understand*, 107.

64. Wright, *The God I Don't Understand*, 106–7.

65. Rauser, "Let Nothing That Breathes Remain Alive," 40.

66. For a trenchant critique of all attempts to justify Canaanite genocide, see Thom Stark, *The Human Faces of God: What Scripture Reveals When It Gets God Wrong (and Why Inerrancy Tries to Hide It)* (Eugene, OR: Wipf & Stock, 2011), 100–150. See also Hector Avalos, *Fighting Words: The Origins of Religious Violence* (Amherst, NY: Prometheus, 2005), 159–70.

67. Consider the reasons given earlier in this chapter for concluding that God did not command Canaanite genocide. For an extended discussion that calls into question the assumption that God said and did everything the Old Testament claims, see Eric A. Seibert, *Disturbing Divine Behavior: Troubling Old Testament Images of God* (Minneapolis: Fortress Press, 2009), chapters 5–8.

68. Derek Flood, "Does Defending the Bible Mean Advocating Violence?", *Huffington Post (Religion)* (November 21, 2011), http://www.huffingtonpost.com/derek-flood/defending -violence-in-the-bible_b_1088517.html.

69. Charles Kimball, *When Religion Becomes Evil* (San Francisco: HarperSanFrancisco, 2002), 156. A similar quote appears on page 1 of Kimball's book.

70. Richard D. Nelson, "Josiah in the Book of Joshua," *JBL* 100 (1981): 531–40. Nelson regards Joshua as a thinly veiled King Josiah.

71. Not everyone would see this as the primary function of the book of Joshua. Lori Rowlett, for example, believes the real focus of the book is to generate loyalty for Josiah among Israelites, not to justify acts of violence against outsiders. See Lori Rowlett, *Joshua*

and the Rhetoric of Violence: A New Historicist Analysis, JSOTSup 226 (Sheffield: Sheffield Academic, 1996), 11–15, 183.

72. For an interesting discussion of how political leaders have used the Bible in American politics, see Jacques Berlinerblau, *Thumpin' It: The Use and Abuse of the Bible in Today's Presidential Politics* (Louisville, KY: Westminster John Knox, 2008). On the dangers of civil religion, see Gregory A. Boyd, *The Myth of a Christian Nation: How the Quest for Political Power Is Destroying the Church* (Grand Rapids, MI: Zondervan, 2005), 111–15, and Michael J. Gorman, *Reading Revelation Responsibly: Uncivil Worship and Witness: Following the Lamb into the New Creation* (Eugene, OR: Cascade, 2011), 40–54.

73. Hawk, *Joshua in 3-D*, xii.

74. Hawk, *Joshua in 3-D*, xxxii.

75. Hawk, *Joshua in 3-D*, xxxii.

76. Hawk, *Joshua in 3-D*, 35.

77. Douglas S. Earl, *The Joshua Delusion? Rethinking Genocide in the Bible* (Eugene, OR: Cascade, 2010).

78. While Earl's reading is not allegorical, it shares the same impulse to look beyond the literal details of the story in order to find other layers of meaning.

79. Earl, *Joshua Delusion?*, 138.

80. While Earl's symbolic approach critiques certain problems occasioned by a literal reading of the conquest narrative (pp. 128–32), I think something more explicit is needed to deal with the problem of "virtuous" violence here.

81. Stark, *Human Faces of God*, 209.

82. Stark, *Human Faces of God*, 140.

83. Peter C. Craigie, *The Problem of War in the Old Testament* (Grand Rapids, MI: Eerdmans, 1978), 10, emphasis mine.

Chapter 8: Keeping the Old Testament from Being Used to Justify War

1. Quoted in Terry L. Brensinger, "War in the Old Testament: A Journey toward Nonparticipation" in *A Peace Reader*, ed. E. Morris Sider and Luke Keefer Jr. (Nappanee, IN: Evangel, 2002), 23.

2. Norman K. Gottwald, "Holy War in Deuteronomy: Analysis and Critique," *RevExp* 61 (1964): 310.

3. Peter C. Craigie, *The Problem of War in the Old Testament* (Grand Rapids, MI: Eerdmans, 1978).

4. Craigie, *Problem of War*, 11, emphasis in original. The other two problems Craigie identifies are (1) the problem of God (How can warlike images of God be reconciled with the characterization of God in the New Testament "as loving and self-giving"?), and (2) the problem of revelation (Why is so much warlike material preserved in the pages of the Bible?).

5. Craigie, *Problem of War*, 11.

6. Quoted in Adolph L. Harstad, *Joshua*, Concordia Commentary (St. Louis: Concordia, 2004), 265.

7. Quoted in Willard W. Swartley, *Slavery, Sabbath, War, and Women* (Scottdale, PA: Herald, 1983), 97.

8. Darrell Cole, *When God Says War Is Right: The Christian's Perspective on When and How to Fight* (Colorado Springs: Waterbrook, 2002), 28.

9. Cole, *When God Says War Is Right*, 36.

10. Cole, *When God Says War Is Right*, 36.

11. Cole, *When God Says War Is Right*, 48.

12. Michael R. Cosby, *Interpreting Biblical Literature: An Introduction to Biblical Studies* (Grantham, PA: Stony Run, 2009), 236–43. The phrase in quotes is from p. 238.

13. For a discussion of various "ideologies" of war in the Old Testament, see Susan Niditch, *War in the Hebrew Bible: A Study in the Ethics of Violence* (New York: Oxford University Press, 1993).

14. See, for example, Sa-Moon Kang, *Divine War in the Old Testament and in the Ancient Near East*, BZAW 177 (Berlin: de Gruyter, 1989).

15. The depiction of the god Chemosh in the Mesha Stele is particularly instructive in this regard, and a number of intriguing parallels could be noted. See Eric A. Seibert, *Disturbing Divine Behavior: Troubling Old Testament Images of God* (Minneapolis: Fortress Press, 2009), 157–59, for a brief discussion.

16. See Siebert, *Disturbing Divine Behavior*, 156–60.

17. See William G. Dever, *Who Were the Early Israelites and Where Did They Come From?* (Grand Rapids, MI: Eerdmans, 2003), 37–74; and Israel Finkelstein and Neil Asher Silberman, *The Bible Unearthed: Archaeology's New Vision of Ancient Israel and the Origin of Its Sacred Texts* (New York: Free Press, 2001), 72–96.

18. See John Rogerson et al., *Beginning Old Testament Study* (St. Louis: Chalice, 1998), 58–76 and 94–113; and Seibert, *Disturbing Divine Behavior*, 145–66.

19. See Kang, *Divine War*.

20. This language of revealing and distorting God's character is from Jack Nelson-Pallmeyer, *Jesus against Christianity: Reclaiming the Missing Jesus* (Harrisburg, PA: Trinity Press International, 2001). See, for example, pp. 16, 65, 88, and 137.

21. Terence E. Fretheim and Karlfried Froehlich, *The Bible as Word of God: In a Postmodern Age* (Minneapolis: Fortress Press, 1998), 116–17. For further discussion of this point, see Seibert, *Disturbing Divine Behavior*, 169–81.

22. See Seibert, *Disturbing Divine Behavior*, 183–207, where I propose utilizing a Christocentric hermeneutic to determine the degree of correspondence.

23. See Seibert, *Disturbing Divine Behavior*, 209–22.

24. In fact, some even argue that God's violence is what motivates and sustains our commitment to nonviolence. See Elmer A. Martens, "Toward Shalom: Absorbing the Violence," in *War in the Bible and Terrorism in the Twenty-First Century*, ed. Richard S. Hess and Elmer A. Martens, BBRSup 2 (Winona Lake, IN: Eisenbrauns, 2008), 33–57, esp. 50–56. "That God is a warrior," writes Martens, "means . . . that his people need not be warlike" (53). Compare Miroslav Volf, *Exclusion and Embrace: A Theological Exploration of Identity, Otherness, and Reconciliation* (Nashville: Abingdon: 1996), 301–4.

25. Eugene H. Merrill, "The Case for Moderate Discontinuity," in *Show Them No Mercy: Four Views on God and Canaanite Genocide*, ed. C. S. Cowles et al. (Grand Rapids, MI: Zondervan, 2003), 92–93.

26. See, for example, Tremper Longman III, *Making Sense of the Old Testament: 3 Crucial Questions* (Grand Rapids, MI: Baker, 1998), 71–86.

27. Seibert, *Disturbing Divine Behavior*, 69–88. See also Eryl W. Davies, *The Immoral Bible: Approaches to Biblical Ethics* (London: T & T Clark, 2010).

28. John Goldingay, *Israel's Life*, vol. 3 of *Old Testament Theology* (Downers Grove, IL: InterVarsity, 2009), 554.

29. The same would be true if we were reading war stories from Egypt, Babylon, Assyria, or any other ancient Near Eastern country. We would be expected to see warfare through their eyes and from their perspective.

30. For an interesting discussion of biblical and more recent views of Philistines, see David Jobling, *1 Samuel* (Berit Olam. Collegeville: Liturgical, 1998), 195–243. This is based upon David Jobling and Catherine Rose, "Reading as a Philistine: The Ancient and Modern History of a Cultural Slur," in *Ethnicity and the Bible*, ed. Mark G. Brett (Leiden: Brill, 1996), 381–417.

31. William Morris, ed., *The American Heritage Dictionary*, 2nd college ed. (Boston: Houghton Mifflin, 1985), 931.

32. For an overview of the Philistines and their culture, see David M. Howard Jr., "Philistines," in *Peoples of the Old Testament World*, ed. Alfred J. Hoerth, Gerald L. Mattingly, and Edwin M. Yamauchi (Grand Rapids, MI: Baker, 1994), 231–50.

33. In an intriguing article written by Susan Ackerman titled, "What If Judges Had Been Written by a Philistine?" (*BibInt* 8 [2000]: 33–41), she surmises that a Philistine author might have made Delilah a heroine in the tradition of Jael rather than the villainess the Bible makes her out to be (p. 41). If so, Ackerman believes it is quite possible Delilah might "bear the epithet otherwise given to Jael in Judg. 5:24, 'most blessed of women'" since she was instrumental in delivering Samson into the hands of the Philistines (p. 41).

34. For a collection of essays devoted to the intersection of Levinasian thought and the Bible, see Tamara Cohn Eskenazi, Gary A. Phillips, and David Jobling, eds., *Levinas and Biblical Studies*, Semeia Studies 43 (Atlanta: Society of Biblical Literature, 2003).

35. Carolyn J. Sharp, *Wrestling the Word: The Hebrew Scriptures and the Christian Believer* (Louisville, KY: Westminster John Knox, 2010), 37.

36. Sharp, *Wrestling the Word*, 37.

37. Sharp, *Wrestling the Word*, 42.

38. Sharp, *Wrestling the Word*, 42.

39. Sharp, *Wrestling the Word*, 42.

40. Sharp, *Wrestling the Word*, 41.

41. Sharp, *Wrestling the Word*, 42.

42. T. R. Hobbs, *A Time for War: A Study of Warfare in the Old Testament* (Wilmington, DE: Michael Glazier, 1989), 166.

43. T. R. Hobbs, *2 Kings*, WBC 13 (Waco, TX: Word, 1985), 197.

44. Hobbs, *Time for War*, 180–81.

45. To be sure, there are some rather graphic descriptions in the Old Testament of what happens to people in times of war. For example, the fat king Eglon is run through with a sword, causing "the dirt" to come out (Judg. 3:22); Jael pins Sisera to the ground with a tent peg (Judg. 4:21); and King Nahash gouges out the right eyes of those he was oppressing (1 Sam. 10:27). These kinds of gruesome details, while not absent from the Old Testament, are the exception rather than the norm.

46. The most we get is a verse or two, as in the case of both Abimelech (Judg. 9:50-54) and Saul (1 Sam. 31:1-4). We get to hear from them briefly after they are mortally wounded in combat, but it does little to help us feel the real pathos of war.

47. For an extensive treatment of this issue as it relates to modern warfare, see Dave Grossman, *On Killing: The Psychological Cost of Learning to Kill in War and Society*, rev. ed. (New York: Back Bay, 2009).

48. See Brensinger, "War in the Old Testament," 26–28, esp. 27.

49. This phrase is from Brensinger, "War in the Old Testament," 26.

50. This phrase is from Brensinger, "War in the Old Testament," 26.

51. For other texts that critique various aspects of war, see Susan Niditch, *War in the Hebrew Bible: A Study in the Ethics of Violence* (New York: Oxford University Press, 1993), 134–49.

Chapter 9: Preventing Violence against Women

1. Pamela J. Milne, "No Promised Land: Rejecting the Authority of the Bible," in Phyllis Trible et al., *Feminist Approaches to the Bible: Symposium at the Smithsonian Institution, September 24, 1994* (Washington, DC: Biblical Archaeology Society, 1995), 47.

2. Nancy R. Bowen, "Women, Violence, and the Bible," in *Engaging the Bible in a Gendered World: An Introduction to Feminist Biblical Interpretation in Honor of Katharine Doob Sakenfeld*, ed. Linda Day and Carolyn Pressler (Louisville, KY: Westminster John Knox, 2006), 186.

3. Susan B. Thistlethwaite, "Every Two Minutes: Battered Women and Feminist Interpretation," in *Feminist Interpretation of the Bible*, ed. Letty Russell (Philadelphia: Westminster, 1985), 106.

4. Linda Day and Carolyn Pressler, "Introduction," in *Engaging the Bible in a Gendered World: An Introduction to Feminist Biblical Interpretation in Honor of Katharine Doob Sakenfeld*, ed. Linda Day and Carolyn Pressler (Louisville, KY: Westminister John Knox, 2006), xxiv.

5. Bowen, "Women, Violence, and the Bible," 193.

6. Bowen, "Women, Violence, and the Bible," 193, emphasis mine.

7. Milne, "No Promised Land," 49. See, further, Eryl W. Davies, *The Dissenting Reader: Feminist Approaches to the Hebrew Bible* (Aldershot, UK: Ashgate, 2003), 11.

8. Written by an undergraduate student from one of my Old Testament Literature classes.

9. Adapted from Eric A. Seibert, *Disturbing Divine Behavior: Troubling Old Testament Images of God* (Minneapolis: Fortress Press, 2009), 228.

10. Day and Pressler ("Introduction," xvii) claim that many "experience the Bible as both patriarchal and liberating."

11. Elisabeth Schüssler Fiorenza, *Bread Not Stone: The Challenge of Feminist Biblical Interpretation* (Boston: Beacon, 1984), x.

12. Schüssler Fiorenza, *Bread Not Stone*, xiii.

13. As Jacqueline Lapsley (*Whispering the Word: Hearing Women's Stories in the Old Testament* [Louisville, KY: Westminster John Knox, 2005], 6) observes: "Lest the gravity and force of feminist biblical scholarship make it appear as though the Bible has only had a negative impact on women's lives, we need to recall that the Bible has also been an enormous source of power and inspiration to women throughout history."

14. For an example of this latter view see, for example, Wayne Grudem, *Evangelical Feminism: A New Path to Liberalism?* (Wheaton, IL: Crossway, 2006).

15. Katharine Doob Sakenfeld, "Feminist Perspectives on Bible and Theology: An Introduction to Selected Issues and Literature," *Int* 42 (1988): 5. Or, if you prefer the cheekier bumper sticker definition: "Feminism is the radical notion that women are people."

16. As we proceed, it will become evident that this chapter depends heavily on feminist biblical scholarship, and I am deeply grateful for the work they have done.

17. Kathleen M. O'Connor, "The Feminist Movement Meets the Old Testament: One Woman's Perspective," in *Engaging the Bible in a Gendered World: An Introduction to Feminist Biblical Interpretation in Honor of Katharine Doob Sakenfeld*, ed. Linda Day and Carolyn Pressler (Louisville, KY: Westminister John Knox, 2006), 12–15.

18. Elisabeth Schüssler Fiorenza, "The Will to Choose or to Reject: Continuing Our Critical Work," in *Feminist Interpretation of the Bible*, ed. Letty Russell (Philadelphia: Westminster, 1985), 130.

19. For a more positive assessment of our ability to hear women's voices and perspectives in the text, see Athalya Brenner and Fokkelien van Dijk-Hemmes, *On Gendering Texts: Female and Male Voices in the Hebrew Bible* (Leiden: Brill, 1993).

20. Carole E. Fontaine, "The Abusive Bible: On the Use of Feminist Method in Pastoral Contexts," in *A Feminist Companion to Reading the Bible: Approaches, Methods and Strategies*, ed. Athalya Brenner and Carole Fontaine (Sheffield: Sheffield Academic, 1997), 98.

21. For an effort to understand what life was actually like for women in ancient Israel, see Carol Meyers, *Discovering Eve: Ancient Israelite Women in Context* (New York: Oxford University Press, 1988).

22. J. Cheryl Exum, "Feminist Criticism: Whose Interests Are Being Served?" in *Judges and Method: New Approaches in Biblical Studies*, ed. Gale A. Yee, 2nd ed. (Minneapolis: Fortress Press, 2007); and Esther Fuchs, *Sexual Politics in the Biblical Narrative: Reading the Hebrew Bible as a Woman*, JSOTSup 310 (Sheffield: Sheffield Academic, 2000).

23. See Brenner and van Dijk-Hemmes, *On Gendering Texts*.

24. Exum, "Feminist Criticism," 66.

25. Day and Pressler, "Introduction," xvii

26. Fuchs, *Sexual Politics*, 14.

27. Bowen, "Women, Violence, and the Bible," 190, emphasis mine.

28. Fontaine, "Abusive Bible," 93, emphasis in original.

29. Schüssler Fiorenza, *Bread Not Stone*, xi.

30. Julia M. O'Brien, *Challenging Prophetic Metaphor: Theology and Ideology in the Prophets* (Louisville, KY: Westminster John Knox, 2008), 67.

31. O'Brien, *Challenging Prophetic Metaphor*, 68.

32. O'Brien, *Challenging Prophetic Metaphor*, 72.

33. O'Brien, *Challenging Prophetic Metaphor*, 71.

34. Cheryl B. Anderson, *Ancient Laws and Contemporary Controversies: The Need for Inclusive Biblical Interpretation* (Oxford: Oxford University Press, 2009), 145. This point is argued in her earlier work, *Women, Ideology, and Violence: Critical Theory and the Construction of Gender in the Book of the Covenant and the Deuteronomic Law* (London: T & T Clark, 2004), 101–17.

35. Anderson, *Ancient Laws*, 46, emphasis mine.

36. Phyllis Trible, *Texts of Terror: Literary-Feminist Readings of Biblical Narratives*, OBT 13 (Philadelphia: Fortress Press, 1984).

37. For a recent study, see Susanne Scholz, *Sacred Witness: Rape in the Hebrew Bible* (Minneapolis: Fortress Press, 2010).

38. Carol Lakey Hess, *Caretakers of Our Common House: Women's Development in Communities of Faith* (Nashville: Abingdon, 1997), 196, emphasis mine.

39. Scholz (*Sacred Witness*, 181) identifies the cities as Jerusalem, Babylon, Nineveh, Sidon, and Edom

40. J. Cheryl Exum, "The Ethics of Violence against Women," in *The Bible in Ethics: The Second Sheffield Colloquium*, ed. John W. Rogerson, Margaret Davies, and Mark Daniel Carroll R., JSOTSup 207 (Sheffield: Sheffield Academic, 1995), 248. She explores Hosea 2:9-10; Isa. 3:16-26; Jer. 2:33—3:20, 4:30; 13:20-27, 22:20-23; Ezekiel 16 and 23; and Lam. 1:8-10. For an extensive study of this image of God in prophetic literature, see Renita J. Weems, *Battered Love: Marriage, Sex, and Violence in the Hebrew Prophets* (Minneapolis: Fortress Press, 1995).

41. For a discussion of problems related to the notion of a "marriage metaphor," including the terminology itself, see Athalya Brenner, "Some Reflections on Violence against Women and the Image of God in the Hebrew Bible," in *On the Cutting Edge: The Study of Women in Biblical Worlds: Essays in Honor of Elisabeth Schüssler Fiorenza*, ed. Jane Schaberg, Alice Bach, and Esther Fuchs (New York: Continuum, 2003), 69–81, esp. 69–74.

42. Scholz, *Sacred Witness*, 191. She examines four texts: Isa. 3:16-17; Jer. 13:22, 26; and Ezekial 16 and 23.

43. Scholz, *Sacred Witness*, 182.

44. Brenner ("Some Reflections," 79) writes: "I regard the violent description of YHWH as a professional soldier and dissatisfied husband who tortures his 'wife' as unacceptable on general humanistic-ethical as well as theological and social-gendered grounds. I regard the relevant passages as pornographic and beyond salvation not only for feminists but also for any objector to violence, be that violence divine or religious or otherwise."

45. Katheryn Pfisterer Darr, "Ezekiel's Justifications of God: Teaching Troubling Texts," *JSOT* 55 (1992): 115.

46. Exum, "Ethics of Violence," 249, emphasis mine.

47. Scholz, *Sacred Witness*, 187.

48. Scholz, *Sacred Witness*, 187.

49. Gracia Fay Ellwood, *Batter My Heart*, Pendle Hill Pamphlet 252 (Wallingford, PA: Pendle Hill Publications, 1988), 19.

50. Judith E. Sanderson, "Nahum," in *The Women's Bible Commentary*, ed. Carol A. Newsome and Sharon H. Ringe (Louisville, KY: Westminster John Knox, 1992), 220–21.

51. Exum, "Ethics of Violence," 259–60.

52. Brenner, "Some Reflections," 72.

53. Mary Ann Tolbert, "Defining the Problem: The Bible and Feminist Hermeneutics," in *The Bible and Feminist Hermeneutics*, ed. Mary Ann Tolbert, Semeia 28 (Chico, CA: Scholars, 1983), 125. Tolbert is referring here to "the hermeneutical and theological dilemma" Bultmann faced and is suggesting that feminists face a similar problem.

54. For an overview of different approaches feminist biblical scholars have taken in an effort to read the Bible faithfully as women, see Tolbert, "Defining the Problem"; Carolyn Osiek, "The Feminist and the Bible: Hermeneutical Alternatives," in *Feminist Perspectives on Biblical Scholarship*, ed. Adela Yarbro Collins, SBLBSNA 10 (Chico, CA: Scholars Press, 1985), 93–105; Sakenfeld, "Feminist Perspectives"; Katharine Doob Sakenfeld, "Feminist Uses of Biblical Materials," in *Feminist Interpretation of the Bible*, ed. Letty Russell (Philadelphia: Westminster, 1985), 55–64; and Heather A. McKay, "On the Future of Feminist Biblical Criticism," in *A Feminist Companion to Reading the Bible: Approaches, Methods and Strategies*, ed. Athalya Brenner and Carole Fontaine (Sheffield: Sheffield Academic, 1997), 61–83. For an excellent overview of feminism and feminist interpretive approaches, particularly as they pertain to the Old Testament, see O'Connor, "Feminist Movement Meets the Old Testament," 3-24.

55. Lapsley, *Whispering the Word*, 37. Her reading of this narrative is found on pp. 35–67 in a chapter titled, "A Gentle Guide: Attending to the Narrator's Perspective in Judges 19–21."

56. See the discussion in chapters 5 and 6 on "interruption" as a reading strategy.

57. Schüssler Fiorenza, "Will to Choose," 130, emphasis in original.

58. David J. A. Clines, *Interested Parties: The Ideology of Writers and Readers of the Hebrew Bible*, JSOTSup 205, (Sheffield: Sheffield Academic, 1995), 21.

59. Schüssler Fiorenza, "Will to Choose," 130.

60. Exum, "Feminist Criticism," 69. Exum explores the "encoded messages" in several narratives involving women in the book of Judges, messages she regards as being detrimental to women in various ways.

61. For attempts to exonerate the Old Testament from charges of sexism and misogyny, see the recent efforts by David T. Lamb, *God Behaving Badly: Is the God of the Old Testament*

Angry, Sexist, and Racist? (Downers Grove, IL: InterVarsity, 2011), 47–70; and Paul Copan, *Is God a Moral Monster?: Making Sense of the Old Testament God* (Grand Rapids, MI: Baker, 2011), 101–9. For a devastating critique of Copan's attempt to deny that certain Old Testament texts are misogynistic, see Thom Stark, "Is God a Moral Compromiser? A Critical Review of Paul Copan's 'Is God a Moral Monster?'" 2nd ed. (2011), 94–115, http://thomstark.net/copan/stark_copan-review.pdf.

62. Hess, *Caretakers of Our Common House*, 195. Hess labels this first strategy "Correcting distortions in interpretation."

63. Hess, *Caretakers of Our Common House*, 195–97.

64. Quoted Pamela J. Milne, "Eve and Adam: A Feminist Reading," in *Approaches to the Bible: The Best of Bible Review*, vol. 2, *A Multitude of Perspectives*, ed. Harvey Minkoff (Washington, DC: Biblical Archaeology Society, 1995), 261.

65. Hess, *Caretakers of Our Common House*, 197.

66. Fontaine, "Abusive Bible," 111.

67. Scholz, *Sacred Witness*, 210. As Scholz notes, the final phrase is from Marie M. Fortune, *Sexual Violence: The Unmentionable Sin* (Cleveland: Pilgrim, 1983).

68. Scholz, *Sacred Witness*, 210.

69. Linda Day, "Rhetoric and Domestic Violence in Ezekiel 16," *BibInt* 8 (2000): 214–16.

70. Weems, *Battered Love*, 68–83, esp. 72; and Katharine Doob Sakenfeld, *Just Wives? Stories of Power and Survival in the Old Testament and Today* (Louisville, KY: Westminster John Knox, 2003), 103–6.

71. Keree Louise Casey, "What Part of 'No' Don't You Understand? Talking the Tough Stuff of the Bible: A Creative Reading of the Rape of Tamar: 2 Sam. 13:1-22," *Feminist Theology* 18 (2010): 170.

72. John L. Thompson, *Reading the Bible with the Dead: What You Can Learn from the History of Exegesis That You Can't Learn from Exegesis Alone* (Grand Rapids, MI: Eerdmans, 2007), 1.

73. Thompson, *Reading the Bible with the Dead*, 5.

74. Trible, *Texts of Terror*, 3.

75. Tikva Frymer-Kensky, review of Phyllis Trible, *Texts of Terror: Literary-Feminist Readings of Biblical Narratives*, *BR* 1 (February 1985): 7.

76. Hess, *Caretakers of Our Common House*, 202. Hess (27–29) imagines Vashti and Esther scheming together through the night at Vashti's hideout to concoct the plan that saves the Jews.

77. Schüssler Fiorenza, *Bread Not Stone*, 20.

78. Schüssler Fiorenza, *Bread Not Stone*, 21.

79. Bowen, "Women, Violence, and the Bible," 195–96.

80. Bowen, "Women, Violence, and the Bible," 196–99.

81. Hess, *Caretakers of Our Common House*, 26.

82. Hess, *Caretakers of Our Common House*, 27.

83. For a collection of retellings in the midrashic tradition, see Norma Rosen, *Biblical Women Unbound: Counter Tales* (Philadelphia: Jewish Publication Society, 1996). For a best-selling, book-length treatment exploring the story of Dinah (Genesis 34), see Anita Diamant, *The Red Tent*, 2nd ed. (New York: Picador/St. Martin's, 1997). For a retelling that subverts some common perceptions about Gomer, see the story written by Mary Caroline Jonah in Sakenfeld, *Just Wives?*, 107–14. See also a number of examples in Philip R. Davies, ed., *First Person: Essays in Biblical Autobiography* (Sheffield: Sheffield Academic, 2002).

84. John L. Thompson, *Writing the Wrongs: Women of the Old Testament among Biblical Commentators from Philo through the Reformation* (Oxford: Oxford University Press, 2001), 6.

85. Alice Bach, "Rereading the Body Politic: Women and Violence in Judges 21," in *Women in the Hebrew Bible: A Reader*, ed. Alice Bach (New York: Routledge, 1999), 398.

86. O'Connor, "Feminist Movement Meets the Old Testament," 21. This quote comes at the end of a paragraph in which O'Connor favorably summarizes Jacqueline Lapsley's work (*Whispering the Word*), so it may be intended to represent Lapsley's thinking, though I suspect O'Connor fully shares this perspective.

87. Bowen, "Women, Violence, and the Bible," 193, emphasis mine.

88. This tendency is especially pronounced in conservative evangelical traditions. See Susanne Scholz, "The Christian Right's Discourse on Gender and the Bible," *JFSR* 21 (Spring 2005): 81–100.

89. See Exum, "Ethics of Violence," 263, esp. note 35.

Chapter 10: The Necessity and Urgency of Reading the Old Testament Nonviolently

1. William W. Emilsen and John T. Squires, "Introduction," in *Validating Violence—Violating Faith? Religion, Scripture and Violence*, ed. William W. Emilsen and John T. Squires (Adelaide: ATF, 2008), xiii.

2. Julia M. O'Brien, *Challenging Prophetic Metaphor: Theology and Ideology in the Prophets* (Louisville, KY: Westminster John Knox, 2008), xxi.

3. For a helpful effort to read the Bible nonviolently, with considerable emphasis on the New Testament, see Jack Nelson-Pallmeyer, *Jesus against Christianity: Reclaiming the Missing Jesus* (Harrisburg, PA: Trinity Press International, 2001).

4. See chapter 2.

5. Emilsen and Squires, "Introduction," xiii.

6. Philip Jenkins, *Laying Down the Sword: Why We Can't Ignore the Bible's Violent Verses* (New York: HarperOne, 2011), 21. As Jenkins observes: "Pretending that . . . troubling texts do not exist poses dangers, because extremists revive them in times of conflict" (19).

7. O'Brien, *Challenging Prophetic Metaphor*, 51, emphasis mine.

8. See chapter 4.

9. Carolyn J. Sharp, *Wrestling the Word: The Hebrew Scriptures and the Christian Believer* (Louisville, KY: Westminster John Knox, 2010), 2.

10. William H. Bellinger Jr., "The Hebrew Scriptures and Theology: Resources and Problems," *PRSt* 31 (2004): 124. See also William L. Holladay, *Long Ago God Spoke: How Christians May Hear the Old Testament Today* (Minneapolis: Fortress Press, 1995), 13–14. Obviously, discomfort with the more violent parts of the Old Testament is not limited to "contemporary believers." Christians and Jews have grappled with the problem of violence in the Bible for centuries. For some discussion of this as it relates to violent portrayals of God, see Eric A. Seibert, *Disturbing Divine Behavior: Troubling Old Testament Images of God* (Minneapolis: Fortress Press, 2009), 53–68.

11. O'Brien, *Challenging Prophetic Metaphor*, 101.

12. See Judges 4 (Jael), 1 Samuel 25 (Abigail), 1 Samuel 17 (David), and Genesis 45 and 50 (Joseph).

13. As Marion J. Benedict (*The God of the Old Testament in Relation to War* [New York: AMS 1972; orig. published 1927], 182) observes: "One viewpoint with regard to ethical and religious values should be consistently expressed in a series of lessons if they are to be effective. If a character is lauded for kindness to enemies in one lesson, and in the same series men

become heroes by virtue of wholesale slaughter, the point of either must be largely negatived by the other."

14. We desperately need curriculum for children and resources for teachers that can help facilitate these kinds of conversations. Unfortunately, to my knowledge, very little material like this exists. Nor has much been written about how to teach the Old Testament to children and youth in ethically responsibly ways. It is an area begging for attention. For an older treatment of this issue, though one with some very valuable insights, see Benedict, *The God of the Old Testament*, 163–84. See also Francis Landy, "Do We Want Our Children to Read This Book?," in *Bible and Ethics of Reading*, ed. Danna Nolan Fewell and Gary A. Phillips, Semeia 77 (Atlanta: Society of Biblical Literature, 1997), 157–76; Valerie A. Stein, "Know*Be*Do: Using the Bible to Teach Ethics to Children," *SBL Forum* 7.2 (2009), http://www.sbl-site .org/publications/article.aspx?articleId=799; Christopher Evans, *Is "Holy Scripture" Christian? And Other Questions* (London: SCM, 1971), 37–50.

15. Eryl W. Davies, "Morally Dubious Passages of the Hebrew Bible: An Examination of Some Proposed Solutions," *Currents in Biblical Research* 3 (2005): 220, emphasis mine.

16. See David J. A. Clines, *Interested Parties: The Ideology of Writers and Readers of the Hebrew Bible*, JSOTSup 205 (Sheffield: Sheffield Academic, 1995), 19–21, and Eryl W. Davies, *The Immoral Bible: Approaches to Biblical Ethics* (London: T & T Clark, 2010), 122–25.

17. For some helpful pedagogical considerations in teaching violent texts, see Amy C. Cottrill, "Reading Textual Violence as 'Real' Violence in the Liberal Arts Context," in *Teaching the Bible in the Liberal Arts Classroom*, ed. Jane S. Webster and Glenn S. Holland (Sheffield: Sheffield Phoenix, forthcoming 2012).

18. Davies, *The Immoral Bible*, 124.

19. For two excellent and very readable introductions to nonviolence that incorporate biblical, theological, and practical perspectives, see Walter Wink, *The Powers That Be: Theology for a New Millennium* (New York: Doubleday, 1998); and John D. Roth, *Choosing against War: A Christian View* (Intercourse, PA: Good Books, 2002).

20. Gene Sharp, *The Politics of Nonviolent Action* (Boston: Porter Sargent, 1973). See part 2, "The Methods of Nonviolent Action," for 198 different nonviolent strategies.

21. See, for example, Peter Ackerman and Jack DuVall, *A Force More Powerful: A Century of Nonviolent Conflict* (New York: St. Martin's, 2000); and Gene Sharp, *Waging Nonviolent Struggle: 20th Century Practice and 21st Century Potential* (Boston: Extending Horizons, 2005).

22. There are also numerous texts within the Bible that help readers imagine alternatives to violence, and these too can help in demonstrating the viability of reading—and living—nonviolently. For a brief overview, see Daniel L. Buttry, *Christian Peacemaking: From Heritage to Hope* (Valley Forge, PA: Judson, 1994), 7–38. For longer treatments on the Old and New Testaments, respectively, see David A. Leiter, *Neglected Voices: Peace in the Old Testament* (Scottdale, PA: Herald, 2007); and Willard M. Swartley, *Covenant of Peace: The Missing Peace in New Testament Theology and Ethics* (Grand Rapids, MI: Eerdmans, 2006).

Appendix: A Brief Word about Biblical Authority

1. Walter Brueggemann, *The Book that Breathes New Life: Scriptural Authority and Biblical Theology* (Minneapolis: Fortress Press, 2005), 20.

2. Eric A. Seibert, *Disturbing Divine Behavior: Troubling Old Testament Images of God* (Minneapolis: Fortress Press, 2009), 263–80.

3. For a broad range of views on this issue, see the various contributions in William P. Brown, *Engaging Biblical Authority: Perspectives on the Bible as Scripture* (Louisville:

Westminster John Knox, 2007). See also the recent work by Kenton L. Sparks, *Sacred Word, Broken Word: Biblical Authority and the Dark Side of Scripture* (Grand Rapids, MI: Eerdmans, 2012).

4. Elsewhere (Seibert, *Disturbing Divine Behavior*, 276–77) I have argued that the content of the Bible is, in fact, a source of its authority. While I stand by that claim, I would reiterate a point made there, namely, that only *some* of the content functions authoritatively. That is why it is so crucial to develop and utilize a principled approach to determine what parts function as normative in this way. In chapter 10 of that book I argue for using a Christocentric hermeneutic.

5. For a discussion of ancient historiography, see Seibert, *Disturbing Divine Behavior*, 131–44.

6. On this point, see the recent study by Christian Smith, *The Bible Made Impossible: Why Biblicism Is Not a Truly Evangelical Reading of Scripture* (Grand Rapids, MI: Brazos, 2011), 3–26.

7. For a convenient sampling, see Paul J. Achtemeier, *Inspiration and Authority: Nature and Function of Christian Scripture*, rev. and exp. ed. (Peabody, MA: Hendrickson, 1999), 50–54.

8. Carole E. Fontaine, "The Abusive Bible: On the Use of Feminist Method in Pastoral Contexts," in *A Feminist Companion to Reading the Bible: Approaches, Methods and Strategies*, ed. Athalya Brenner and Carole Fontaine (Sheffield: Sheffield Academic, 1997), 92.

9. As Carole Fontaine ("The Abusive Bible," 97) views it: "The very nature of the Bible, then—human words in fancy divine dress—has worked to undercut critique of its violence."

10. Terry Brensinger, ("The Inspiration and Authority of Scripture," unpublished paper presented at the Theological Colloqium, Lancaster, PA, September 2010), emphasizes the importance of understanding biblical authority in this way, and I am grateful to him for providing me with a copy of his paper and helping me think along these lines.

Bibliography

Achtemeier, Paul J. *Inspiration and Authority: Nature and Function of Christian Scripture*. Rev. and exp. ed. Peabody, MA: Hendrickson, 1999.

Ackerman, Peter, and Jack DuVall. *A Force More Powerful: A Century of Nonviolent Conflict*. New York: St. Martin's, 2000.

Ackerman, Susan. "What If Judges Had Been Written by a Philistine?" *BibInt* 8 (2000): 33–41.

Adam, A. K. M. *Handbook of Postmodern Biblical Interpretation*. St. Louis: Chalice, 2000.

Anderson, Cheryl B. *Ancient Laws and Contemporary Controversies: The Need for Inclusive Biblical Interpretation*. Oxford: Oxford University Press, 2009.

———. *Women, Ideology, and Violence: Critical Theory and the Construction of Gender in the Book of the Covenant and the Deuteronomic Law*. London: T & T Clark, 2004.

Anderson, Craig A., and Brad J. Bushman. "The Effects of Media Violence on Society." *Science* 295 (2002): 2377, 2379.

Archer, Gleason L. *New International Encyclopedia of Bible Difficulties*. Grand Rapids, MI: Zondervan, 1982.

Ateek, Naim Stifan. *Justice and Only Justice: A Palestinian Theology of Liberation*. Maryknoll, NY: Orbis, 1989.

———. "A Palestinian Perspective: The Bible and Liberation." Pages 394–99 in *Biblical Studies Alternatively: An Introductory Reader*. Edited by Susanne Scholz. Upper Saddle River, NJ: Prentice Hall, 2003.

Avalos, Hector. *Fighting Words: The Origins of Religious Violence*. Amherst, NY: Prometheus, 2005.

———. "The Letter Killeth." *Journal of Religion, Conflict, and Peace* 1 (2007). http://www.religionconflictpeace.org/node/17

Augustine, Saint. *On Christian Doctrine, in Four Books*. Grand Rapids, MI: Christian Classics Ethereal Library. http://www.ccel.org/ccel/augustine/doctrine.html.

Bach, Alice. "Rereading the Body Politic: Women and Violence in Judges 21." Pages 389–401 in *Women in the Hebrew Bible: A Reader*. Edited by Alice Bach. New York: Routledge, 1999.

Bainton, Roland H. *Christian Attitudes toward War and Peace: A Historical Survey and Critical Re-evaluation*. Nashville: Abingdon, 1960.

Baker, Sharon L. *Razing Hell: Rethinking Everything You've Been Taught about God's Wrath and Judgment*. Louisville, KY: Westminster John Knox, 2010.

Bakhtin, M. M. *The Dialogic Imagination: Four Essays*. Edited by Michael Holquist. Translated by Caryl Emerson and Michael Holquist. Austin: University of Texas Press, 1981.

Bal, Mieke. *On Story-Telling: Essays in Narratology*. Edited by David Jobling. Sonoma, CA: Polebridge, 1981.

Barr, James. *Biblical Faith and Natural Theology: The Gifford Lectures for 1991*. Oxford: Clarendon, 1993.

Barrett, Rob. *Disloyalty and Destruction: Religion and Politics in Deuteronomy and the Modern World*. LHBOTS 511. New York: T & T Clark, 2009.

Barton, John. *How the Bible Came to Be*. Louisville, KY: Westminster John Knox, 1997.

———. *Understanding Old Testament Ethics: Approaches and Explorations*. Louisville, KY: Westminster John Knox, 2003.

Beal, Timothy. *The Rise and Fall of the Bible: The Unexpected History of an Accidental Book*. Boston: Houghton Mifflin Harcourt, 2011.

Bellinger, William H., Jr. "The Hebrew Scriptures and Theology: Resources and Problems." *PRSt* 31 (2004): 123–33.

Bellis, Alice Ogden. *Helpmates, Harlots, and Heroes: Women's Stories in the Hebrew Bible*. 2nd ed. Louisville, KY: Westminster John Knox, 2007.

Benedict, Marion J. *The God of the Old Testament in Relation to War*. New York: Teachers College, Columbia University, 1927. Repr., New York: AMS, 1972.

Berlinerblau, Jacques. *Thumpin' It: The Use and Abuse of the Bible in Today's Presidential Politics*. Louisville, KY: Westminster John Knox, 2008.

Bernardin, Joseph Cardinal. "A Consistent Ethic of Life: An American-Catholic Dialogue." Gannon Lecture. Fordham University, New York, December 6, 1983, 1–6.

Bicksler, Harriet Sider. "Pursuing Peace." Pages 129–44 in *Focusing Our Faith: Brethren in Christ Core Values*. Edited by Terry L. Brensinger. Nappanee, IN: Evangel, 2000.

Birch, Bruce C. *Let Justice Roll Down: The Old Testament, Ethics, and Christian Life*. Louisville, KY: Westminster John Knox, 1991.

Bowen, Nancy R. "Women, Violence, and the Bible." Pages 186–99 in *Engaging the Bible in a Gendered World: An Introduction to Feminist Biblical Interpretation in Honor of Katharine Doob Sakenfeld*. Edited by Linda Day and Carolyn Pressler. Louisville, KY: Westminster John Knox, 2006.

Boyarin, Daniel. *Intertextuality and the Reading of Midrash*. Bloomington: Indiana University Press, 1990.

Boyd, Gregory A. *The Myth of a Christian Nation: How the Quest for Political Power Is Destroying the Church*. Grand Rapids, MI: Zondervan, 2005.

Brenner, Athalya. "Some Reflections on Violence against Women and the Image of God in the Hebrew Bible." Pages 69–81 in *On the Cutting Edge: The Study of Women in Biblical Worlds: Essays in Honor of Elisabeth Schüssler Fiorenza*. Edited by Jane Schaberg, Alice Bach, and Esther Fuchs. New York: Continuum, 2003.

Brenner, Athalya, and Fokkelien van Dijk-Hemmes. *On Gendering Texts: Female and Male Voices in the Hebrew Bible*. Leiden: Brill, 1993.

Brensinger, Terry L. "The Inspiration and Authority of Scripture." Unpublished paper. Presented at the Theological Colloquium, Lancaster, PA, September 2010.

———. "War in the Old Testament: A Journey toward Nonparticipation." Pages 22–31 in *A Peace Reader*. Edited by E. Morris Sider and Luke Keefer Jr. Nappanee, IN: Evangel, 2002.

Brown, William P., ed. *Engaging Biblical Authority: Perspectives on the Bible as Scripture*. Louisville: Westminster John Knox, 2007.

Brueggemann, Walter. *The Book that Breathes New Life: Scriptural Authority and Biblical Theology*. Minneapolis: Fortress Press, 2005.

———. *Theology of the Old Testament: Testimony, Dispute, Advocacy*. Minneapolis: Fortress Press, 1997.

Bunge, Marcia J., Terence E. Fretheim, and Beverly Roberts Gaventa, eds. *The Child in the Bible*. Grand Rapids, MI: Eerdmans, 2008.

Bushman, Brad J., and Craig A. Anderson. "Media Violence and the American Public: Scientific Facts versus Media Misinformation." *American Psychologist* 56 (2001): 477–89.

Bushman, Brad J., et al. "When God Sanctions Killing: Effect of Scriptural Violence on Aggression." *Psychological Science* 18 (2007): 204–7.

Buttry, Daniel L. *Christian Peacemaking: From Heritage to Hope*. Valley Forge, PA: Judson, 1994.

Byron, John. *Cain and Abel in Text and Tradition: Jewish and Christian Interpretations of the First Sibling Rivalry*. Leiden: Brill, 2011.

Casey, Keree Louise. "What Part of 'No' Don't You Understand? Talking the Tough Stuff of the Bible: A Creative Reading of the Rape of Tamar: 2 Sam. 13:1-22." *Feminist Theology* 18 (2010): 160–74.

Clines, David J. A. "Ethics as Deconstruction, and the Ethics of Deconstruction." Pages 77–106 in *The Bible in Ethics: The Second Sheffield Colloquium*. Edited by

John W. Rogerson, Margaret Davies, and M. Daniel Carroll R. JSOTSup 207. Sheffield: Sheffield Academic, 1995.

———. *Interested Parties: The Ideology of Writers and Readers of the Hebrew Bible.* JSOTSup 205. Sheffield: Sheffield Academic, 1995.

Cole, Darrell. *When God Says War Is Right: The Christian's Perspective on When and How to Fight.* Colorado Springs: Waterbrook, 2002.

Collins, John J. *The Bible after Babel: Historical Criticism in a Postmodern Age.* Grand Rapids, MI: Eerdmans, 2005.

———. *Does the Bible Justify Violence?* Minneapolis: Fortress Press, 2004.

Comstock, Gary David. *Violence against Lesbians and Gay Men.* New York: Columbia University Press, 1991.

Copan, Paul. *Is God a Moral Monster?: Making Sense of the Old Testament God.* Grand Rapids, MI: Baker, 2011.

———. "Is Yahweh a Moral Monster? The New Atheists and Old Testament Ethics." *Philosophia Christi* 10 (2008): 7–37.

Cosby, Michael R. *Interpreting Biblical Literature: An Introduction to Biblical Studies.* Grantham, PA: Stony Run, 2009.

Cosgrove, Charles H. *Appealing to Scripture in Moral Debate: Five Hermeneutical Rules.* Grand Rapids, MI: Eerdmans, 2002.

Cottrill, Amy C. "Reading Textual Violence as 'Real' Violence in the Liberal Arts Context." In *Teaching the Bible in the Liberal Arts Classroom.* Edited by Jane S. Webster and Glenn S. Holland. Sheffield: Sheffield Phoenix, forthcoming 2012.

Cowles, C. S. "A Response to Eugene H. Merrill." Pages 97–101 in C. S. Cowles et al., *Show Them No Mercy: Four Views on God and Canaanite Genocide.* Grand Rapids, MI: Zondervan, 2003.

Cowles, C. S., et al. *Show Them No Mercy: Four Views on God and Canaanite Genocide.* Grand Rapids, MI: Zondervan, 2003.

Craigie, Peter C. *The Problem of War in the Old Testament.* Grand Rapids, MI: Eerdmans, 1978.

Darr, Katheryn Pfisterer. "Ezekiel's Justifications of God: Teaching Troubling Texts." *JSOT* 55 (1992): 97–117.

Davies, Eryl W. *The Dissenting Reader: Feminist Approaches to the Hebrew Bible.* Aldershot, UK: Ashgate, 2003.

———. *The Immoral Bible: Approaches to Biblical Ethics.* London: T & T Clark, 2010.

———. "The Morally Dubious Passages of the Hebrew Bible: An Examination of Some Proposed Solutions." *Currents in Biblical Research* 3 (2005): 197–228.

Davies, Philip R., ed. *First Person: Essays in Biblical Autobiography.* Sheffield: Sheffield Academic, 2002.

Davis, Ellen F. *Getting Involved with God: Rediscovering the Old Testament.* Cambridge, MA: Cowley, 2001.

———. "Losing a Friend: The Loss of the Old Testament to the Church." Pages 83–94 in *Jews, Christians, and the Theology of the Hebrew Scriptures*. Edited by Alice Ogden Bellis and Joel S. Kaminsky. SBL Symposium Series 8. Atlanta: Society of Biblical Literature, 2000.

Dawkins, Richard. *The God Delusion*. Boston: Houghton Mifflin, 2006.

Day, Linda. "Rhetoric and Domestic Violence in Ezekiel 16." *BibInt* 8 (2000): 205–30.

Day, Linda, and Carolyn Pressler. "Introduction." Pages ix–xxvii in *Engaging the Bible in a Gendered World: An Introduction to Feminist Biblical Interpretation in Honor of Katharine Doob Sakenfeld*. Edited by Linda Day and Carolyn Pressler. Louisville, KY: Westminster John Knox, 2006.

De La Torre, Miguel A. *Reading the Bible from the Margins*. Maryknoll, NY: Orbis, 2002.

Desjardins, Michel. *Peace, Violence and the New Testament*. Sheffield: Sheffield Academic, 1997.

Dever, William G. *Who Were the Early Israelites and Where Did They Come From?* Grand Rapids, MI: Eerdmans, 2003.

Diamant, Anita. *The Red Tent*. 2nd ed. New York: Picador/St. Martin's, 1997.

Donaldson, Laura E. "Postcolonialism and Biblical Reading: An Introduction." Edited by Laura E. Donaldson and R. S. Sugirtharajah. *Semeia* 75 (1996): 1–14.

Doré, Gustave. *The Doré Bible Illustrations*. Mineola, NY: Dover, 1974.

Driver, John. *How Christians Made Peace with War: Early Christian Understandings of War*. Scottdale, PA: Herald, 1988.

Earl, Douglas S. *The Joshua Delusion? Rethinking Genocide in the Bible*. Eugene, OR: Cascade, 2010.

Ellerbe, Helen. *The Dark Side of Christian History*. Windermere, FL: Morningstar and Lark, 1995.

Ellwood, Gracia Fay. *Batter My Heart*. Pendle Hill Pamphlet 282. Wallingford, PA: Pendle Hill Publications, 1988.

Emilsen, William W., and John T. Squires. "Introduction." Pages xiii–xvi in *Validating Violence—Violating Faith? Religion, Scripture and Violence*. Edited by William W. Emilsen and John T. Squires. Adelaide: ATF, 2008.

Engelhardt, Christopher R., et al. "This Is Your Brain on Violent Video Games: Neural Desensitization to Violence Predicts Increased Aggression following Violent Video Game Exposure." *Journal of Experimental Social Psychology* 47 (2011): 1033–36.

Epp-Tiessen, Esther. "Conquering the Land." Pages 62–74 in *Under Vine and Fig Tree: Biblical Theologies of Land and the Palestinian-Israeli Conflict*. Edited by Alain Epp Weaver. Telford, PA: Cascadia, 2007.

Eskenazi, Tamara Cohn, Gary A. Phillips, and David Jobling, eds. *Levinas and Biblical Studies*. Semeia Studies 43. Atlanta: Society of Biblical Literature, 2003.

Evans, Christopher. *Is "Holy Scripture" Christian? And Other Questions*. London: SCM, 1971.

Evans, James H., Jr. *We Have Been Believers: An African American Systematic Theology*. Minneapolis: Fortress Press, 1992.

Everts, Don. *God in the Flesh: What Speechless Lawyers, Kneeling Soldiers, and Shocked Crowds Teach Us about Jesus*. Downers Grove, IL: InterVarsity, 2005.

Exum, J. Cheryl. "The Ethics of Violence against Women." Pages 248–71 in *The Bible in Ethics: The Second Sheffield Colloquium*. Edited by John W. Rogerson, Margaret Davies, and M. Daniel Carroll R. JSOTSup 207. Sheffield: Sheffield Academic, 1995.

———. "Feminist Criticism: Whose Interests Are Being Served?" Pages 65–89 in *Judges and Method: New Approaches in Biblical Studies*. Edited by Gale A. Yee. 2nd ed. Minneapolis: Fortress Press, 2007.

———. "Second Thoughts about Secondary Characters: Women in Exodus 1.8—2.10." Pages 75–87 in *A Feminist Companion to Exodus and Deuteronomy*. Edited by Athalya Brenner. Sheffield: Sheffield Academic, 1994.

———. "'You Shall Let Every Daughter Live': A Study of Exodus 1:8—2:10." In *The Bible and Feminist Hermeneutics*. Edited by Mary Ann Tolbert. Semeia 28. Chico, CA: Scholars, 1983, 63–82. Repr., *A Feminist Companion to Exodus and Deuteronomy*. Pages 37–61. Edited by Athalya Brenner. Sheffield: Sheffield Academic, 1994.

Fewell, Danna Nolan. *The Children of Israel: Reading the Bible for the Sake of Our Children*. Nashville: Abingdon, 2003.

———. "Deconstructive Criticism: Achsah and the (E)razed City of Writing." Pages 115–37 in *Judges and Method: New Approaches in Biblical Studies*. Edited by Gale A. Yee. 2nd ed. Minneapolis: Fortress Press, 2007.

———. "Reading the Bible Ideologically: Feminist Criticism." Pages 268–82 in *To Each Its Own Meaning: An Introduction to Biblical Criticisms and Their Application*. Edited by Steven L. McKenzie and Stephen R. Haynes. Rev. and exp. ed. Louisville, KY: Westminster John Knox, 1999.

Fewell, Danna Nolan, ed. *Reading between Texts: Intertextuality and the Hebrew Bible*. Louisville, KY: Westminister John Knox, 1992.

Finkelstein, Israel, and Neil Asher Silberman. *The Bible Unearthed: Archaeology's New Vision of Ancient Israel and the Origin of Its Sacred Texts*. New York: Free Press, 2001.

Fish, Stanley E. *Self-Consuming Artifacts: The Experience of Seventeenth Century Literature*. Berkeley: University of California Press, 1972.

Flannery, Frances. "'Go Back the Way You Came': An Internal Textual Critique of Elijah's Violence in 1 Kings 18–19." Pages 161–73 in *Writing and Reading War: Rhetoric, Gender, and Ethics in Biblical and Modern Contexts*. Edited by Brad

E. Kelle and Frank Ritchel Ames. SBLSymS 42. Atlanta: Society of Biblical Literature, 2008.

Flood, Derek. "Does Defending the Bible Mean Advocating Violence?" *Huffington Post (Religion)*. November 21, 2011. http://www.huffingtonpost.com/derek-flood/defending-violence-in-the-bible_b_1088517.html.

———. "The Way of Peace and Grace: How Paul Wrestled with Violent Passages in the Hebrew Bible." *Sojourners* 41 (January 2012): 34–37, 46.

Fontaine, Carole E. "The Abusive Bible: On the Use of Feminist Method in Pastoral Contexts." Pages 84–113 in *A Feminist Companion to Reading the Bible: Approaches, Methods and Strategies*. Edited by Athalya Brenner and Carole Fontaine. Sheffield: Sheffield Academic, 1997.

Fortune, Marie M. *Sexual Violence: The Unmentionable Sin*. Cleveland, OH: Pilgrim, 1983.

Fowl, Stephen. "Texts Don't Have Ideologies." *BibInt* 3 (1995): 15–34.

Fretheim, Terence E. *First and Second Kings*. Louisville: Westminster John Knox, 1999.

———. "'God Was with the Boy' (Genesis 21:20): Children in the Book of Genesis." Pages 3–23 in *The Child in the Bible*. Edited by Marcia J. Bunge, Terence E. Fretheim, and Beverly Roberts Gaventa. Grand Rapids, MI: Eerdmans, 2008.

Fretheim, Terence E., and Karlfried Froehlich. *The Bible as Word of God: In a Postmodern Age*. Minneapolis: Fortress Press, 1998.

Frymer-Kensky, Tikva. Review of Phyllis Trible, *Texts of Terror: Literary-Feminist Readings of Biblical Narratives*. *BR* 1 (February 1985): 6–7. Repr. in *Approaches to the Bible: The Best of Bible Review*. Vol. 2, *A Multitude of Perspectives*, ed. Harvey Minkoff, 301–4. Washington, DC: Biblical Archaeology Society, 1995.

Fuchs, Esther. *Sexual Politics in the Biblical Narrative: Reading the Hebrew Bible as a Woman*. JSOTSup 310. Sheffield: Sheffield Academic Press, 2000.

Goldingay, John. *Israel's Life*. Vol. 3 of *Old Testament Theology*. Downers Grove, IL: InterVarsity, 2009.

Gomes, Peter J. *The Good Book: Reading the Bible with Mind and Heart*. New York: Avon, 1996.

Gorman, Michael J. *Reading Revelation Responsibly: Uncivil Worship and Witness: Following the Lamb into the New Creation*. Eugene, OR: Cascade, 2011.

Gottwald, Norman K. "Holy War in Deuteronomy: Analysis and Critique." *RevExp* 61 (1964): 296–310.

Grossman, Dave. *On Killing: The Psychological Cost of Learning to Kill in War and Society*. Rev. ed. New York: Back Bay, 2009.

Grudem, Wayne. *Evangelical Feminism: A New Path to Liberalism?* Wheaton, IL: Crossway, 2006.

Gunn, David M. "Colonialism and the Vagaries of Scripture: Te Kooti in Canaan: (A Story of Bible and Dispossession in Aotearoa/New Zealand)." Pages 127–42 in *God in the Fray: A Tribute to Walter Brueggemann*. Edited by Tod Linafelt and Timothy K. Beal. Minneapolis: Fortress Press, 1998.

Gunn, David M., and Danna Nolan Fewell. *Gender, Power, and Promise: The Subject of the Bible's First Story*. Nashville: Abingdon, 1993.

———. *Narrative in the Hebrew Bible*. Oxford: Oxford University Press, 1993.

Hamilton, Jeffries. "How to Read an Abhorrent Text: Deuteronomy 13 and the Nature of Authority." *HBT* 20 (1998): 12–32.

Harstad, Adolph L. *Joshua*. Concordia Commentary. St. Louis: Concordia, 2004.

Hawk, L. Daniel. "Conquest Reconfigured: Recasting Warfare in the Redaction of Joshua." Pages 145–60 in *Writing and Reading War: Rhetoric, Gender, and Ethics in Biblical and Modern Contexts*. Edited by Brad E. Kelle and Frank Ritchel Ames. SBLSymS 42. Atlanta: Society of Biblical Literature, 2008.

———. "The God of the Conquest: The Theological Problem of the Book of Joshua." *TBT* 46 (2008): 141–47.

———. *Joshua in 3-D: A Commentary on Biblical Conquest and Manifest Destiny*. Eugene, OR: Cascade, 2010.

Haynes, Stephen R. *Noah's Curse: The Biblical Justification of American Slavery*. New York: Oxford, 2002.

Hays, Richard B. *The Moral Vision of the New Testament: Community, Cross, New Creation: A Contemporary Introduction to New Testament Ethics*. San Francisco: HarperSanFrancisco, 1996.

———. "Salvation by Trust? Reading the Bible Faithfully." *ChrCent* 114 (1997): 218–23.

Heard, Chris. "Hearing the Children's Cries: Commentary, Deconstruction, Ethics, and the Book of Habakkuk." In *Bible and Ethics of Reading*. Edited by Danna Nolan Fewell and Gary A. Phillips. *Semeia* 77 (1997): 75–89.

Herion, Gary A. "Why God Rejected Cain's Offering: The Obvious Answer." Pages 52–65 in *Fortunate the Eyes That See: Essays in Honor of David Noel Freedman in Celebration of His Seventieth Birthday*. Edited by Astrid B. Beck et al. Grand Rapids, MI: Eerdmans, 1995.

Hess, Carol Lakey. *Caretakers of Our Common House: Women's Development in Communities of Faith*. Nashville: Abingdon, 1997.

Hess, Richard S. "The Jericho and Ai of the Book of Joshua." Pages 33–46 in *Critical Issues in Early Israelite History*. Edited by Richard S. Hess, Gerald A. Klingbeil, and Paul J. Ray, Jr. BBRSup 3. Winona Lake, IN: Eisenbrauns, 2008.

Hill, Jim, and Rand Cheadle. *The Bible Tells Me So: Uses and Abuses of Holy Scripture*. New York: Doubleday, 1996.

Hobbs, T. R. *2 Kings*. WBC 13. Waco, TX: Word, 1985.

———. *A Time for War: A Study of Warfare in the Old Testament*. Wilmington, DE: Michael Glazier, 1989.

Holben, L. R. *What Christians Think about Homosexuality: Six Representative View-points*. North Richland Hills, TX: BIBAL, 1999.

Holladay, William L. *Long Ago God Spoke: How Christians May Hear the Old Testament Today*. Minneapolis: Fortress Press, 1995.

Hoskins, Richard Kelly. *Vigilantes of Christendom: The Story of the Phineas Priesthood*. Lynchburg, VA: Virginia Publishing, 1990.

Howard, David M., Jr. "Philistines." Pages 231–50 in *Peoples of the Old Testament World*. Edited by Alfred J. Hoerth, Gerald L. Mattingly, and Edwin M. Yamauchi. Grand Rapids, MI: Baker, 1994.

Hunter, Alastair G. "(De)nominating Amalek: Racist Stereotyping in the Bible and the Justification of Discrimination." Pages 92–108 in *Sanctified Aggression: Legacies of Biblical and Post Biblical Vocabularies of Violence*. Edited by Jonneke Bekkenkamp and Yvonne Sherwood. London: T & T Clark, 2003.

Jenkins, Philip. *Laying Down the Sword: Why We Can't Ignore the Bible's Violent Verses*. New York: HarperOne, 2011.

Jersak, Brad. "Nonviolent Identification and the Victory of Christ." Pages 18–53 in *Stricken by God? Nonviolent Identification and the Victory of Christ*. Edited by Brad Jersak and Michael Hardin. Grand Rapids, MI: Eerdmans, 2007.

Jobling, David. *1 Samuel*. Berit Olam. Collegeville: Liturgical, 1998.

Jobling, David and Catherine Rose, "Reading as a Philistine: The Ancient and Modern History of a Cultural Slur." Pages 381–417 in *Ethnicity and the Bible*. Edited by Mark G. Brett. Leiden: Brill, 1996.

Johnson, Sylvester. "New Israel, New Canaan: The Bible, the People of God, and the American Holocaust." *Union Seminary Quarterly Review* 59 (2005): 25–39.

Jones, Gwilym H. *1 and 2 Kings*. Vol. 2. Grand Rapids: Eerdmans, 1984.

Kang, Sa-Moon. *Divine War in the Old Testament and in the Ancient Near East*. BZAW 177. Berlin: de Gruyter, 1989.

Kille, D. Andrew. "'The Bible Made Me Do It': Text, Interpretation, and Violence." Pages 8–24 in *The Destructive Power of Religion: Violence in Judaism, Christianity, and Islam*. Edited by J. Harold Ellens. Condensed and updated ed. Westport, CT: Praeger, 2007.

Kimball, Charles. *When Religion Becomes Evil*. San Francisco: HarperSanFrancisco, 2002.

Kirk-Duggan, Cheryl A. *Violence and Theology*. Nashville: Abingdon, 2006.

Kirsch, Jonathan. *The Harlot by the Side of the Road: Forbidden Tales of the Bible*. New York: Ballantine, 1997.

Klassen, William. "The Authenticity of the Command: 'Love Your Enemies.'" Pages 385–407 in *Authenticating the Words of Jesus*. Edited by Bruce Chilton and Craig A. Evans. Boston: Brill, 2002.

———. "Love Your Enemy: A Study of New Testament Teaching on Coping with an Enemy." Pages 153–83 in *Biblical Realism Confronts the Nation: Ten Christian*

Scholars Summon the Church to the Discipleship of Peace. Edited by Paul Peachey. Scottdale, PA: Herald, 1963.

Klawans, Jonathan (with contributions by David A. Bernat). "Introduction: Religion, Violence, and the Bible." Pages 1–15 in *Religion and Violence: The Biblical Heritage*. Edited by David A. Bernat and Jonathan Klawans. Sheffield: Sheffield Phoenix, 2007.

Knust, Jennifer Wright. *Unprotected Texts: The Bible's Surprising Contradictions about Sex and Desire*. New York: HarperOne, 2011.

Kruer, Matthew. "Red Albion: Genocide and English Colonialism, 1622–1646." M.A. thesis, Graduate School of the University of Oregon, 2009.

Kugel, James L. *Traditions of the Bible: A Guide to the Bible As It Was at the Beginning of the Common Era*. Cambridge: Harvard University Press, 1998.

Lamb, David T. *God Behaving Badly: Is the God of the Old Testament Angry, Sexist, and Racist?* Downers Grove, IL: InterVarsity, 2011.

Landy, Francis. "Do We Want Our Children to Read This Book?" In *Bible and Ethics of Reading*. Edited Danna Nolan Fewell and Gary A. Phillips. *Semeia* 77 (1997): 157–76.

Lapsley, Jacqueline E. *Whispering the Word: Hearing Women's Stories in the Old Testament*. Louisville, KY: Westminster John Knox, 2005.

Leiter, David A. *Neglected Voices: Peace in the Old Testament*. Scottdale, PA: Herald, 2007.

Lemche, Niels Peter. *The Canaanites and Their Land: The Tradition of the Canaanites*. JSOTSup 110. Sheffield: JSOT, 1991. Repr., Sheffield: Sheffield Academic, 1999.

Linafelt, Tod. "Taking Women in Samuel: Readers/Responses/Responsibility." Pages 99–113 in *Reading between Texts: Intertextuality and the Hebrew Bible*. Edited by Danna Nolan Fewell. Louisville, KY: Westminster John Knox, 1992.

Longman, Tremper, III. "The Case for Spiritual Continuity." Pages 161–87 in C. S. Cowles et al., *Show Them No Mercy: Four Views on God and Canaanite Genocide*. Grand Rapids, MI: Zondervan, 2003.

———. *Making Sense of the Old Testament: 3 Crucial Questions*. Grand Rapids, MI: Baker, 1998.

Longman, Tremper, III, and Daniel G. Reid. *God Is a Warrior*. Grand Rapids, MI: Zondervan, 1995.

Love, Gregory Anderson. *Love, Violence, and the Cross: How the Nonviolent God Saves Us through the Cross of Christ*. Eugene, OR: Cascade, 2010.

Lynch, Joseph H. "The First Crusade: Some Theological and Historical Context." Pages 23–36 in *Must Christianity Be Violent? Reflections on History, Practice, and Theology*. Edited by Kenneth R. Chase and Alan Jacobs. Grand Rapids, MI: Brazos, 2003.

Martens, Elmer A. "Toward Shalom: Absorbing the Violence." Pages 33–57 in *War in the Bible and Terrorism in the Twenty-First Century*. Edited by Richard S. Hess and Elmer A. Martens. BBRSup 2. Winona Lake, IN: Eisenbrauns, 2008.

Martin, Dale B. *Sex and the Single Savior: Gender and Sexuality in Biblical Interpretation*. Louisville, KY: Westminster John Knox, 2006.

Matthews, Shelly, and E. Leigh Gibson, eds. *Violence in the New Testament*. New York: T & T Clark, 2005.

Matties, Gordon H. *Joshua*. BCBC. Harrisonburg, VA: Herald, 2012.

McEntire, Mark. *The Blood of Abel: The Violent Plot in the Hebrew Bible*. Macon, GA: Mercer University Press, 1999.

McKay, Heather A. "On the Future of Feminist Biblical Criticism." Pages 61–83 in *A Feminist Companion to Reading the Bible: Approaches, Methods and Strategies*. Edited by Athalya Brenner and Carole Fontaine. Sheffield: Sheffield Academic, 1997.

McKenzie, Steven L. *King David: A Biography*. New York: Oxford University Press, 2000.

McKenzie, Steven L., and Stephen R. Haynes, eds. *To Each Its Own Meaning: An Introduction to Biblical Criticisms and Their Application*. Rev. and exp. ed. Louisville, KY: Westminster John Knox, 1999.

Merrill, Eugene H. "The Case for Moderate Discontinuity." Pages 63–94 in C. S. Cowles et al., *Show Them No Mercy: Four Views on God and Canaanite Genocide*. Grand Rapids, MI: Zondervan, 2003.

Merton, Thomas. *Opening the Bible*. Collegeville: Liturgical, 1986.

Meyers, Carol. *Discovering Eve: Ancient Israelite Women in Context*. New York: Oxford University Press, 1988.

Michel, Andreas. "Sexual Violence against Children in the Bible." Pages 51–60 in *The Structural Betrayal of Trust*. Edited by Regina Ammicht-Quinn, Hille Haker, and Maureen Junker-Kenny. Concilium 2004/3. London: SCM, 2004.

Miller, Patrick D. "What I Have Learned from My Sisters." Pages 238–52 in *Engaging the Bible in a Gendered World: An Introduction to Feminist Biblical Interpretation in Honor of Katharine Doob Sakenfeld*. Edited by Linda Day and Carolyn Pressler. Louisville, KY: Westminster John Knox, 2006.

Miller, Robert J. *Both Prayed to the Same God: Religion and Faith in the American Civil War*. Lanham, MD: Lexington, 2007.

Milne, Pamela J. "Eve and Adam: A Feminist Reading." Pages 259–69 in *Approaches to the Bible: The Best of Bible Review*. Vol. 2, *A Multitude of Perspectives*. Edited by Harvey Minkoff. Washington, DC: Biblical Archaeology Society, 1995. Repr., *BR* 4 (June 1988): 12–21, 39.

———. "Labouring with Abusive Biblical Texts: Tracing Trajectories of Misogyny." Pages 267–83 in *The Labour of Reading: Desire, Alienation, and Biblical Interpretation*. Edited by Fiona C. Black, Roland Boer, and Erin Runions. Semeia Studies 36. Atlanta: Society of Biblical Literature, 1999.

———. "No Promised Land: Rejecting the Authority of the Bible." Pages 47–73 in Phyllis Trible et al., *Feminist Approaches to the Bible: Symposium at the Smithsonian*

Institution, September 24, 1994. Washington, DC: Biblical Archaeology Society, 1995.

Morris, William, ed. *The American Heritage Dictionary*. 2nd college ed. Boston: Houghton Mifflin, 1985.

Mouw, Richard J. *Uncommon Decency: Christian Civility in an Uncivil World*. Downers Grove, IL: InterVarsity, 1992.

Nelson, Richard D. "Josiah in the Book of Joshua." *JBL* 100 (1981): 531–40.

Nelson-Pallmeyer, Jack. *Is Religion Killing Us? Violence in the Bible and the Quran*. Harrisburg, PA: Trinity Press International, 2003.

———. *Jesus against Christianity: Reclaiming the Missing Jesus*. Harrisburg, PA: Trinity Press International, 2001.

Neufeld, Thomas R. Yoder, *Killing Enmity: Violence and the New Testament*. Grand Rapids, MI: Baker, 2011.

Niditch, Susan. *War in the Hebrew Bible: A Study in the Ethics of Violence*. New York: Oxford University Press, 1993.

Noll, Mark A. *The Civil War as a Theological Crisis*. Chapel Hill: University of North Carolina Press, 2006.

O'Brien, Julia M. *Challenging Prophetic Metaphor: Theology and Ideology in the Prophets*. Louisville, KY: Westminster John Knox, 2008.

O'Connor, Kathleen M. "The Feminist Movement Meets the Old Testament: One Woman's Perspective." Pages 3–24 in *Engaging the Bible in a Gendered World: An Introduction to Feminist Biblical Interpretation in Honor of Katharine Doob Sakenfeld*. Edited by Linda Day and Carolyn Pressler. Louisville, KY: Westminster John Knox, 2006.

Ollenburger, Ben C. "Introduction: Gerhard von Rad's Theory of Holy War." Pages 1–33 in Gerhard von Rad, *Holy War in Ancient Israel*. Translated and edited by Marva J. Dawn. Grand Rapids, MI: Eerdmans, 1991.

Ortberg, John. *Stepping Out in Faith: Life-Changing Examples from the History of Israel*. Grand Rapids, MI: Zondervan, 2003.

Osiek, Carolyn. "The Feminist and the Bible: Hermeneutical Alternatives." Pages 93–105 in *Feminist Perspectives on Biblical Scholarship*. Edited by Adela Yarbro Collins. SBLBSNA 10. Chico, CA: Scholars, 1985.

Paris, Jenell Williams. *The End of Sexual Identity: Why Sex Is Too Important to Define Who We Are*. Downers Grove, IL: InterVarsity, 2011.

Patte, Daniel, et al., eds. *Global Bible Commentary*. Nashville: Abingdon, 2004.

Patterson, Linda J. *Hate Thy Neighbor: How the Bible Is Misused to Condemn Homosexuality*. West Conshohocken, PA: Infinity, 2009.

Peterson, Eugene H. *Eat This Book: A Conversation in the Art of Spiritual Reading*. Grand Rapids, MI: Eerdmans, 2006.

Phillips, Gary A. "The Killing Fields of Matthew's Gospel." Pages 249–65 in *The Labour of Reading: Desire, Alienation, and Biblical Interpretation*. Edited by

Fiona C. Black, Roland Boer, and Erin Runions. Semeia Studies 36. Atlanta: Society of Biblical Literature, 1999.

Pippin, Tina. "Ideology, Ideological Criticism, and the Bible." *CurBS* 4 (1996): 51–78.

Plotz, David. *Good Book: The Bizarre, Hilarious, Disturbing, Marvelous, and Inspiring Things I Learned When I Read Every Single Word of the Bible.* New York: Harper, 2009.

Powery, Emerson B. "Reading the Bible as a Minority." *Brethren in Christ History and Life* 33 (April 2010): 177–94.

Presbyterian Understanding and Use of Holy Scripture. Louisville, KY: Office of the General Assembly, 1992.

Pressler, Carolyn. "The 'Biblical View' of Marriage." Pages 200–211 in *Engaging the Bible in a Gendered World: An Introduction to Feminist Biblical Interpretation in Honor of Katharine Doob Sakenfeld.* Edited by Linda Day and Carolyn Pressler. Louisville, KY: Westminster John Knox, 2006.

Prior, Michael. *The Bible and Colonialism: A Moral Critique.* Sheffield: Sheffield Academic, 1997.

———. "The Bible as Instrument of Oppression," *ScrB* 25 (1995): 2–14.

Provan, Iain, V. Philips Long, and Tremper Longman III. *A Biblical History of Israel.* Louisville, KY: Westminster John Knox, 2003.

Pui-lan, Kwok. *Discovering the Bible in the Non-Biblical World.* Maryknoll, NY: Orbis, 1995.

———. "Racism and Ethnocentrism in Feminist Biblical Interpretation." Pages 101–16 in *Searching the Scriptures.* Vol. 1, *A Feminist Introduction.* Edited by Elisabeth Schüssler Fiorenza. New York: Crossroad, 1993.

Rauser, Randal. "Let Nothing that Breathes Remain Alive': On the Problem of Divinely Commanded Genocide." *Philosophia Christi* 11 (2009): 27–41.

Reeder, Caryn A. *The Enemy in the Household: Family Violence in Deuteronomy and Beyond.* Grand Rapids, MI: Baker, 2012.

Reimer, David J. "Stories of Forgiveness: Narrative Ethics and the Old Testament." Pages 359–78 in *Reflection and Refraction: Studies in Biblical Historiography in Honour of A. Graeme Auld.* Edited by Robert Rezetko, Timothy H. Lim, and W. Brian Aucker. VTSup 113. Leiden: Brill, 2007.

Riley-Smith, Louise, and Jonathan Riley-Smith. *The Crusades: Idea and Reality, 1095–1274.* London: Edward Arnold, 1981.

Rogers, Jack. *Jesus, the Bible, and Homosexuality: Explode the Myths, Heal the Church.* Rev. and exp. ed. Louisville, KY: Westminster John Knox, 2009.

Rogerson, John, et al. *Beginning Old Testament Study.* St. Louis: Chalice, 1998.

Rosen, Norma. *Biblical Women Unbound: Counter-Tales.* Philadelphia: Jewish Publication Society, 1996.

Roth, John D. *Choosing against War: A Christian View.* Intercourse, PA: Good Books, 2002.

Rowlett, Lori L. *Joshua and the Rhetoric of Violence: A New Historicist Analysis.* JSOT-Sup 226. Sheffield: Sheffield Academic, 1996.

Ruether, Rosemary Radford. *Sexism and God-Talk: Toward a Feminist Theology.* Boston: Beacon, 1983.

Said, Edward W. "Michael Walzer's *Exodus and Revolution*: A Canaanite Reading." Pages 161–78 in *Blaming the Victims: Spurious Scholarship and the Palestinian Question.* Edited by Edward W. Said and Christopher Hitchens. London: Verso, 1988.

Sakenfeld, Katharine Doob. "Feminist Perspectives on Bible and Theology: An Introduction to Selected Issues and Literature." *Int* 42 (1988): 5–18.

———. "Feminist Uses of Biblical Materials." Pages 55–64 in *Feminist Interpretation of the Bible.* Edited by Letty Russell. Philadelphia: Westminster, 1985.

———. *Just Wives? Stories of Power and Survival in the Old Testament and Today.* Louisville, KY: Westminster John Knox, 2003.

Sanderson, Judith E. "Nahum." Pages 217–21 in *The Women's Bible Commentary.* Edited by Carol A. Newsome and Sharon H. Ringe. Louisville, KY: Westminster John Knox, 1992.

Scholz, Susanne. "The Christian Right's Discourse on Gender and the Bible." *JFSR* 21 (Spring 2005): 81–100.

———. *Sacred Witness: Rape in the Hebrew Bible.* Minneapolis: Fortress Press, 2010.

Schüssler Fiorenza, Elisabeth. Bread Not Stone: The Challenge of Feminist Biblical Interpretation. Boston: Beacon, 1984.

———. "The Ethics of Biblical Interpretation: Decentering Biblical Scholarship." JBL 107 (1988): 3–17.

———. "The Will to Choose or to Reject: Continuing Our Critical Work." Pages 125–36 in Feminist Interpretation of the Bible. Edited by Letty Russell. Philadelphia: Westminster, 1985.

Schwager, Raymund. *Must There Be Scapegoats? Violence and Redemption in the Bible.* Translated by Maria L. Assad. New York: Crossroad, 2000.

Schwartz, Regina. *The Curse of Cain: The Violent Legacy of Monotheism.* Chicago: University of Chicago Press, 1997.

Segal, Charles M., and David C. Stineback. *Puritans, Indians, and Manifest Destiny.* New York: G. P. Putnam's Sons, 1977.

Segovia, Fernando F., and Mary Ann Tolbert. *Reading from This Place.* Vol. 2, *Social Location and Biblical Interpretation in Global Perspective.* Minneapolis: Fortress Press, 1995.

Seibert, Eric A. *Disturbing Divine Behavior: Troubling Old Testament Images of God.* Minneapolis: Fortress Press, 2009.

———. "Jonah, the 'Whale,' and Dr. Seuss: Asking Historical Questions without Alienating Conservative Students." *CGR* 28 (Spring 2010): 62–76.

———. *Subversive Scribes and the Solomonic Narrative: A Rereading of 1 Kings 1–11.* LHBOTS 436. New York: T & T Clark, 2006.

Seuss, Dr. *Fox in Socks*. New York: Beginner Books, 1965.

Sharp, Carolyn J. *Irony and Meaning in the Hebrew Bible*. Bloomington: Indiana University Press, 2009.

———. *Wrestling the Word: The Hebrew Scriptures and the Christian Believer*. Louisville, KY: Westminster John Knox, 2010.

Sharp, Gene. *The Politics of Nonviolent Action*. Boston: Porter Sargent, 1973.

———. *Waging Nonviolent Struggle: 20th Century Practice and 21st Century Potential*. Boston: Extending Horizons, 2005.

Shedinger, Robert F. "Who Killed Goliath? History and Legend in Biblical Narrative." Pages 27–38 in *Who Killed Goliath? Reading the Bible with Heart and Mind*. Edited by Robert F. Shedinger and Deborah J. Spink. Valley Forge, PA: Judson, 2001.

Shields, Mary E. "An Abusive God? Identity and Power/Gender and Violence in Ezekiel 23." Pages 129–51 in *Postmodern Interpretations of the Bible: A Reader*. Edited by A. K. M. Adam. St. Louis: Chalice, 2001.

Smith, Christian. *The Bible Made Impossible: Why Biblicism Is Not a Truly Evangelical Reading of Scripture*. Grand Rapids, MI: Brazos, 2011.

Sparks, Kenton L. *God's Word in Human Words: An Evangelical Appropriation of Critical Biblical Scholarship*. Grand Rapids, MI: Baker, 2008.

———. *Sacred Wood, Broken Wood: Biblical Authority and the Dark Side of Scripture*. Grand Rapids, MI: Eerdmans, 2012.

Spong, John Shelby. *The Sins of Scripture: Exposing the Bible's Texts of Hate to Reveal the God of Love*. San Francisco: HarperSanFrancisco, 2005.

Stark, Thom. *The Human Faces of God: What Scripture Reveals When It Gets God Wrong (and Why Inerrancy Tries to Hide It)*. Eugene, OR: Wipf & Stock, 2011.

———. *Is God a Moral Compromiser? A Critical Review of Paul Copan's "Is God a Moral Monster?"* 2nd ed. 2011. http://thomstark.net/copan/stark_copan-review.pdf.

Stassen, Glen H., and Michael L. Westmoreland-White. "Defining Violence and Nonviolence." Pages 17–36 in *Teaching Peace: Nonviolence and the Liberal Arts*. Edited by J. Denny Weaver and Gerald Biesecker-Mast. Lanham, MD: Rowman and Littlefield, 2003.

Stein, Valerie A. "Know*Be*Do: Using the Bible to Teach Ethics to Children." *SBL Forum* 7.2 (2009). http://www.sbl-site.org/publications/article.aspx?articleId=799.

Stiebing, William H., Jr. *Out of the Desert? Archaeology and the Exodus/Conquest Narratives*. Amherst, NY: Prometheus, 1989.

Stone, Lawson G. "Ethical and Apologetic Tendencies in the Redaction of the Book of Joshua." *CBQ* 53 (1991): 25–36.

Sugirtharajah, R. S. *Voices from the Margin: Interpreting the Bible in the Third World*. 3rd ed. Maryknoll, NY: Orbis, 2006.

Swartley, Willard M. *Covenant of Peace: The Missing Peace in New Testament Theology and Ethics*. Grand Rapids, MI: Eerdmans, 2006.

———. *Slavery, Sabbath, War, and Women*. Scottdale, PA: Herald, 1983.

Switzer, David K. *Pastoral Care of Gays, Lesbians and Their Families*. Minneapolis: Fortress Press, 1999.

Taylor, Barbara Brown. "Hard Words." *ChrCent* 118 (May 2001): 24.

Thatcher, Adrian. *The Savage Text: The Use and Abuse of the Bible*. Malden, MA: Wiley-Blackwell, 2008.

Thistlethwaite, Susan B. "Every Two Minutes: Battered Women and Feminist Interpretation." Pages 96–107, 159–160, in *Feminist Interpretation of the Bible*. Edited by Letty Russell. Philadelphia: Westminster, 1985.

Thompson, John L. *Reading the Bible with the Dead: What You Can Learn from the History of Exegesis That You Can't Learn from Exegesis Alone*. Grand Rapids, MI: Eerdmans, 2007.

———. *Writing the Wrongs: Women of the Old Testament among Biblical Commentators from Philo through the Reformation*. Oxford: Oxford University Press, 2001.

Tite, Philip L. *Conceiving Peace and Violence: A New Testament Legacy*. Dallas: University Press of America, 2004.

Tolbert, Mary Ann. "Defining the Problem: The Bible and Feminist Hermeneutics." In *The Bible and Feminist Hermeneutics*. Edited by Mary Ann Tolbert. *Semeia* 28 (1983): 113–26.

Trible, Phyllis. *Texts of Terror: Literary-Feminist Readings of Biblical Narratives*. OBT 13. Philadelphia: Fortress Press, 1984.

Tripp, Tedd. *Shepherding a Child's Heart*. 2nd ed. Wapwallopen, PA: Shepherd, 2005.

Tyerman, Christopher. *God's War: A New History of the Crusades*. Cambridge, MA: Harvard University Press, 2008.

Van Winkle, Dwight. "Canaanite Genocide and Amalekite Genocide and the God of Love." 1989 Winifred E. Weter Faculty Award Lecture. Seattle Pacific University, Washington, April 6, 1989, 1–45.

Volf, Miroslav. *Exclusion and Embrace: A Theological Exploration of Identity, Otherness, and Reconciliation*. Nashville: Abingdon: 1996.

Wallis, Jim. *God's Politics: Why the Right Gets It Wrong and the Left Doesn't Get It*. San Francisco: HarperSanFrancisco, 2005.

Warrior, Robert Allen. "Canaanites, Cowboys, and Indians: Deliverance, Conquest, and Liberation Theology Today." *Christianity and Crisis* 49 (1989): 261–65.

Webb, William J. *Corporal Punishment in the Bible: A Redemptive-Movement Hermeneutic for Troubling Texts*. Downers Grove, IL: InterVarsity, 2011.

———. *Slaves, Women and Homosexuals: Exploring the Hermeneutics of Cultural Analysis*. Downers Grove, IL: InterVarsity, 2001.

Weems, Renita J. *Battered Love: Marriage, Sex, and Violence in the Hebrew Prophets.* Minneapolis: Fortress Press, 1995.

———. "Reading Her Way through the Struggle: African American Women and the Bible." Pages 55–77 in *Stony the Road We Trod: African American Biblical Interpretation.* Edited by Cain Hope Felder. Minneapolis: Fortress Press, 1991.

West, Gerald O. *The Academy of the Poor: Towards a Dialogical Reading of the Bible.* Sheffield: Sheffield Academic, 1999.

Wink, Walter. *Engaging the Powers: Discernment and Resistance in a World of Domination.* Minneapolis: Fortress Press, 1992.

———. *The Powers That Be: Theology for a New Millennium.* New York: Doubleday, 1998.

Wink, Walter, ed. *Homosexuality and Christian Faith: Questions of Conscience for the Churches.* Minneapolis: Fortress Press, 1999.

Wright, Christopher J. H. *The God I Don't Understand: Reflections on Tough Questions of Faith.* Grand Rapids, MI: Zondervan, 2008.

———. *Old Testament Ethics for the People of God.* Downers Grove, IL: InterVarsity, 2004.

Yancey, Philip. *The Bible Jesus Read.* Grand Rapids, MI: Zondervan, 1999.

Yee, Gale A., ed. *Judges and Method: New Approaches in Biblical Studies.* 2nd ed. Minneapolis: Fortress Press, 2007.

Yoder, Perry B. *Shalom: The Bible's Word for Salvation, Justice, and Peace.* Nappanee, IN: Evangel, 1987.

Younger, K. Lawson, Jr. *Ancient Conquest Accounts: A Study in Ancient Near Eastern and Biblical History Writing.* JSOTSup 98. Sheffield: JSOT Press, 1990.

Index of Biblical References

Index of Modern Authors

Cosgrove, Charles H., 172
Cottrill, Amy C., 191
Cowles, C. S., 107, 182,
Craigie, Peter C., 111, 113, 165, 183

D

Darr, Katheryn Pfisterer, 137, 188
Davies, Eryl W., 61, 63, 66, 70–71, 95,
    155, 171, 172, 173, 174, 176, 177, 180,
    184, 186, 191
Davies, Philip R., 181, 189
Davis, Ellen F., 164, 171
Dawkins, Richard, 24, 168
Day, Linda, 130, 133, 142, 186, 187, 189
De La Torre, Miguel A., 85, 178
Desjardins, Michel, 163
Dever, William G, 97, 180, 184
Diamant, Anita, 189
Dijk-Hemmes, Fokkelien van, 186, 187
Donaldson, Laura E., 1, 103, 163, 181
Driver, John, 165
DuVall, Jack, 191

E

Earl, Douglas S., 110, 111, 165, 183
Ellerbe, Helen, 167
Ellwood, Gracia Fay, 138, 188
Emilsen, William W., 147, 148, 190
Engelhardt, Christopher R., 172
Epp-Tiessen, Esther, 1, 18, 85, 163, 166,
    178, 181
Eskenazi, Tamara Cohn, 185
Evans, Christopher, 191
Evans, James H., Jr., 19, 166
Everts, Don, 75, 176
Exum, J. Cheryl, 73, 137, 138, 140, 176,
    187, 188, 190

F

Fetterley, Judith, 66, 174
Fewell, Danna Nolan, 15, 50–51, 63,
    64–65, 80, 83, 165, 166–67, 172, 174,
    177, 178
Finkelstein, Israel, 184

Fish, Stanley E., 171
Flannery, Frances, 78, 176–77
Flood, Derek, 109, 177, 182
Fontaine, Carole E., 133, 134, 142, 161,
    169, 187, 189, 192
Fortune, Marie M., 189
Fowl, Stephen, 171
Fretheim, Terence E., 25–26, 117, 167,
    169, 170, 184
Froehlich, Karlfried, 169, 184
Frymer-Kensky, Tikva, 143, 189
Fuchs, Esther, 133–34, 187

G

Gaventa, Beverly Roberts, 167
Gibson, E. Leigh, 164
Goldingay, John, 52, 119, 173, 184
Gomes, Peter J., 40, 170
Gorman, Michael J., 183
Gottwald, Norman K., 113, 183
Grossman, Dave, 185
Grudem, Wayne, 186
Gunn, David M., 15, 50–51, 80, 165, 166,
    172, 177

H

Hamilton, Jeffries, 170
Harstad, Adolph L., 183
Hawk, L. Daniel, 95, 99–100, 101, 106–7,
    110, 179, 181, 182, 183
Haynes, Stephen R., 19, 166, 176
Hays, Richard B., 17, 18, 165, 166, 175–76
Heard, Chris, 84-85, 178
Herion, Gary A., 169
Hess, Carol Lakey, 61, 64, 136, 141, 144,
    145, 173, 174, 187, 189
Hess, Richard S., 97, 180, 184
Hill, Jim, 163
Hobbs, T. R., 123, 185
Holben, L. R., 167
Holladay, William L., 65, 174, 190
Hoskins, Richard Kelly, 168
Howard, David M., Jr., 185
Hunter, Alastair G., 73, 176